Life-Span Development

This thorough revision of the highly successful first edition of *Life-Span Development*, offers the reader a wide-ranging and thought provoking account of human development throughout the life-span. The life-span perspective emphasises that development does not stop when we cease to be adolescents but goes on throughout adulthood and into old age.

In initial chapters Léonie Sugarman outlines the issues surrounding the notion of development and how it can be studied, including reviews of the work of key theorists Erikson, Levinson and Gould. She goes on to consider the different ways in which the life course can be construed; as a series of age-related stages; as a cumulative sequence; as a series of developmental tasks; as a series of key life events and transitions or as a narrative construction which creates a sense of dynamic continuity. A final chapter looks at how people cope, the resources that are available and the theoretical and practical issues regarding interventions to assist them in the process.

New to the book is increased coverage of the topical issue of successful ageing and a new chapter on the increasingly popular narrative approach to life-span development. This edition is also more student-friendly with exercises in self-reflection that encourage the reader to look at the development of their own lives or those of their current or future clients. Boxed material highlighting major theories and clarifying concepts is also included. This book will be invaluable for students of developmental and occupational psychology and professionals in the fields of health management, education and social work.

Léonie Sugarman is a Chartered Occupational Psychologist, specialising in the area of adult development. She is a Senior Lecturer in Psychology at St Martin's College, Lancaster, where she teaches aspects of life-span development, stress management and individual change to students and practitioners in a range of professions.

Life-Span Development

Frameworks, accounts and strategies

Second edition

Léonie Sugarman

First edition published 1986
by Methuen & Co Ltd.

First edition reprinted 1990, 1993, 1995, 1996 and 2000
by Routledge

This edition first published 2001 by Psychology Press Ltd,
27 Church Rd, Hove, East Sussex, BN3 2FA

http://www.psypress.co.uk

Simultaneously published in the USA and Canada
by Taylor & Francis Inc.,
29 West 35th Street, New York, NY 10001

Psychology Press is a part of the Taylor & Francis Group

Typeset in Times by
Florence Production Ltd, Stoodleigh, Devon
Printed and bound in the UK by TJ International Ltd,
Padstow, Cornwall

British Library Cataloguing in Publication Data
A catalogue record for this book is available from the
British Library

Library of Congress Cataloging-in-Publication Data
Sugarman, Leonie, 1950–
Life-span development: frameworks, accounts, and strategies /
Leonie Sugarman — 2nd ed.

p. cm.
Previous ed. published under title: Life-span development.
Includes bibliographical references and index.
ISBN 0–415–19264–1 — ISBN 0–145–19265–X
1. Developmental psychology. I.Sugarman, Leonie, 1950–
Life-span development. II. Title.
BF713. S84 2001
155—dc210 2001031826

ISBN 0–415–19264–1 (hbk)
ISBN 0–415–19265-X (pbk)

Contents

Tables

Figures

Boxes

Activities

Preface to second edition

Since publication of the first edition of this book in 1986, the topic of life-span development has become incorporated not only into the main stream of psychology courses but also into the training for a range of human services professions, including nursing, counselling, social work, and occupational therapy. A plethora of textbooks has appeared – primarily emanating from North America – some of which have already reached their sixth edition. These tend to adopt a chronological structure, devoting one or more chapters to some or all of the following life stages: infancy and childhood, adolescence, adulthood, and old age. Adulthood is often subdivided into early, middle, and late substages, and several texts distinguish between different aspects of each stage, for example, the cognitive, personal, and social dimensions. How then to revise *Life-span development: Theories, concepts and interventions* so that it was reasonably comprehensive and yet did not merely replicate what was becoming increasingly available in other texts?

As with the first edition, the book opens with a chapter outlining the broad-based, inclusive stance that characterises the life-span perspective. Recognising that life-span developmental psychology is an empirical as well as a theoretical discipline. This is followed by a chapter on data collection and allied research issues. I succumb to the conventional organisation of material in Chapter 3 by organising discussion of the life course, first, around different life stages and, second, around developmental threads that run through a number of stages. The emphasis of the next four chapters, however, is on meta-models, that is, largely metaphorical images of the life course that convey its overall shape and rhythm rather than the specifics of particular life stages or domains. In recognition of the applied nature of the topic, the final chapter focuses on issues of intervention and the facilitation of life-span development. The result is a book that gives relatively scant attention to some of the traditional bastions of developmental psychology – Freud and Piaget, for example – and that brings into the foreground some of the less ubiquitously mentioned work of others. Thus, whilst Erikson's concept of the adolescent identity crisis is well known, the present text gives equal emphasis to the other stages in his schema. Similarly, the account of Levinson's work goes beyond the frequently reproduced diagram outlining the approximate age bands of different "seasons" in the evolution of a person's life structure.

The result is, I hope, a book whose ideas can contribute to a "working knowledge" of life-span development that readers can call on in both their professional and personal lives. I have also altered the subtitle of the book. Being somewhat tautological, "theories and concepts" are now subsumed under the heading of "frameworks". "Accounts" has been added to signpost an increasing emphasis on participant-led approaches to the study of psychological development, and "interventions" has been replaced by "strategies" to incorporate better the informal and self-generated efforts to promote what can be termed successful ageing.

I acknowledge with thanks and appreciation the range of professional, practical, and personal support provided by Nell Bridges MA, Dr Christine Doyle, Dr Neil Kendra, Dr Ian Rivers, Professor David Sugarman, and Ruth Wright MA. The book is dedicated to my husband David, and to my daughters, Erica and Clare, whose life-span development I find endlessly fascinating.

Léonie Sugarman
February 2001

1 Life-span developmental psychology

> It is interesting to note how rarely the term *development* is used to describe changes in the later years. Despite current emphasis on a lifespan perspective, change in later years is still typically described as *aging*. In the same way, although the word *day* can refer to the twenty-four-hour span, we normally use it to refer to only the brighter hours. *Aging* has come to refer to the darker side of growing old. To make changes in later life one must fight against all sorts of popular mindsets.
>
> (Langer, 1989)

Life-span development is about every one of us. In keeping with this, the text of the present book is interspersed with activities that encourage you to reflect on both the ideas introduced in the text and their place in your own life and the lives of others. You are invited to complete these exercises as you read through the book, working alone or using them as the basis of class discussions. Beginning as you mean to go on, can I ask you first of all to turn your attention to Activity 1.1.

Activity 1.1 Lifeline

Take a blank sheet of paper and, allowing the left and right hand edges of the page to represent the beginning and end of your life respectively, draw a line across the page (in the manner of a temperature chart) to depict the peaks and troughs experienced in your life so far, and those you would predict for the future.

When finished, sit back and ask yourself some questions about this graph – your "lifeline":

- What is its general shape? Does it continue to rise throughout life? Does it depict peaks and troughs around some arbitrary mean? Alternatively, is there a plateau and subsequent fall in the level of the curve? Is it punctuated with major or only relatively minor peaks and troughs?

- The horizontal axis represents time; but how about the vertical axis – what dimension does that reflect?
- What (or who) triggered the peaks and troughs in the graph? Why did they occur at the time that they did?
- What might have been done (or was done) to make the peaks higher and the troughs shallower? How might the incidence and height of the peaks be increased in the future? And the incidence and depth of the troughs decreased?
- What positive results emerged from the troughs and what were the negative consequences of the peaks?

Consideration of questions such as those in Activity 1.1 form the subject matter of life-span developmental psychology. It is to questions such as these that the present book is directed. Whilst life-span developmental psychology is an area that has, as it were, come of age during the last two decades, it is founded on the work of theorists such as Jung (Staude, 1981), Bühler (Bühler & Massarik, 1968), Havighurst (1972), and Erikson (1980). None the less, it was not until 1980 that the *Annual Review of Psychology* included its first review of life-span developmental psychology, defining it as a discipline concerned with the description, explanation, and modification (optimisation) of within-individual change and stability from birth (or possibly from conception) to death and of between-individual differences and similarities in within-individual change (Baltes, Reese, & Lipsitt, 1980). Since the publication of this review the area has been accepted into the mainstream of psychology and its aims have remained largely unchanged.

Change and continuity

To live is to change. This truism is implicit in the notion of life-span development. We are each palpably different from the person we were 10 years ago and the person we will be in 10, 20, or 30 years' time. Life-span developmental psychology is concerned with documenting, explaining, and influencing these changes. In Activity 1.2 you are asked to think about your own life in a different way to the Lifeline exercise – a way that will probably direct attention to how different we all are at different ages.

However, despite the changes that beset all of us as we grow up and grow older, we do not become totally different people. The life course is characterised by continuity as well as change, and we operate on the assumption that past behaviour and temperament are reliable guides to the future. Thus,

Activity 1.2 Changes or consistencies?

- Think of yourself as you are, were, or imagine you will be, at the ages of 7, 17, 27, 37, 47, 57, 67, 77, and 87 years.
- Now think of your priorities, your skills, your worries, your relationships, your enjoyments:
  - what changes?
  - what remains the same?

we might talk about someone acting "out of character" and in writing a job reference might strive to predict future performance on the basis of past and present achievements. The tension between change and continuity is taken up in more detail elsewhere – through an overview of change, consistency and chaos as concepts for organising life-span data (in Chapter 3), and through discussion of the concepts of dynamic continuity and narrative construction (in Chapter 7).

Development

This book is not merely about change. It is about development. Not all change across the life course would necessarily be described as developmental. "Development" is not an empirical term (Reese & Overton, 1970), although on occasions it is used as though it were (Kaplan, 1983). No matter how much data we were able to collect about the course of an individual's life this, of itself, would not enable us to define what is meant by the term "development", unless, that is, we were to say that whatever happens across the life span is what constitutes development. This, however, would reduce developmental psychology to a largely atheoretical data-collection exercise. Furthermore, because such a perspective makes no judgements as to what is better or preferable, it negates the notion of development-enhancing interventions. As, from this viewpoint, any life course is as good (or as developed) as any other, there are no grounds for attempting to influence it.

As an alternative, we might try to define development empirically by reference to norms – saying that development is what happens to the majority of people across the life course. This, however, would also be flawed. It represents a conflation of the "is" and the "ought", seeing them as synonymous. The intervention implications would be that people should be encouraged to be like the average, discouraging both individuality and the exceptional.

Rather than emerging in some self-evident way from empirical data, the concept of development requires the initial postulation of assumptions,

Activity 1.3 How would you define development?

- How would you define development? How would you distinguish it from mere change?
- Jot down some ideas of your own and, if possible, discuss them with a group of colleagues.
- Think about the extent to which your ideas concur with those of the authors quoted below.

underlying premises or value judgements as to its defining characteristics. The concept of development centres on a value-based notion of improvement. These standards of comparison precede empirical observation. Changes in amount and in quality are evaluated against some implicit or explicit standard as to what constitutes the "good" or the "ideal". In other words, we begin with a definition of development and then examine data to see whether they meet our criteria. For example, whether or not it is viewed as development when adolescents challenge the received wisdom of their elders depends on what we mean by the term. Opinions on such matters can vary. Value judgements are involved. Use Activity 1.3 to help you decide what *you* think of when you think of development. Box 1.1 provides some suggestions on how to structure your ideas.

The definitions in Box 1.1 paint a picture of a person learning and benefiting from experience; accomplishing tasks characterising different stages

Box 1.1 Defining development

Thomas (1990, p. 50) emphasises the value-laden basis of concepts of development when he writes:

> People are developing normally (properly, desirably, satisfactorily, acceptably) when:
>
> - they feel that they are fulfilling their own needs at least moderately well,
> - their behavior does not unduly encroach upon other people's rights and opportunities,
> - they fulfil the responsibilities typically held as reasonable for people of their ability (physical and mental) and social environment, and
> - their personal characteristics do not cause others to treat them in ways which harm them physically, psychologically, or socially or which deny them opportunities [equal to those of their peers of the same age, gender, and physical, intellectual, and/or social behaviour] to pursue their ambitions.

Chaplin (1988, p. 45) focuses on the process of development, rejecting the idea of directional movement toward an explicit, coherent "end-state":

> We grow and change in more of a spiral than in a straight line. We go backwards as well as forwards. Perhaps we can only go forwards if we go backwards and regress into childlike feelings first. Growth is working with the rhythms, not proceeding from some depressing reality to a perfect harmonious self in the future.

Rogers (1980, p. 80), in contemplating his own life, sees development as the personal expansion that comes from learning, itself the outcome of risk taking:

> Perhaps the major reason I am willing to take chances is that I have found that in doing so, whether I succeed or fail, I *learn*. Learning, especially learning from experience, has been a prime element in making my life worthwhile. Such learning helps me to expand. So I continue to take risks.

In an otherwise fairly abstract and technical discussion, Ford and Lerner (1992, p. 42) use the metaphor of a sea journey to capture the adaptive nature of human development. Although maps and charts can help us on our travels, there is always the chance that we will meet the unexpected, the unforeseeable and the unfamiliar. They see development as:

> . . . a continuous and sometimes unpredictable voyage throughout life, sailing from seas that have become familiar into oceans as yet uncharted toward destinations to be imagined, defined, and redefined as the voyage proceeds, with occasional, often unpredictable transformations of one's vessel and sailing skills and the oceans upon which one sails resulting from unforeseen circumstances.

of the life course and on which later development, at least to some extent, rests; and working through the implications of significant life events to emerge a stronger, more mature, more "developed" person (Sugarman, 1996).

In the past, developmental psychology was, with a few exceptions, synonymous with child development. The term development was applied only to physical, cognitive, personal, or social changes that met a number of criteria, such as being sequential, unidirectional, universal, irreversible, and end-state or goal-directed. Because these criteria are met by few of the life changes of the adult years, if adulthood is not to be construed as a period largely devoid of development, then this restrictive definition must be challenged.

How, though, should we proceed with the task of defining development? First, a good place to begin is by following Kaplan's (1983) advice to distinguish between development as an ideal process and the realities of what actually happens during the course of a life. Development, "pertains to a rarely, if ever, attained ideal, not the actual" (Kaplan, 1983, p. 188). With this in mind, empirical studies can then furnish data concerning the extent to which individuals do or do not develop and may provide information concerning factors that facilitate or impede development.

Second, development is better thought of as a process than as a state. Thus, we ask not whether a person has reached some ideal end-state or *telos*, but rather (assuming such an end-state exists, even in theory) the extent to which he or she is moving in its direction. In this vein, Kaplan (1983) defines development as movement in the direction of perfection, although he acknowledges that what we mean by perfection is neither transparent nor easy to articulate. None the less, from a variety of theoretical perspectives come common themes if not of perfection, then at least of successful ageing (Ryff, 1989). Thus, accounts of personal growth and ways of being that "surpass the average" (Jourard, 1974) include descriptions of self-actualisation (Maslow, 1970), the healthy personality (Jourard, 1974), and the mature personality (Allport, 1964). Rogers' (1961) concept of the fully functioning person – summarised in Box 1.2 – serves to illustrate the notion of development as a process towards a theoretical ideal.

Box 1.2 The fully functioning person (Kirschenbaum & Henderson, 1989; Rogers, 1961)

It is somewhat misleading to talk of "the" fully functioning person because Rogers does not see it as an achievable, "developed" state. Rather, development is denoted by the process of moving in the direction of becoming more fully functioning. It is a process with some discernible, universal qualities: an increasing openness to experience, increasingly existential living, and an increasing trust in one's own organism.

1. *An increasing openness to experience*. To become more open to experience involves becoming less defensive – the polar opposite of openness. Defensiveness is where experiences are distorted in awareness or are denied awareness because they are perceived as threatening. In this way they are temporarily rendered harmless. Movement from the pole of defensiveness towards the pole of openness to experience allows people to become more able to listen to themselves and to experience what is going on within them. It is movement towards greater emotional self-awareness and acceptance. Feelings – be they positive or negative – are experienced more fully.
2. *Increasingly existential living*. As a person becomes more open to experience he or she tends to live less in the past or the future and more in the present moment. This is what Rogers means by increasingly existential living. To live fully in the moment, "means an absence of

rigidity, of tight organization, of the imposition of structure on experience. It means instead a maximum of adaptability, a discovery of structure *in* experience, a flowing, changing organization of self and personality." (Rogers, 1961, p. 189).

3. *An increasing trust in one's own organism.* Rather than depending on abstract principles, codes of action or previous experience for guidance, people who are open to their own experience and are living fully in the present are able to trust and be guided by their "total organismic reaction" to situations. They are confident that their own experience provides a sufficient and satisfactory basis for deciding how to respond to a particular situation.

The process of becoming a fully functioning person is rarely smooth. Rather, it tends to occur unevenly, by what Rogers (1961) refers to as "moments of movement" occurring in situations where people (who are often, but not always, in therapy) feel themselves to be fully accepted and "received". The good life that results from this movement is not a fixed state of virtue, contentment, or happiness in which the person is adjusted, fulfilled or actualised. Indeed, it is not a state at all. It is a movement from fixity towards changingness, from rigid structure towards flow, and from stasis to process. It is a continuing process of being in which people discover that, if they are open to their experiences, then doing what "feels right" is "a competent and trustworthy guide to behavior which is truly satisfying" (Rogers, 1961, p. 189).

Age

The question "What is your age?" might seem to have a simple, unambiguous answer – you are 18 years and 6 months, 30 years and 2 months, 89 years and 11 months, or whatever. However, our chronological age is an incomplete statement of "how old we are" (see Activity 1.4), as is indicated when we describe someone as being "young for their age", as "old before their time", or as "having aged 10 years in the last 3 weeks". At any one time we are both old and young – the 15-year-old is "too young" to vote and "too old" for primary school.

Non-chronological concepts of age, that is, our psychological, social, functional, and biological ages (see Box 1.3), all contribute to the question of how old we are. None the less, it is chronological age that is almost universally used in developmental psychology as either a main or subsidiary criterion in anchoring accounts of change over the life course. Such categorisation of people and processes according to age serves to facilitate the organisation of knowledge, individuals, and society, and provides a framework in relation to which we can order much of our daily lives. However, age norms are inevitably averages, with many, if not most,

Activity 1.4 How old are you?

How old are you? I am ______ years old. But are you?

- I *look* as if I am ______ years old.
- I *feel* as if I am ______ years old
- I *behave* as if I am ______ years old.

Complete the following sentences:

- The best thing about my current age is . . .
- At my age I should . . .
- At my age I should not . . .
- I will be old when . . .
- In ten years' time I will . . .
- In ten years' time I won't be able to . . .
- I feel I'm already too old to . . .
- The best age to be is . . .

If possible, compare your answers with those of other people of different ages. You might find that notions of "old" and "young" bear very little relation to chronological age. I once overheard my 3-year-old daughter describing her babysitter to a friend as being "Really, really old – at least twelve". In fact the babysitter was fifteen, and my concern was that she might be "too young".

individuals deviating from them to some degree. An "age-irrelevant" concept of development (Baer, 1970) focuses not on the age at which particular experiences occurred, but at their point in a sequence of experiences.

Ageism

Because the topic of age is almost inevitably implicated in discussions of life-span development, it is important constantly to be on the alert for evidence of ageism in our own or others' thinking. However, in the same way as we asked what is meant by the concept of age, so, too, we need to ask what we mean by ageism. Perhaps you could spend a few moments reflecting on and jotting down what you understand by the term.

Over a quarter of a century ago the term ageism was invoked to express concern about the condition and treatment of older people during the 1960s

Box 1.3 Non-chronological age variables

Key "non-chronological" age variables (Barak & Schiffman, 1981; Birren & Renner, 1977) include:

- *Subjective (or psychological) age* – people's sense of their own age as, for example, "young", "middle-aged" or "grown up", irrespective of their chronological age. Subjective age is reflected in the adage, "You're as old as you feel".
- *Social age* – the extent to which a person's social roles, lifestyle, and attitudes conform to the norms and the social expectations for someone of their chronological age. Are they "acting their age", or perhaps behaving as "mutton dressed up as lamb"?
- *Functional age* – a person's capacities or abilities relative to others of similar age. Functional age can be applied to the condition of an individual's organ and body systems (such as heart and lung capacity) and to his or her intellectual and practical skills.
- *Biological age* – an estimate of the individual's present position in relation to his or her potential life span. The biological age of, say, a fit 70-year-old may be less than that of an unfit 50-year-old.

and 1970s. Thus Butler (1987; Butler & Lewis, 1973) defined ageism as, "a process of systematic stereotyping of and discrimination against people because they are old, just as racism and sexism accomplish this for skin colour and gender" (Butler, 1987, p. 22). This remains the most widely assumed meaning of the term, although it does have certain weaknesses and limitations. Seeing ageism as something that applies only to older people fosters a "them" and "us" view of "the elderly" as a minority group, different and separate from the rest of society (Bytheway, 1995; Johnson & Bytheway, 1993). In this sense, the concept of ageism can itself be seen as ageist. This is perhaps understandable given the prevalence of the view of old age as a period of decline and marginalisation. If old age is seen as inevitably accompanied by decrement and decline then it is not surprising if fear or, at best, ambivalence about ageing leads young and middle-aged people to distance themselves from those who are older. The result is that so-called "enlightened" views of ageing may incorporate a Victorian sense of *noblesse oblige* accompanied by images of a gracious but patronising Lady Bountiful. Kalish (1979, p. 398) expressed this perspective thus:

> You are poor, lonely, weak, incompetent, ineffectual, and no longer terribly bright. You are sick, in need of better housing and transportation and nutrition, and we – the nonelderly and those elderly who align themselves with us – are finally going to turn our attention to you, the deserving elderly, and relieve you from ageism.

However, even if we reject this patronising view of older people, it is also the case that ageing is associated with some decrements that it is not unreasonable to regret. Schonfield (1982) suggested that guilt about our fear or dislike of some aspects of ageing leads us to define as ageist feelings, such as the expression of greater regret for the death of an 18-year-old than on the death of a 75-year-old, that are in fact reasonable and understandable. Fear of our own ageing is not the same as, although it may contribute to, negative attitudes towards older people in general.

Rather than seeing ageism as something applying only to older people (which could, suggests Johnson and Bytheway (1993), be called "old-ageism"), it can be seen as a process affecting all individuals from birth onwards, "at every stage putting limits and constraints on experience, expectations, relationships and opportunities" (Itzin, 1986, p. 114). From this perspective, ageism is prejudice based on age, not specifically old age (Johnson & Bytheway, 1993). Setting a lower minimum wage for workers less than 25 years old can, from this perspective, be defined as ageist practice. Whilst our experiences of racism and sexism will generally have a degree of continuity throughout our life, the nature of any ageism we experience will vary, depending on our chronological age at the time (Bytheway, 1995). The analogy between ageism and these other forms of prejudice is therefore imperfect.

Although prejudice based on age can affect us at any point in life, this does not mean it is distributed evenly across the life course. Age-based limits and restrictions do tend to be greatest for "the young" and "the old", a reflection of the (perhaps implicit) adoption of the growth–maintenance–decline model of the life course – whereby the middle years are seen to represent the peak of maturity (with the young being "too young" and the old being "too old"). It also reflects a power structure within society where the reins of power are typically held by those in midlife (Pilgrim, 1997).

Ageism is not only manifested in explicit age-based restrictions. Of at least equal importance as institutionalised ageism is internalised ageism – the frequently implicit or internalised notions of age-appropriate behaviour that comprise a society's age-grade system. It is reflected in inappropriate attitudes and behaviour towards one age group or generation by another. It encompasses both overtly offensive standpoints (for example calling someone an "old bag") and also the kindly but patronising exercising of benevolent patronage (for example, "keeping an eye on the old dears") that is described by Johnson and Bytheway (1993) as perhaps the most pervasive form of ageism.

It is also important to realise that we can apply ageist attitudes towards ourselves as well as others. Whilst societal constraints to life course timing and sequencing might be more relaxed than previously – career change in our 30s, becoming a grandparent at 35 or 75 – and the variability of individual life-course patterns has increased (Neugarten, 1979; Rindfuss, Swicegood, & Rosenfeld, 1987), internalised conceptions of age-appropriate behaviours and achievements still influence our aspirations and sense of success and failure. Such normative assumptions provide us with a degree of security – helping to confer a sense of order and predictability on our lives. However, they can also be a major constraint to our life-course development (Heckhausen, 1999). Langer (1989, pp. 94–5) eloquently makes this point with regard to old age:

> When we are young and answer questions about old age, we do so with the feeling that we will never grow old. In the meantime, we form mindsets about the relationship between debilitated performance and old age. Once we awaken to an old self, those relationships become threatening and the fears begin. Such fears are inhibiting and likely to discourage older people from trying to extend themselves in new ways.

A significant role for life-span developmental interventions lies in the identification and countering of ageism, including the raising of consciousness about internalised age-related norms. When age-normative conceptions about the life course are shared by members of a given society they can be experienced as "natural" and, therefore, as largely inevitable and unchangeable. It is important always to look past the age variable to the individual beyond and to strive, in the words of one commentator, "to develop a society that encourages people to stop acting their age and start being themselves" (Ponzo, 1978, pp. 143–4).

Different views of the life course

Accounts of people's lives are not told merely as lists of incidents. They are woven together into a story (Cohler, 1982). Your lifeline can be thought of as a graphical representation of your life story, with the number of "ups and downs" indicating eventfulness, and the degree of slope representing the amount of dramatic tension (Gergen, 1988). The "plot" of this story can be represented in a number of ways, for example, as a series of turning points or transitions (Schlossberg, Waters, & Goodman, 1995), as a sequential pattern or series of stages (Erikson, 1980; Levinson, Darrow, Klein, Levinson, & McKee, 1978), or as the occupancy of an age-based series of culturally determined roles (Neugarten & Datan, 1973; Neugarten, Moore, & Lowe, 1965). The range of forms your lifeline could have taken represents alternative models of the life course.

A more formal definition of the life course would be, "the sequence of events and experiences in a life from birth until death, and the chain of personal states and encountered situations which influence, and are influenced by this sequence of events" (Runyan, 1978, p. 570). The danger of such an umbrella definition is that it can seem to be all things to all people. Indeed, life-span developmental psychology has been described as just that – as a, "motley and monolithic movement" in which, "everyone is invited to contribute his/her voice to the songfest without any restrictions on melody, lyrics and arrangements" (Kaplan, 1983, p. 193).

Box 1.4 Tenets of a life-span perspective (Baltes, 1987)

Development is:

- *A lifelong process*. Development is not restricted to childhood. Both quantitative and qualitative development can occur at all stages of the life course.
- *Multidimensional and multidirectional*. Development occurs in a number of different domains, at different rates, and in a number of directions.
- A process that *shows plasticity*. An individual's developmental course can, at least to some degree, be modified through life conditions and experience.
- A process *involving both gains and losses*. As well as involving growth and gain, development also involves coming to terms with decline and loss.
- An *interactive process*. Development is the outcome of interactions between individual and environment, both of which can influence its course.
- *Culturally and historically embedded*. Developmental rates and courses vary across different cultures and historical periods.
- A *multidisciplinary field of study*. Life-span development is not concerned merely with psychological factors. Biological, sociological, anthropological, and environmental factors can all interact with and influence individual development.

Adherents of a life-span perspective have risen to the challenge of such a barb by distinguishing different types of theoretical orientations to the life course. Key dimensions (several of them overlapping) on which theories vary include:

- the degree to which stages can be identified
- the origin of these stages within either the individual or the environment
- the extent to which stages are universal, or at least shared by people of a particular time and place
- a concern with the continuities and consistencies that characterise particular lives across time
- the extent to which life-span development is directed at a universal end-point
- the balance of emphasis between a concern with the process of development and the content of the life course

- a focus on the life course as a whole, on particular points or stages, or on the nature of the process of change.

The theories of life-span development discussed in this book can be located at different points on the above dimensions. Few theorists, however, are totally dismissive of opposing viewpoints – disagreements tend to focus on the *relative* importance of different factors, nature versus nurture, predetermined versus variable, continuity versus change, for example. Life-span developmental psychology is an inclusive discipline, characterised by a set of gradually emerging tenets (Baltes, 1987; Magnusson, 1989; Rutter, 1989) as summarised in Box 1.4 and discussed in the following section.

Tenets of a life-span perspective

In their 1980 landmark paper, Baltes et al. (1980) described the life-span approach as a general orientation to development rather than a particular theory. As such, it is characterised by a number of propositions. Although the number and emphasis of these assumptions is not fixed, Baltes et al. did identify four that had received what they described as "some primacy":

1. Development is a lifelong process.
2. Development is an expression of biological, socialisation, historical, and cultural processes.
3. Restricted and monolithic definitions of the nature of development are inappropriate.
4. Life-span developmental psychology offers a potentially integrative umbrella under which different aspects of development can be explored and understood.

These assumptions were later refined into seven tenets (Baltes, 1987), which are used as the framework for the following overview of what might be termed the life-span philosophy.

1. Development is a lifelong process

As should already be apparent, the life-span perspective assumes that the potential for development extends throughout life. It rejects the traditional assumption that childhood is the main, or only, period of growth and development. There is no assumption that the lifeline must reach a plateau and/or decline during adulthood and old age. Instead, it is assumed that there is, throughout the life course, the potential both for continuous growth (which is gradual, incremental, cumulative, and quantitative) and discontinuous development (which is rapid, innovative, substantial, and qualitative).

Life-span developmental psychology challenges the frequently implicit assumption of a growth–maintenance–decline model of development. To what extent did your own lifeline (see Activity 1.1) follow this pattern? Such a pattern, whilst generally applicable to biological and physical functioning, may not, it is suggested, be an appropriate model for the psychological, social, and spiritual realms. Development through change and adaptation continues throughout life (Datan, Rodeaver, & Hughes, 1987).

2. *Development is multidimensional and multidirectional*

To be concerned with the "whole person" is to attempt to grapple with, "something round, large, undifferentiated and thus difficult to manipulate, analyse, study or write about" (McCandless & Evans, 1973, p. 3). Distinguishing between different dimensions of development imposes some form and order (Loevinger, 1976) on what might otherwise appear an amorphous mass, and acknowledges that development does not necessarily advance simultaneously or in the same form on all fronts. In other words, development is both multidimensional and multidirectional.

Typically, distinction is made within developmental psychology between the physical, cognitive, personal, and social domains (Box 1.5), although other dimensions could be included, for example, spiritual development (Assagioli, 1986; Fowler, 1981; Wilber, 1979) or career development (Dalton, Thompson, & Price, 1977; Super, 1984, 1990). It is recognised, however, that these domains do not operate in isolation from each other. Thus, for example, "baby walkers", designed to promote independent mobility (physical development) in infants, can also, by giving the child some choice over where he or she goes, can encourage the development of a sense of control over one's environment (personal development). By the same token, concentration of efforts in one domain may restrict developments in another, as, for example, when the development of musical or athletic talent is at the expense of a broad range of social activities.

Box 1.5 Dimensions of human development (adapted from Rice, 1995)

- *Physical development.* Includes the physical growth of all components of the body and changes in motor development, the senses, and in bodily systems.
- *Cognitive development.* Includes all changes in the intellectual processes of thinking, learning, remembering, judging, problem solving, and communicating.
- *Personal development.* Includes the development of the concept of self; the development of attachment, trust, security, love, and affection; and the development a variety of emotions, feelings, and personality traits.
- *Social development.* Includes the development of interpersonal relationships with family members, peers, and other members of the community.

Other bases for distinguishing different developmental domains could be used. Thus, Schlossberg et al. (1995) distinguish between transitions experienced in three different areas of life: (1) internally; (2) in close interpersonal relationships; and (3) in relation to work or other areas of endeavour. Recurring issues in internal or intrapsychic transitions are those of identity, autonomy, and making meaning. For interpersonal transitions, recurring themes centre around intimacy, mattering, and belonging. With regard to the work arena, questions of work saliency (the centrality of work in people's lives), resilience (career adaptability), mastery (self-efficacy), and balance tend to predominate. Again, it must be accepted that such classifications are somewhat arbitrary and, also, that there is considerable overlap among the categories. Transitions in one area can have an impact both on other areas of the person's life and on the lives of those with whom he or she comes into contact.

Another possible approach centres on the different roles assumed by an individual across the life course. Thus, Super (1980, 1990) employs the notion of a "life-career rainbow" (Box 1.6) to represent a "total life space, total life span" view of the person. He distinguishes nine roles that together describe, "most of the life space of most people during the course of a lifetime" (Super, 1980, p. 283). At first the life space contains only one role, that of child; but it may later contain seven or eight, as when a person is pursuing an occupation; maintaining a home; being a spouse, a parent and the supporting child of ageing parents; engaging in civic activities; and following hobbies or further education. Everyone's life-career rainbow contains some universal, some unique, and some shared but not universal features. Other roles could be identified. Not everyone necessarily occupies all roles depicted in Box 1.6 and, furthermore, the sequencing of roles may vary.

Box 1.6 The life-career rainbow (Super, 1980)

Super's depiction of the life course is not unusual in invoking an image from the natural world – a rainbow (Figure 1.1). The arc reflects the life stages identified by Super – initially in relation to career choice and development – namely: growth, exploration, establishment, maintenance, and decline. It should be noted that this represents the traditional, but now challenged, growth–maintenance–decline model of the life course. Also note how Super places the life course in the context of situational and personal influences – in keeping with the interactional perspective on development and change.

Super (1980) considers more than mere occupancy of roles. He elaborates two further characteristics – emotional salience (how important a role is to us) and time demands (the proportion of our life spent in that role). These two characteristics need not vary in tandem. Thus, an unmotivated student might spend a lot of time in the student role but accord it low emotional

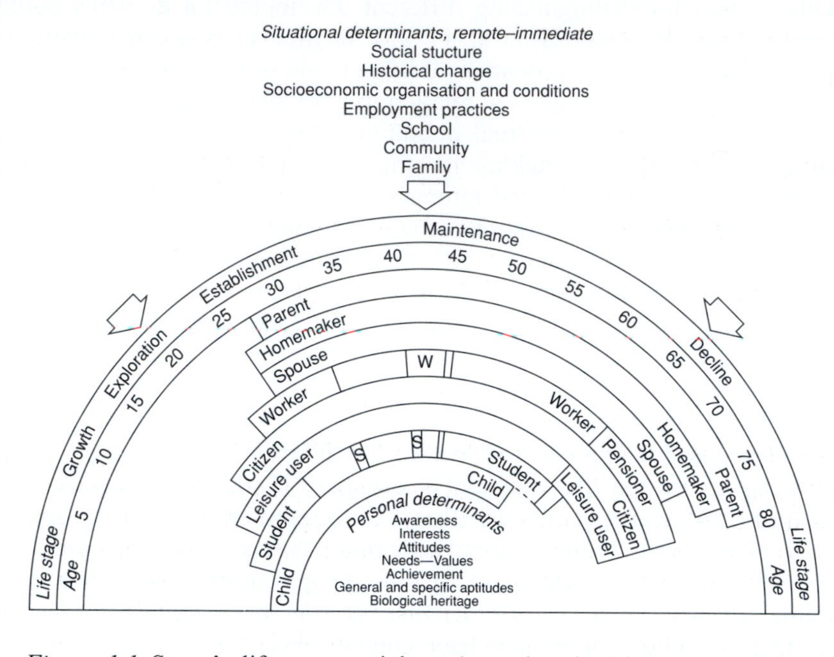

Figure 1.1 Super's life-career rainbow (reproduced with permission from Super, D.E. (1980). A life-span, life-space approach to career development. *Journal of Vocational Behavior, 16*, 282–298. Copyright © 1980 by Academic Press).

salience, whilst the non-resident parent in a divorced couple might spend only short amounts of time in the parent role but this time could be of great personal significance. Emotional saliency could be represented on the life-career rainbow by varying the depth of colour of the different bands, and time demands could be represented by varying the bandwidths.

As well as being multidimensional, developmental trajectories can also be multidirectional. This is something that is not incorporated into a life-career rainbow but is reflected in lifelines of differing shapes. It contradicts the notion that development always follows an "onwards and upwards" path and also links in with another tenet of the life-span perspective – that development involves managing losses as well as gains.

One reason why you might have found the earlier lifeline exercise hard is that it requires the integration of all the different developmental domains to produce some sort of global assessment. It might be more feasible, and more meaningful, to draw several lifelines, each representing a different developmental domain. This would allow the depiction of lines of differing shapes and degrees of incline. Points of interaction between different developmental domains could be identified (see Activity 1.5 and Box 1.7).

Activity 1.5 Return to the lifeline

- Following on from Activity 1.1, now draw a series of lifelines to distinguish between the different developmental domains – perhaps physical, cognitive, personal, and social.
- To what extent do these lifelines follow different paths?
- Try to identify points where something in one domain strongly influenced or was influenced by something in another domain. The information in Box 1.7 might help you to convey this.

Box 1.7 The interaction of different development domains

Rapoport and Rapoport (1980) used the image of a triple helix (Figure 1.2) to depict the intertwined nature of different developmental trajectories. Points where the different threads cross mark occasions where two developmental paths impact on each other. Rapoport and Rapoport distinguished between occupational, family, and leisure careers – an alternative might be the distinction between physical, cognitive, personal, and social development made by (for example) Rice (1995), or that between internal, interpersonal, and work transitions advocated by Schlossberg et al. (1995).

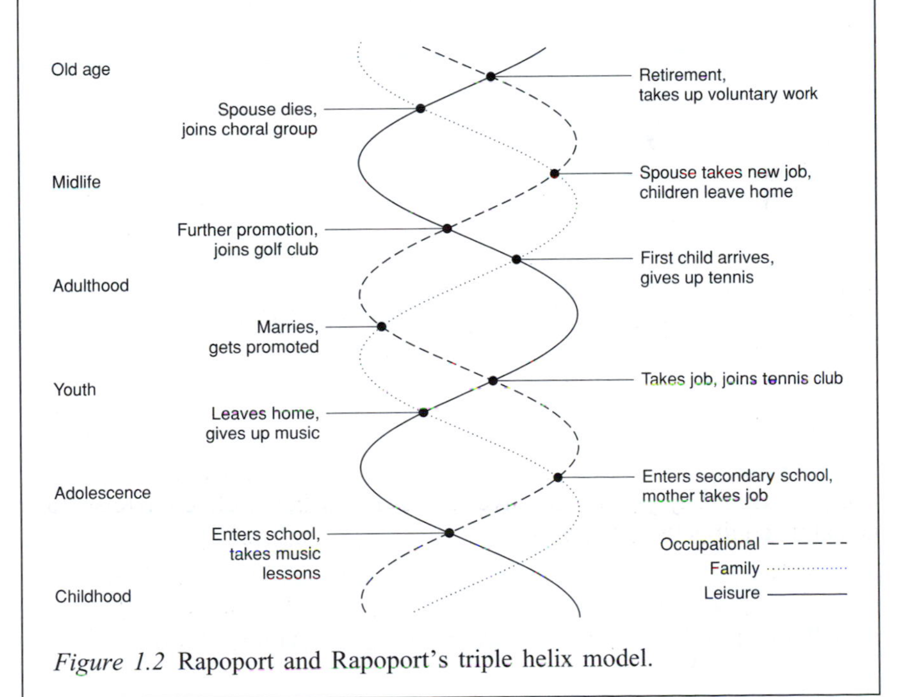

Figure 1.2 Rapoport and Rapoport's triple helix model.

3. Development shows plasticity

Plasticity refers to the modifiability of individual developmental trajectories. Not only is development multidimensional and multidirectional but its path may also, to a greater or lesser degree, be redirected by life conditions and experiences. Plasticity is distinguished from multidirectionality in that whereas the latter looks at potential individual differences, plasticity is concerned with the potential for directional change within an individual – the extent to which a developmental path can be altered once it has began. Thus, improved diet and an emotionally, intellectually and socially enriching environment can ameliorate much thwarted development in a child whose life has been characterised by multiple deprivations.

There will, however, be limits to plasticity within any particular developmental domain. Thus, some strands of development, for example, career development, will show greater potential plasticity than others, such as speech development. None the less, the emphasis on plasticity is both optimistic (we may be able to overcome or undo the effects of early problems) and cautionary (it warns against complacency because "living happily ever after" can never be assumed – we need continually to work at it).

4. Development involves both gains and losses

Development is not simply the cumulative amassing of ever more attributes and capacities. Rather, it is a joint expression of both growth (gain) and decline (loss) at all points in the life course. Thus, throughout early childhood a range of infantile reflexes and skills disappear – they have served their purpose and are replaced by other, more currently relevant faculties (Rutter & Rutter, 1993). Thus, for example, as infants grow, their body proportions change, facilitating the acquisition and refinement of walking and running skills but making it harder for them to suck their toes with ease. However, because such a skill is of doubtful long-term adaptive value, its disappearance would not usually be regretted as a loss. More generally, the process of decision making inevitably requires choosing between different options – if only between doing something and doing nothing – and, therefore, the loss of what pursuing other alternatives would have provided. Transitions – both positive and negative – almost inevitably involve severing links with aspects of our past, such that Schlossberg (1981) suggests it is generally preferable to think in terms of role exchange rather than role gain or loss. None the less, the balance between developmental gains and losses is not consistent across the life course (Baltes, 1987). Losses may become increasingly predominant relative to gains as we age because, for example, of social norms and decreases in biological and/or mental resources (Baltes & Baltes, 1990).

5. *Development is the outcome of interaction between the individual and the environment*

An informative metaphor of the life course is the image of a river that, whilst having a force and momentum of its own, is also shaped and modified by the terrain over and through which it flows. In turn, the river exerts its own influence on its surroundings. Indeed, it is somewhat artificial to separate the river from its habitat; a more accurate picture is obtained when they are considered as a single unit. Whilst it is similarly artificial to separate the individual from the context in which he or she is embedded, for ease and clarity of analysis they are often treated as separate entities and psychologists have traditionally focused their attention on only one or the other, that is, on either the person or their environment (Pervin & Lewis, 1978). This dichotomy between person and environment appears in a number of forms throughout developmental psychology (Lerner, 1976), underpinning, for example, debates between maturation and learning or between inherited and acquired characteristics. Whatever terms are used, the basic thrust of the issue remains the same. It is the question of nature versus nurture.

Whilst we can concentrate on either the person or the environment as the locus of the developmental imperative, we will gain a complete picture of life-span development only if we consider the interaction between the two. Psychology, with its traditional emphasis on the individual, has developed fewer tools for analysing environment contexts than for analysing the person (Kindermann & Valsiner, 1995). However, Bronfenbrenner (1977, 1979, 1992), drawing on the theories of Kurt Lewin, takes a broad and differentiated ecological view of the environment – a perspective that has also found acceptance in, for example, family process (Bronfenbrenner, 1986) and health psychology (Hancock & Perkins, 1985).

Defining the environment (Bronfenbrenner & Crouter, 1983, p. 359) as, "any event or condition outside the organism that is presumed to influence, or be influenced by, the person's development", Bronfenbrenner (1977, p. 514) depicts the environment hierarchically as, "a nested arrangement of structures, each contained within the next". At the broadest and most encompassing level of influence are the general cultural carriers of the values and priorities of a particular society (the macrosystem). The next system comprises the major institutions of a society (the exosystem), followed by the network of interacting personal systems of which the individual is a part (the mesosystem). At the most specific level of cultural or social influence are the interactions between individuals and their immediate physical and social environment (the microsystems). These relationships are shown diagrammatically and summarised more fully in Box 1.8. Activity 1.6 suggests you create a diagram of the environmental influences in your own life.

Rather than being seen as a static framework, Bronfenbrenner's model should be seen as a dynamic model in which the various elements vary

Box 1.8 Bronfenbrenner's nested model of the environment

Bronfenbrenner's model of the environment goes beyond the immediate situation or situations that contains the individual. It considers the relations within and between the different settings in which the individual operates, and also the larger social contexts, both formal and informal, in which such settings are embedded. The model can be presented diagrammatically, as shown in Figure 1.3.

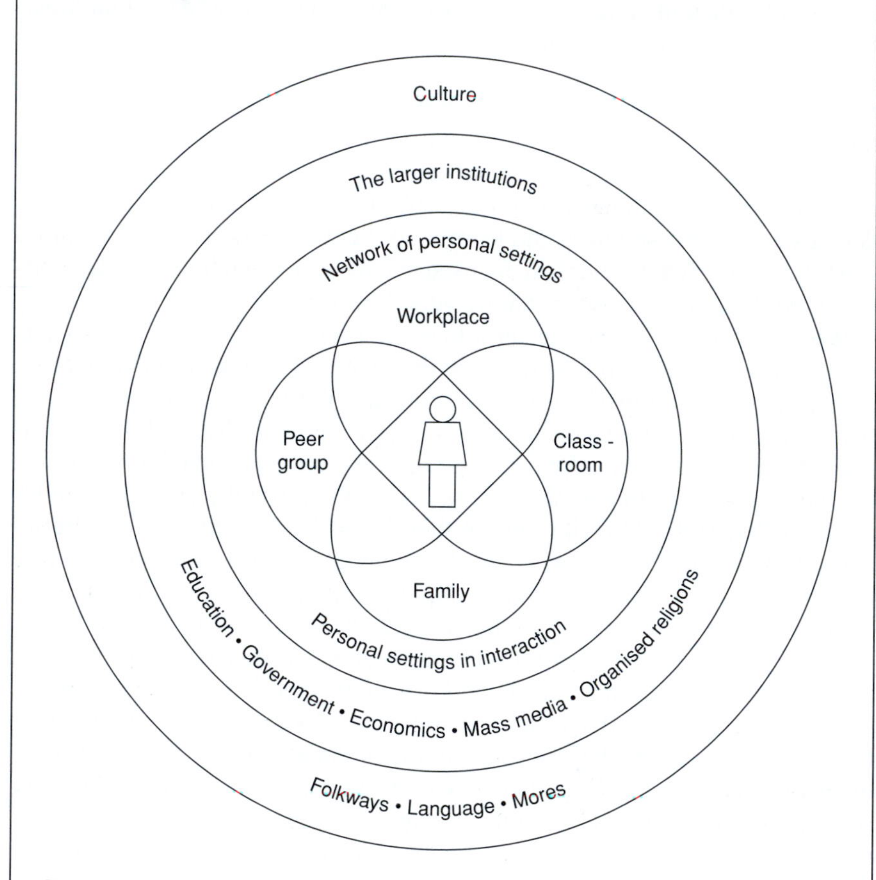

Figure 1.3 Diagrammatic representation of Bronfenbrenner's nested model of the environment (reproduced with permission from Egan, G.E., & Cowan, M.A. (1979). *People in systems: A model for development in the human service professions and education*. Monterey, CA: Brooks/Cole).

Employing terminology derived from Brim (1975), Bronfenbrenner distinguishes between four environmental systems located at different levels: microsystems, mesosystems, exosystems, and macrosystems:

- A microsystem is "the complex of relations between the developing person and environment in an immediate setting containing the person" (Bronfenbrenner, 1977, p. 514). The setting can be defined by a number of physical and personal elements: place (e.g. home, college, office), time, physical features, activities, participants, and roles. A primary setting for most of us is our family but, through the course of life, we move into and out of a range of different settings – peer group, classroom, and workplace are singled out in Egan and Cowan's diagram above.
- A mesosystem is the relationships within a collection of interacting microsystems, "the interrelations among major settings containing the person at a particular point in his or her life" (Bronfenbrenner, 1977, p. 514). Thus, home life and work life interact when a particular career (such as in the armed forces) results in a particular style of social life, or when considerations concerning a child's education influence whether or not a job offer in a new location is accepted or rejected.
- An exosystem is an influence system that contains microsystems, mesosystems and also specific social structures, both formal and informal, which impinge on or encompass the settings in which the person is found. "These structures include the major institutions of the society, both deliberately structured and spontaneously evolving, as they operate at the concrete level" (Bronfenbrenner, 1977, p. 515). Thus, we are not a part of the local public transport system (unless, let us say, we work for the district bus company), but the nature of that system influences the mesosystems and microsystems of which we are a part. Other exosystems include the labour market, government agencies, medical services, and the mass media.
- Macrosystems are the blueprints of micro-, meso-, and exosystems. They are "the overarching institutional patterns of the culture or subculture" (Bronfenbrenner, 1977, p. 515). Carriers of information and ideology, macrosystems are generally informal and implicit, but are made explicit through a society's recorded laws, regulations, and rules. A reflection of the values and priorities of a society, they include the principles of a society's economic, social, educational, legal, and political systems. Such manifestations of a society's culture are transmitted as norms and values through exo-, meso-, and microsystems to individuals, thereby influencing their thoughts, behaviours and opportunities.

Activity 1.6 Environmental forces

Read Box 1.8 and then draw a diagram similar to Figure 1.3 to map the environmental forces influencing your own life-span development.

in nature and significance across time and culture, and also in the course of an individual's life. Not only this, but the individual is also changing in ways that alter the meaning of the environment to him or her (Vygotsky, 1994). Environmental factors that had one meaning and played a certain role at a given age, can, over a period of time, begin to have a different meaning and to play a different role because the person has changed. Furthermore, the influence is reciprocal – the individual influences the environment as well as the environment influencing the individual. This awareness has facilitated a developing interest in exploring person–environment relations rather than exploring the person or the environment as separate entities (Lerner, 1995).

6. Development is culturally and historically embedded

The tenet that development is culturally and historically embedded follows from the proposition that development is the outcome of individual–environment interaction. This interaction can actuate changes in the individual, the environment, and the nature of their relationship. Social and cultural environments change over time, both as a result of specific events such as wars, geographic disasters, or economic recessions, which will be experienced by some generations but not by others, and also as a result of more incremental changes associated with industrialisation and postindustrialisation, such as technological developments and changing social trends. Baltes et al. (1980) refer to these as normative history-graded influences on development in that they have a strong relationship with historical time rather than chronological age. They give rise to the dubbing of eras as "the roaring 20s", "the swinging 60s" or "the caring 90s"; the "renaissance", "industrial", or "technological" age. They make the past an uncertain guide to the future.

Stewart and Healy (1989) suggest a model of how historical events might affect differentially those at different stages of individual development, thereby creating psychologically distinct cohorts. They propose that social historical events occurring during a person's childhood will influence the individual's background assumptions about life and the world, whilst those occurring during late adolescence will have an impact on conscious identity. Social historical events occurring during a person's adult years, it is suggested, will have less effect on a person's values or identity but will influence the opportunities available to them.

A focus on how influences on development change across cohorts or generations represents a longitudinal perspective on patterns of influence. Taking more of a cross-sectional stance leads to the recognition that human development varies across cultures, social class, racial, and ethnic groups. All societies rationalise the passage of life time by dividing it into socially relevant units that are expressed in normative age grade systems whereby particular duties, rights and rewards are distributed according to chronological age or life stage (Neugarten & Datan, 1973). Despite the increasing fluidity of life cycles (Hirschhorn, 1977) and age grade systems in developed Western societies, some roles, responsibilities, and obligations remain tied to chronological age, either legally (for example, eligibility to vote, drive a car, or serve on a jury) or through social convention and expectation.

Much knowledge of life-span psychological development is limited historically and culturally to studies of adults and children in twentieth century, Western societies. Within these societies it is the middle class, white males who were first examined most thoroughly and taken as the norm against which other groups were compared. Acceptance of the historical and cultural embeddedness of much development implies caution when transferring concepts of development from one cultural group to another.

7. Life-span development is a multidisciplinary field of study

The adoption of a life-span perspective implies recognising the contribution of many academic disciplines. Psychological development needs to be seen as resulting from the impact of a number of different influence systems, each with associated fields of study. Table 1.1 details some of the most important of these disciplines, along with their major, although not necessarily sole, focus and the kinds of questions they typically raise about human development. They can, following Bronfenbrenner's model (see Box 1.8), be ordered roughly according to their proximity to the individual and, except for biology, be seen as directed at the micro-, meso-, exo- or macrosystem level. This list is not complete, however. Thus, many journalistic or literary texts and poems address questions of human development. Many, if not most, life-span psychologists adopt a broader perspective than the traditional focus indicated in Table 1.1, venturing into the other areas listed in this table and directing analysis at different levels in Bronfenbrenner's nested arrangement of influence systems. In sum, the above tenets can be described as an inclusive philosophy of "both/and" rather than "either/or". Together, they form what Baltes (1987, p. 612) refers to as a "family of perspectives" that, "together specify a coherent metatheoretical view on the nature of development". Taken separately, none of the tenets listed in Box 1.6 is unique to the life-span orientation. Their significance lies in the overall pattern, ethos, or world view that they give rise to.

Whilst all life stages are of relevance to life-span developmental psychology, there are two topics that have been especially important in the generation of a developmental psychology that covers the total life-span – first, the study of the midlife period, and second, the framework from which the experiences of old age are viewed. Both are, therefore, considered in more detail in the next two sections, although the emphasis in each section is rather different. Whilst the discussion of the midlife

Table 1.1 The contribution of different disciplines to the study of human development (adapted from Sigelman & Shaffer, 1995)

Discipline	*Major focus*	*Sample questions of interest*
Anthropology	Macrosystem: the effects of culture on development	How much do cultural practices such as child rearing methods or care for the frail elderly differ across societies, and what are the implications? Are there aspects of development that are universal, or evident in all known cultures?
History	Exo-, meso-, or microsystem: changes in human development over the centuries	What has it been like to be a child or an elderly person in different historical periods? How is the family of today different from the family of the nineteenth century? How do major historical events affect people's lives?
Sociology	Exosystem: the nature of society and the individual's relationship to society	What does society expect of us at different ages? What roles do we play in the larger social system as we progress through life? How are we affected by social institutions and changes in these institutions?
Social psychology	Meso- or micro-system: develop-ment within its family and societal context	What is the nature of the family as an institution? How do family relationships contribute to the individual's development and adjustment?
Psychology	Microsystem: the functioning of the individual	How do mental abilities, personality traits, and social skills typically change with age? How stable or changeable are each individual's qualities, and why?
Biology	The growth and ageing of cells and organs (not included- in Bronfenbrenner's model)	How does one fertilised egg become a fully developed human being? How does the functioning of human organs change as we age?

period gives most attention to *what* happens during this phase, the discussion of old age is primarily concerned with our *interpretation* of what happens. This reflects, on the one hand, our previous ignorance about the tasks of midlife, and, on the other hand, narrow and ageist assumptions concerning the nature of old age.

Perspectives on midlife

I imagine that most of you have been asked over the years, "What are you going to be when you grow up?" I wonder if you yet know the answer. I wonder if any of us ever knows the answer. Similarly, I expect many of you have heard, or indeed made, comments about what a particular older person "used to be" or "used to do" – generally a reference to their paid occupation. Implicit in such questions and comments is the notion of adulthood as a plateau – a period of relative equilibrium and uneventfulness. It also reflects the stereotype of adulthood as the pinnacle of development, preceded by childhood – a period of preparation or apprenticeship – and followed by old age – a period of descent from this height.

Despite both this privileging of adulthood as the high point of development and the fact that adulthood is the longest phase of the life course, it has, until the last few decades, been the phase least researched by psychologists. In 1978 Levinson et al. were still able to describe adulthood as, "one of the best kept secrets in our society, and probably in history generally" (p. ix). Since that time, however, it has become the focus of academic, media, and popular attention. In retrospect it can be seen that Jaques' (1965) paper was perhaps a landmark, coining the phrase "midlife crisis" – a concept that has since found its way into an alternative stereotype of the middle years. Central to the concept of the midlife crisis is the sense of actual or impending loss – of health and vigour, of professional status, of the parental role, of life itself. However, there is evidence that it is only a minority of people who experience serious psychological problems during midlife (Chiriboga, 1989; McCrae & Costa, 1984). Change there may be, but this is often experienced as a challenge rather than a crisis. The "empty nest" stage of life – when children leave the family home – may be looked forward to with eager anticipation rather than dread (Lowenthal & Chiriboga, 1972) as a time conferring greater personal freedom and the opportunity to share more time and activities with one's partner. Far from being perceived as narrowing, a person's interests and activities in contemporary Western societies may broaden and branch out at this time (Maas, 1989), in particular allowing for an expansion of involvement in community-based and socially responsible activities. The slip in the logic of the midlife crisis concept is to equate "change" with "crisis" – a conflation that "seems to either inflate the importance of the former concept or weaken the latter" (Chiriboga, 1989, p. 117). It is better to think of midlife as a potential psychological turning point, defined by Wethington, Cooper, and Holmes (1997, p. 217) as, "a period or point in time in which a person has undergone a major transformation in views about the self, commitments to important relationships, or involvement in significant life roles".

Even the picture of the midlife as a period of challenge and change (rather than crisis) may, however, be an exaggeration. To be defined as a turning point (Wethington et al., 1997), there needs to have been both a fundamental shift in the meaning, purpose, or direction of a person's life and also a self-reflective awareness of, or insight into, the significance of the change. Not all experiences of midlife meet these criteria and it may be that, "continuities of love, relationships, family commitments, work involvements, and personality patterns often seem more salient than any changes that occur" (Berger, 1994, p. 559). If the midlife is not to be depicted as either a plateau or a crisis, then a pivot might be a more appropriate image: the person balances, as it were, on the fulcrum of a see-saw, which may tip either way (towards decline or towards continued growth) or, alternatively, maintain its somewhat precarious equilibrium. This is the image of the midlife period that fits best within the framework of a life-span developmental psychology.

Perspectives on old age

Consistent with the view of old age as a period of descent from the peak of midlife – being "over the hill", we might say – is disengagement theory (Cumming, 1975; Cumming & Henry, 1961), in its time a very influential model. It developed out of the Kansas City Studies of Adult Life that had been launched at the University of Chicago in the mid-1950s. In the end, more that 700 subjects were studied. They were described as "stereotypical" American adults (that is, white, middle-class men and women between 40 and 90 years of age) living in a "typical" American city (Kansas, Missouri). Subjects were followed up for a period of 6 years, thus providing cross-sectional and some limited longitudinal data. Disengagement theory rests on two strands of data – one relating to changes in people's "personality" (that is, to a person's internal world) as they age, and the other to people's interaction with their environment. First, the researchers observed increasing interiority with age. As people aged they seemed to lose interest in the outside world and become more preoccupied with themselves. The second key finding prompting the development of disengagement was that by their mid-sixties the number of roles people occupied had decreased dramatically. Month by month people spent more time alone and had ever decreasing contact with other people.

From these findings Cumming and Henry (1961) concluded, first, that in old age a gradual process of disengagement occurs, and, second, that this disengagement is universal, normal and natural – the "right way" to age. A subsequent reformulation of the theory (Cumming, 1975) proposed three elements:

- shrinkage of the life space – a decrease, as we age, in both the number of roles occupied and the number of people with whom we interact
- increased individuality – a decrease in the degree to which remaining roles and relationships are governed by strict rules or expectations
- active initiation and acceptance of these changes.

However, whilst a shrinking of the life space might reflect the reality of many older people's lives, even in the original sample on which disengagement theory is based, not all older people were disengaged (Hochschild, 1975, 1976) – 22 per cent of those between the ages of 70 and 74 had "a large number of roles", over one-third had "high daily interaction with others" and nearly one-fifth had a "large lifespace". These people, however, were not described by Cumming and Henry as "engaged" but as "unsuccessful disengagers". Similarly, the finding that a number of women in their 60s had a larger lifespace than many women in their 50s was explained by the latter being "off time" (that is, early) rather than "on time" disengagers. Such interpretations have the effect of rendering disengagement theory unfalsifiable (Hochschild, 1976).

It is also possible that such social and psychological disengagement as does take place is not triggered internally but is the consequence of role loss stipulated by the rules of the institutions in which the older people participate (Crawford, 1971, 1972; Hochschild, 1975, 1976). Retirement may precipitate social and psychological disengagement (Rose & Peterson, 1965) as a result of economic loss and/or loss of employment-related associations.

Disengagement may not, therefore, be intrinsic, inevitable, or universal. What is even more controversial, however, is the value judgement that such disengagement as does occur is not only statistically normal but also desirable and "healthy". Such a stance lends the stamp of legitimacy to social policies that separate the older person from the rest of society.

In opposition to the notion of disengagement stands activity theory. The activity theory of successful ageing is associated primarily with Robert Havighurst (1963; Havighurst, Neugarten, & Tobin, 1968), but emerged almost immediately Cumming and Henry published their theory (Maddox & Eisdorfer, 1962). It proposed that maximum life satisfaction in old age is achieved when people are able to maintain into old age the activity patterns and values that typify the middle years. If relationships, activities, or roles of middle age are lost, activity theory advocates that they be replaced with new ones. This is the opposite of Cumming and Henry's (1961) position. Older people are, therefore, encouraged by activity theory to deny the onset of old age and, by disengagement theory, to embrace the restrictions of their life space that old age frequently brings.

Although activity theory encourages social policies that promote older people's involvement in society, it has been criticised as unrealistic (Bond, Briggs, & Coleman, 1993) in its implicit assumption that the maintenance of activity associated with middle age is a feasible option for all, or even the majority, given the biological changes that accompany ageing. Furthermore, the economic, political, legislative, and social structure of society excludes older people from many significant roles, again making maintenance of an activity level associated with the middle years potentially problematic.

Both disengagement theory and activity theory can be criticised for neglecting the meaning of the disengagement or activity to the person concerned. Neugarten (1968) found that continuity of both level and type of activity was associated with high life satisfaction in old age. It could be that two individuals with identical "role counts" apply different meanings to these roles and to any disengagement from them (Hochschild, 1976). The continuity explanation of ageing argues that individuals who disengaged from active social roles and the complexities of everyday life would experience low levels of life satisfaction if they had been socially active in earlier years but not necessarily if they had, by choice, not been socially active at any point in their lives (Dreyer, 1989).

The notion of continuity can be applied to a person's internal sense of themselves as well as to their external role involvement (Atchley, 1989, 1999) – a point discussed in more detail in Chapter 7. From this perspective, optimal ageing comprises the ability to maintain at least a degree of continuity in both external roles and settings and, more importantly, in the inner sense of self and identity. The sense of self can be resilient even in the face of substantial changes in the details of everyday life. The mechanism by which this is achieved, and its role in retaining a sense of life satisfaction, is suggested in the description of successful ageing as involving selective optimisation with compensation. It is an approach that rejects the importance of disengagement or activity *per se* in favour of a focus on the meaning of such processes to the individuals concerned.

Selective optimisation with compensation describes a model of successful ageing that reflects a dynamic interplay between developmental gains and losses and between continuing developmental potential and age-related limitations (Marsiske, Lang, Baltes, & Baltes, 1995). The model, developed by Baltes and Baltes (1980, 1990; Baltes, 1993), describes a general process of adaptation that pertains throughout the life course, but which takes on particular significance during old age.

The first element, selection, refers people's decisions to concentrate their energies on life domains that are of high priority. Such selective investment of resources increases the likelihood of people achieving intended outcomes by their own activity. Environmental demands, personal skills, motivations, and biological capacity will all influence such decisions and, whilst selection implies a reduction in the number of domains in which the individual operates, it does not preclude the adoption of new or transformed domains or the formulation of new life goals. Such selection takes place at all points of decision making – to follow one path inevitably means to turn one's back on other routes.

Optimisation, the second element in the model, refers to the mechanisms and strategies – such as time, effort, and skill – that people use to enhance and enrich their potential and functioning in selected domains.

The third element, compensation, becomes operative when specific capacities are lost or become insufficient for adequate functioning. Failure and losses can be compensated for by investing more external resources in achieving the goal, or by disengaging from the goal and reinterpreting the failure in a self-protective way (Heckhausen & Schultz, 1993, 1995). Psychological compensation might include, for example, the use of new mnemonic strategies to overcome problems of failing memory. The use of hearing aids would, by contrast, be an example of compensation by means of technology. Baltes and Baltes (1990) cite an example of selective optimisation with compensation given by the pianist, Artur Rubinstein, in a television interview. Rubinstein commented on how he conquered weaknesses of ageing in his piano playing by, first, reducing his repertoire and playing a smaller number of pieces (selection); second, practising these pieces more often (optimisation), and third, slowing down his speed of playing prior to fast movements, thereby producing a contrast that enhances the impression of speed in the fast movements (compensation).

Whilst gerontologists have long challenged the decline view of ageing, their work has frequently not been placed in the context of the total life span. The selective optimisation with compensation model is, however, applicable to all life stages. Career specialisation is an example of selection, generally during early or middle adulthood, in order to optimise the chances of career success and advancement. Selection and optimisation do, none the less, have a price. The individual will, through the selection of a particular career path, have closed off other potentially rewarding avenues – like all "developments", career specialisation involves losses as well as gains, although it may be possible to compensate for this by subsequently changing careers or by developing leisure interests in different fields. Despite its applicability to all life stages, the selective optimisation with compensation model is particularly applicable to old age. This is because, first, in old age the relative balance between losses and gains tips towards losses, and, second, because with age the absolute level of physical, psychological and/or social resources available to the individual is likely to decrease (Baltes & Baltes, 1990). For both of these reasons the need for selective optimisation with compensation is likely to increase as we become older.

With the surge of interest in adulthood as a life stage has come the recognition that development is not complete by the end of childhood or adolescence. Adding to this the view of old age as, at least potentially, a period of gain as well as loss, has led to a developmental psychology that includes the whole of the life course. Adopting a life-span perspective encourages the development of theory and research that goes beyond the psychology of particular age groups and offer instead "metamodels" and "metaconcepts" that embrace multiple life stages and events.

Organisation of the present book

The present chapter has sought to introduce readers to the life-span orientation to development and to draw attention to some of the key issues that emerge from adopting this perspective. Chapter 2 addresses some of the issues surrounding data collection that impinge not only on studies of life-span development but on all psychological research. As will be clear from the contents page, the organisation of the present book moves away from the usual age or life stage approach. This is an attempt to avoid emphasising, perhaps unwittingly, the ordered and predictable aspects of the life course. None the less, the first part of Chapter 3 briefly reviews, as a backdrop to the remainder of the book, the main characteristics of eight age stages from infancy to late-late adulthood. The second part of Chapter 3 introduces a range of metamodels for conceptualising the life course that focus on the role of change, consistency or chaos. The central section of the book (Chapters 4 to 7) covers these metamodels in more detail. Chapter 4 deals with cumulative sequences, in particular, the work of Erikson (1980) and McAdams (1997); Chapter 5 with developmental tasks especially as identified by Havighurst (1972), Levinson et al. (1978), and Gould (1978); Chapter 6 with transitions and life events, notably the work of Hopson, Scally, and Stafford (1988), and Schlossberg et al. (1995); and Chapter 7 with dynamic continuity, as discussed by Atchley (1989) and achieved through the process of narrative construction. Undoubtedly, the material could have been organised differently but hopefully the approach adopted makes sense and will sensitise readers to key aspects of a range of theories and models of the life course. The book concludes with a chapter concerned with intervention. It seeks, first, to throw light on some of the key parameters and assumptions inherent in different approaches to life-span interventions, and, second, to raise some important issues concerning the practice and skills of intervention.

2 Collecting data about lives

> As the method of study moves away from the experimental, hypothesis-testing mode and toward the exploratory mode, a corresponding transformation in the posture of the investigator may be seen, from arrogance to humility. With increased interdisciplinarity characterizing the study of the life span, the field has come to embrace as complementary methodologies that were once viewed as mutually exclusive.
>
> (Datan et al., 1987)

Life-span developmental psychology is an empirical field of enquiry, albeit based on a pre-existing (if sometimes implicit) set of assumptions or tenets. To discover how and why people do or do not change and develop we must learn about their lives. Delineating the characteristics and developmental tasks of different life stages can suggest developmental problems or issues that may occur at particular points in the life course (Rodgers, 1984) and can provide what Thomas (1990) describes as a "head-start" for practitioners working with clients of a particular age group, "the data furnish some initial expectations or probabilities which then can be confirmed, revised, or rejected" (Thomas, 1990, p. 17). In sum, a main purpose of research in life-span developmental psychology is to develop and advance a body of knowledge that will guide professional practice (DePoy & Gitlin, 1998).

In keeping with the broad and inclusive scope of life-span developmental psychology, many and varied strategies are employed for collecting and analysing data about the life course. The present chapter reviews the "hows", the "whens" and the "how wells" of this data collection. How to collect data is considered in the section on methods; the questions of when to collect it, and from whom, are discussed under the headings of research design and sampling; and the issue of assessing the quality of this data is discussed under evaluation. Finally, reference is made to the discussion of ethical principles drawn up by the British Psychological Society to direct the conduct of research with human participants.

You will not find in this chapter the same type of self-reflective activities as were included in Chapter 1. It would be well, however, to remember the principles and alternative modes of inquiry outlined in the following pages when reading empirical research on life-span development or, indeed, when conducting your own studies.

Methods

To fulfil the goals of life-span developmental psychology, life-span researchers call upon a range of methodologies involving observations (both naturalistic and manipulated) and/or self-reports by participants (including interviews, questionnaires, and inventories). Studies may vary in scope from large-scale quantitative surveys to in-depth case studies of perhaps only one person. The nature of the researcher–participant relationship may vary from one where the subject is a passive (and perhaps even unknowing) provider of data, to one of shared power and co-operation with an emphasis on the participants' construction and reconstruction of their life story rather than what might be considered a more objective account of what happened (Datan et al., 1987). In keeping with its multidisciplinary orientation, research on life-span development also makes use of data from sources less frequently tapped by psychologists, including autobiography, storytelling, diaries, literature, and fiction (Datan et al., 1987). Each method has its associated strengths and limitations and is appropriate for different research questions.

Observational methods

Observation can take place under conditions that range from naturalistic to highly manipulative. Thus, children may be observed in their homes and schools, or may be brought into laboratories where they can be observed under more controlled conditions.

With naturalistic observation the researcher seeks to understand real lives-in-context, influencing the subjects' behaviour as little as possible and getting as close as possible to how the subject would behave if the researcher were not there at all. "Fly-on-the-wall" television documentaries espouse a similar goal – although it is always difficult to be sure whether the participants are, perhaps unwittingly, playing to the camera (or, indeed, the researcher). With both naturalistic observations and television documentaries there is the need to be selective. The behaviour of interest to researchers is likely to be embedded amongst a great deal of other behaviour, and they may confront difficult problems of deciding what to observe and record, and of how to interpret the findings. Similarly, television programme makers may have to create a 45-minute programme from hours of material recorded over many weeks. Specific methods of naturalistic observation (Wright, 1960) include:

- *Diary description* – that is, the making of fairly regular (often daily or weekly) descriptions of particular behaviours. Thus, the speech of a young child may be observed on a weekly basis in order to monitor increasing vocabulary and use of grammatical rules.
- *Specimen description* – the compiling of detailed descriptions of sequences of behaviour that are as comprehensive as possible rather than focusing selectively on particular aspects of behaviour. Thus, the use made of a particular piece of playground equipment during breaktime at a primary school may be videotaped for later analysis.
- *Time sampling* – observing behaviours intermittently during short but regular periods of time. For example, the behaviour of a school child may be observed for 30 seconds every half-hour.
- *Event sampling* – recording specific behaviours during the observational time whilst other behaviours are ignored. Thus, a researcher might only record examples of antisocial behaviour.

Time and event sampling are often used together (Lefrancois, 1996), with time sampling specifying when observations are to be made and event sampling specifying what is to be observed.

Because of the concern not to influence the situation (or at least to minimise the degree of influence), naturalistic observation cannot provide data on how things might be different under different circumstances. Furthermore, naturalistic observation is an inefficient way of collecting data about events that occur only rarely in the participants' natural environment. Much observational data is, therefore, collected not in naturalistic, but in simulated situations (Wilkinson, 1995) in laboratory settings. This gives the researcher increased control over the situation – some variables are systematically manipulated whilst others are held constant in order to investigate how they influence each other. Control is, however, achieved at the cost of ecological validity, that is, of connection with life outside the laboratory. To know how people behave in an experimental laboratory does not necessarily help us understand how they will behave when embedded in "real life" microsystems and mesosystems (Bronfenbrenner, 1977). Many developmental processes involve multifaceted, reciprocal influences that cannot be reproduced artificially. Furthermore, observation in both naturalistic and simulated situations also conflicts with the notion of involving research participants as active co-researchers rather than as passive providers of data. Methods of data collection involving self-report are capable of affording participants a more active and influential role in the research.

Self-report methods

Observational research, by definition, focuses on overt, observable behaviour. It cannot provide data about internal cognitive or emotional processes, nor about behaviour occurring in the researcher's absence. For this, some sort of self-report is required. The main methods of self-report are interviews, questionnaires and standardised inventories.

Interviews

Interviews (see, for example, Breakwell, 1995) generally involve face-to-face conversation between researcher and participant, although telephone interviews are possible and e-mail conversations can be thought of as midway between an interview and a written survey. Interviews can be highly structured, with all respondents answering the same series of predetermined questions, or very open-ended, with participant and researcher freely discussing a number of broadly defined questions or topics. A main advantage of interviews is the opportunity that they provide to obtain detailed and personal information. Misunderstandings on the part of both interviewee and interviewer can be sorted out and, through the use of follow-up discussion, topics can be explored in depth, taking advantage of the particular perspective of each interviewee. Unstructured or semi-structured interviews are particularly appropriate for exploratory research, where the goal is to understand the world from the interviewee's perspective, also enabling interviewees to play a more active role in shaping the direction of the research. Box 2.1 describes Levinson et al.'s use of such a strategy.

Box 2.1 Levinson et al.'s (1978) biographical interviewing

Daniel Levinson and his colleagues at Yale University (Levinson et al., 1978) collected data for their study of what it means to be an adult primarily through the use of what they termed "biographical interviewing".

Biographical interviewing is an approach to interviewing that aims to combine aspects of the research and the clinical interview. Although certain topics have to be covered, the interviewer is sensitive to the feelings expressed by interviewees and attempts to explore themes in ways that have meaning for each participant – following rather than leading. Whilst both interviewer and participant have a defined role, with the constraints that this implies, the relationship between them is one of equality, both being able to comment on the research, and the interviewer as well as the participant being able to respond on the basis of their own personal experiences:

> What is involved is not simply an interviewing technique or procedure, but a relationship of some intimacy, intensity and duration. Significant work is involved in forming, maintaining and terminating

> the relationship. The recruiting of participants, the negotiation of a research contract, and the course of the interviewing relationship are phases within a single, complex process. Understanding and managing this process is a crucial part of our research method. Managed with sensitivity and discretion, it is a valuable learning experience for the participant as well as the researcher. Although therapy was not a primary aim, the interviews may have had some therapeutic effects. Virtually all of the men [all Levinson et al.'s subjects were male], we believe, found this a worthwhile undertaking.
>
> (Levinson et al., 1978, p. 15)

Each man in Levinson et al.'s study was seen between five and ten times over a period of 2 or 3 months, with most interviews lasting between 1 and 2 hours. All interviews were tape-recorded and subsequently transcribed. This yielded an average of 300 pages of transcript for each participant.

Interviews do have some disadvantages. They are expensive and time consuming to conduct, and can, as with Levinson et al.'s study, yield vast amounts of data that is not necessarily easy to analyse. There are, however, increasingly sophisticated techniques, including computer-assisted procedures, available for the analysis of interviews and other forms of qualitative data (see, for example, Denzin & Lincoln, 1994). Nonetheless, the quality of the data is highly dependent on the skill of the interviewer and on the motivation of the interviewee.

Questionnaires

With questionnaires (see, for example, Fife-Schaw, 1995) respondents are asked for written answers to a set of predetermined questions. The questions may be highly structured (with a number of prescribed responses from which the respondent chooses), highly unstructured (with the respondent being asked for a series of essay-type answers), anything in between, or a combination of different types of question. Questionnaires are cheaper and easier to administer than interviews, and analysis, especially of structured questionnaires, is also more straightforward. However, poorly designed questionnaires, with ambiguous, overlapping, or irrelevant questions, or where important topics have been omitted, will yield only poor quality data. They require careful design and piloting (see, for example, Oppenheim, 1992; Sudman & Bradburn, 1982).

Standardised inventories

Standardised inventories (see, for example, Hammond, 1995) are questionnaires designed to measure a range of psychological constructs such as intelligence and personality, and are used for research and diagnostic purposes. Their use means that researchers do not have to develop all their research instruments from scratch and they allow different researchers to compare their findings. To be useful, however, standardised inventories need to be valid and reliable and to have been developed with appropriate comparison groups.

Triangulation

All methods of data collection have their associated advantages and disadvantages. To capitalise on the former, and compensate for the latter, many research studies employ a range of methods. Using multiple measures of the same variable increases the researcher's confidence that the data reflects the phenomenon under study, rather than being an artefact of the method of data collection. Thus, both quantitative and qualitative data can be collected. Self-reports can be supplemented by observer ratings. Case studies can be selected from within a wider survey, to give depth as well as breadth.

This use of varied types of data concerning the same issue is one example of what has come to be known as triangulation (Denzin, 1978; Smith & Klein, 1986). The term is taken from land surveying (Janesick, 1994), where three points (as in a triangle) are used to locate oneself at particular locations, and radio triangulation (Lincoln & Guba, 1985), whereby directional antennae set up at the two ends of a known baseline are used to identify the point of origin of a radio transmission. Denzin (1978), in a text on sociological methods, identified four basic types of triangulation, to which Janesick (1994) adds a fifth:

- *Source triangulation* – that is, the use of a variety of data sources. Brewin, Andrews, and Gotlib (1993) discuss this as a way of addressing the question of the accuracy of retrospective reports of childhood experience – the issue at the heart of the "recovered" versus "false" memory debate with regard to recollections of childhood sexual abuse. From a review of a range of studies, Brewin et al. (1993) conclude that whilst recollections of childhood experience may be subject to error, their unreliability has been exaggerated. The authors recommend that, where possible, accounts by people about their early experience are supplemented by accounts from other family members and from independent observers. Brewin et al. (1993) report the consistent finding that parents tend to give more positive accounts of their children's early life than do the children themselves, siblings, or independent observers.
- *Investigator triangulation* – namely, the use of several different researchers. Seven people contributed, at various times, to the research team from which Levinson's theory of adult development (reviewed in Chapter 5) emerged, with four of them contributing to the book *The*

season's of a man's life (Levinson et al., 1978). "The research project was a cooperative one. As in all collaborations, it is difficult to sort out the distinctive contributions of all individual members. The five of us feel part of a collective process that yielded a common product" (Levinson et al., 1978, p. xi).

- *Methodological triangulation* – the use of multiple methods to study a single problem. Thus, McAdams' (1997) theory of identity as a personal narrative (discussed in Chapters 4 and 7) emerged primarily out of interviews with "real people, living and describing real lives" (McAdams, 1997, p. 15), but also drew on data from standardised inventories (for example, the Bem Sex-Role Inventory [BSRI]) and projective techniques (including the Thematic Apperception Test [TAT]).
- *Theory triangulation* – the use of multiple perspectives to interpret a single set of data. Schlossberg et al. (1995) review how theorists of the life course have adopted different, albeit overlapping, perspectives on adult development by choosing to emphasise context, maturation, life events, or individual–environmental transactions. Whilst each offers insight into aspects of life-span development, Schlossberg et al. prefer the transactional or, as they term it, the transitional stance and present a model of coping with transitions that is reviewed in Chapter 6.
- *Interdisciplinary triangulation* – the use of sources, investigators, theories, and methods from other disciplines. This facilitates the development of a more complete picture of the phenomenon under investigation, helps to avoid blind spots or tunnel vision, and can enhance creativity and insight. Table 1.1 gives an indication of the wide range of disciplines contributing to our understanding of development across the life-span. Even within disciplines, however, variation in theoretical stance can be valuable – Levinson, for example, pays particular credit to a team member who was of a different disciplinary background to the majority (Levinson et al., 1978).

Triangulation gives researchers and users of research greater confidence in the findings. It is a way of monitoring the validity or trustworthiness of the research. It facilitates the generation of credible research findings.

Research design

As well as choosing *how* to collect data (that is, the research method), researchers must also decide *when* to collect it. This is the question of research design (see Figures 2.1 and 2.2 for a summary of the options to be considered below). Longitudinal and cross-sectional studies are the most frequently employed strategies in developmental research and are represented as, respectively, the columns and rows in the matrix in Figure 2.1. A third design, time-lag studies, is represented by diagonals across this matrix from bottom left to top right. Each design has limitations that can

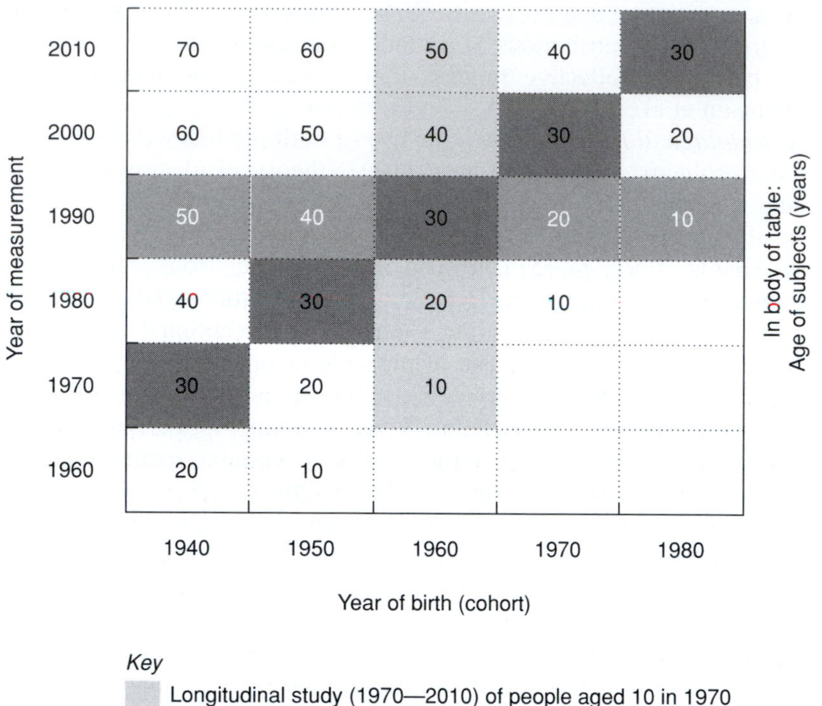

Figure 2.1 Longitudinal, cross-sectional and time-lag research designs.

be mitigated by more comprehensive sequential designs (Schaie, 1965, 1986), as shown in Figure 2.2 on page 41.

Longitudinal research

Perhaps the most obvious research design for developmental psychology is the longitudinal study. A group of subjects is followed over time, with particular emphasis on any changes in the characteristic under investigation. Caution must be exercised, however, before interpreting any changes that are found. Longitudinal research identifies age-related changes for any particular cohort (Nunnally, 1973) but we cannot assume these to be universal across generations or cultures. Time of measurement must also be taken into account. Suppose we had, in 1960, begun a longitudinal study of the career patterns of a group of 20-year-olds. Further suppose that some 30 years later, when the subjects were in their early 50s, we found that the incidence of redundancy and the average time taken to secure a new job had both increased. It would be naive to suppose that this could be accounted for entirely by reference to changes on the part of the individual. At the very least, prevailing economic conditions and national levels of unemployment in the 1960s and the 1990s would need to be considered. So too would social attitudes towards "the unemployed" and towards middle-aged as opposed to young employees.

There are other problems with longitudinal research. We need, for example, to consider the effect that prolonged participation in the research may have on the research subjects. If people are regularly asked about their career plans throughout adulthood then we might reasonably expect this to influence the extent and manner in which they think about their work. Also, at the theoretical level, we might find that advances in the topic under investigation make our original theoretical perspective or criteria for subject selection seem inadequate or outmoded. Vaillant (1977) spoke of the unforgivable omission of women from the longitudinal study of Harvard University graduates that he joined some decades after its inception. Haan (1972) described how data collected earlier in the study with which she worked needed to be re-evaluated in the light of later theoretical developments.

Another problem with longitudinal research is subject attrition. It is almost inevitable that during the course of a study lasting some considerable period of time, a proportion of participants will disappear – they might move home and be impossible to trace, they might die, or they might refuse to continue participating in the study. Those who do continue might not be representative of the total. At the more practical level, there can be difficulties in securing funding for lengthy longitudinal studies and, even if such funding is forthcoming, it is unlikely that there will be continuity of researchers over a 20- or 30-year period.

Cross-sectional research

In longitudinal research the subject group remains the same and the time of measurement is varied. Reversing these characteristics produces the cross-sectional design, whereby individuals of different ages are compared at the same point in time. Such a strategy is expedient. It means, to return to our hypothetical example, that we do not need to wait 30 years to examine the differential employability of 20- and 50-year-olds. It also avoids the necessity of repeatedly studying the same individuals.

However, the cross-sectional design has its own problems. Again, we must be wary of accounting for differences between the different age groups in terms of within-individual change over time. The different groups of subjects are from different generations or cohorts and it may be this, rather than any inherent differences between 20- and 50-year-olds, that accounts for our findings. The two groups will have experienced different amounts and types of education, they will have been prepared for different worlds, with different skills and possibly different values. As with much longitudinal research, we can describe age differences but we cannot necessarily explain them.

Time-lag research

Longitudinal studies follow the same group of people over time and cross-sectional studies investigate people of different ages at the same point in time. Another possibility is to study people of the same age coming from different cohorts. We might, for example, be interested in how 30-year-olds born in 1930 compare with 30-year-olds born in 1950 or in 1970. Known as the time-lag method, this research design requires research projects to extend over many years. In our hypothetical example, data would need to be collected in 1960 for the group born in 1930, in 1980 for the group born in 1950, and in 2000 for those born in 1970. It is an approach that has, therefore, some of the practical disadvantages of longitudinal research but it does not involve repeated study of the same individuals, with all the problems that entails.

The time-lag design is used for investigating cohort differences, as, for example, when it is discovered that children of today are, say, more obese, less active, and less good at maths than they were 20, 30 or 40 years ago. It does not, however, offer an explanation of why such differences have been found and a range of possibilities could be hotly debated – too much fatty food, too much television, too much dependence on car travel, inadequate teaching, the use of calculators, the decline of community sporting facilities, etc., etc. Also, because time-lag studies investigate individuals who are all of the same age (albeit they reach that age at different times), they cannot provide insight into what is the primary concern of developmental psychologists – *individual* change and stability across time.

Sequential research

A single dimension on the matrix in Figure 2.1 can represent each of the three research designs discussed above. To avoid some of their respective disadvantages, Schaie (1965, 1986), in what he termed a general developmental model, proposed a number of more complex sequential research designs. Representing step-wise progression across the matrix in Figure 2.2, these each combine the characteristics of two or more of the linear designs already discussed.

- The *cohort-sequential* design, or longitudinal sequence, as it is termed by Baltes (1968), examines longitudinal sequences for two or more cohorts. In other words, it combines the characteristics of longitudinal and time-lag studies. An example from Figure 2.2 would be a study that sampled two or more of the shaded columns. Thus, we could

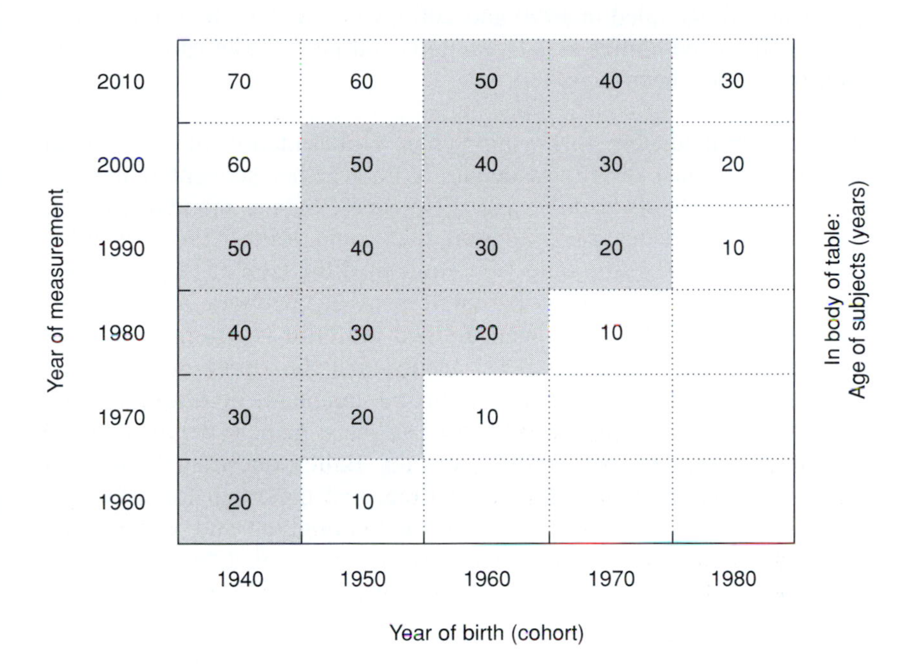

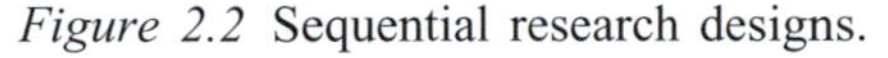

Figure 2.2 Sequential research designs.

both follow the development of individuals as they aged and also compare different cohorts of, say 30- and 40-year-olds.

- The *time-sequential*, or cross-sectional sequence (Baltes, 1968), examines cross-sectional samples on two or more occasions. In other words, it combines the characteristics of cross-sectional and time-lag designs – all ages of interest are sampled at all times of measurement. An example from the matrix in Figure 2.2 would be a study that examined a sample of 30-, 40-, and 50-year-olds in 1990, and a different sample of 30-, 40-, and 50-year-olds in 2000 – in other words, going across two rows in this table but with different subjects on each occasion. Selecting new samples at each time of measurement avoids the disadvantages of repeated measures with the same individuals.
- The *cross-sequential design*, Schaie's third sequential design, combines the characteristics of longitudinal, cross-sectional, and time-lag studies. All cohorts are measured at all times of measurement. With regard to the matrix in Figure 2.2, this would involve examining multiple rows and multiple columns, for example, sampling 30- and 40-year-olds in 1980, 1990, and 2000. This could, however, be merely a longitudinal sequence (cohort-sequential design) or cross-sectional sequence (time-sequential design), depending on whether repeated measurement is used, or whether all groups represent independent samples. A true cross-sequential design would require both. Thus, the

> 40-year-olds sampled in 1990 and 2000 would include both those who had participated earlier as 30-year-olds and new participants who had not previously been involved.

In the years immediately following Schaie's presentation of his general developmental model there was debate as to whether sequential designs can explain as well as describe age differences. Schaie maintained that, with appropriate statistical manipulation, they could. Baltes (1968) disputed this on two counts. His first objection concerned the lack of independence in the definitions of the three parameters of age, cohort, and time of measurement. Once two have been defined the third is determined automatically and Baltes (1968, p. 157) argued that the "existence of these mutual dependencies signifies that the three components do not satisfy the qualifications of three true experimental variables, namely they cannot be defined and varied independently". Second, Baltes questioned Schaie's interpretation of the meanings of age, time, and cohort differences. All three, Baltes argued, are aspects of the time continuum and it is unwarranted to make functional interpretations (for example, that age differences are maturation effects, or that time of measurement differences are environmental effects) of differences in these components. Despite their differences, Baltes and Schaie agree on the importance of recognising the impact on developmental processes of both time of measurement (that is, whether the data was collected in 1970 or 1990, for example) and cohort (that is, whether the participants were born, say, in 1965 or 1985) influences on developmental processes.

Sampling

Along with questions of how, where, what, and when to collect research data comes the issue of *from whom,* within a particular population, the data is to be collected. This is the question of sampling.

A random sample is one in which everyone in the population of interest has an equal chance of being selected. However, it is not always possible to obtain a complete list of a population, and, even if it were, practical constraints may preclude the selection of a truly random sample. Most studies, therefore, focus on a subsection of the total population, chosen through a number of theoretical and/or pragmatic criteria. Box 2.2 describes the sampling procedure used in a 12-year longitudinal study of change and continuity in adulthood.

A sample can be said to be representative if it includes the same proportion of people of different ages and gender and from the different cultural, ethnic, socioeconomic, educational, etc. backgrounds as the population from which the sample is drawn. The variables selected to define the population will depend on the focus of research and, because not all possible variables will be included, care must be taken in generalising findings to

Box 2.2 Selecting a sample – pragmatics and theoretical rationale

Fiske and Chiriboga (1990) describe the selection of the sample for their oft-cited longitudinal study of people facing transitions (Lowenthal, Thurnher, & Chiriboga, 1975). This extract shows how sampling and other research design decisions tend to reflect theoretical interests, practical pragmatics, and serendipity – who happens to be around at the time the research is initiated, and the nature of their expertise:

> Although most of the research team were gerontologists by training, our sampling design was based on the premise that to appreciate fully how a person grows into old age, one must also appreciate how a person grows from adolescence into young adulthood and from young adulthood into middle-age. For this reason we opted for a life-span sample approach. Recognizing that age acts as a spurious or "carrier" variable, . . . Instead of sampling according to age, we sampled according to where people stood in relation to one of four normative (and therefore predictable) life transitions . . . (1) high school seniors who were facing graduation and entry into adult status and (2) men and women whose first marriage was less than one year old and who would presumably be dealing with parenthood within the next few years . . . (3) men and women whose youngest child was a high school senior and who therefore were likely to face the proverbial empty nest and (4) men and women who either were expecting to retire within five years or had a spouse about to retire. . . . One of our major concerns was to study ordinary people. . . . Inasmuch as we planned to do so in depth, and with many variables, we sought to simplify the demographic characteristics by selecting the most homogenous district of one West Coast city: San Francisco. The district we selected was composed at that time (with few exceptions) of lower-middle-class and blue-collar workers. The neighborhood was then almost exclusively white. With the hard-won cooperation of the city's school board, and encouraged by a faculty colleague who happened to be a board member during the planning phase of our study, one sampling base became the senior class of a large high school in that district.
>
> From school records we identified high school seniors who were the youngest members of their families, thereby also locating parents who were about to enter the empty nest phase. With one exception, they were not parents of the high school senior sample. Using public vital statistics, we identified newlyweds of less than a year with at least one of each pair living or having lived in this district; for all this was their first marriage. The oldest people, who planned to retire within two or three years, were located through the other three groups.
>
> (Fiske & Chiriboga, 1990, pp. 3–4)

Fiske and Chiriboga (1990, p. 8) go on to discuss their wish that their research conveys, "both the generalities of gender and phase-of-life differences *and* the uniqueness of individuals" (my emphasis). In addition to the presentation of quantitative analysis of data from the whole sample, important findings were illustrated through the use of vignettes and quotations, and the lives of four individuals were considered in depth. Fiske and Chiriboga describe the selection of these case studies, again illustrating how sampling, whilst grounded in sound theoretical rationale, is also concerned with the "art of the possible":

> In selecting cases to be followed intensively throughout the book, we first had to decide on how many people to use. Anything fewer than four seemed insufficient to illustrate the complex transactions between individual and environment; anything more than four seemed likely to overwhelm the reader: four cases seemed just right. Having settled on four cases, then, our next decision concerned whether we should include a representative from each stage of life. After reviewing the pros and cons, we decided to draw these four people from the two older groups. The reasons were twofold. First, the need to comprehend the "developmental" part of adult development is most evident when we consider the older adult. . . . Second, the entire research team was composed of specialists in the second half of life and thus we felt particularly qualified to delve into the issues of older adulthood in the way these case studies demanded.
>
> The cases were selected on the basis of the interviewees' estimate of their personal self-concern – a category covering preoccupations with the self that ranged from self-protectiveness to a carefree hedonism:
>
> We first identified all of those middle-aged and older people who, at the first contact, ranked self-concern the highest or lowest of their commitments. The next step was to locate subgroups of changers and nonchangers and finally, among the changers, to locate people who had changed in specific ways at subsequent interviews – for example, from low to high to low or from high to low. Since we wished to have one man and one woman in each of the two older groups, the last screening was of stage and sex groups.
>
> Nine people fit our requirements. Of these we selected the four whose, education, marital status, and occupation were most typical of the two older groups as a whole. The remaining five are introduced in later chapters as "alternates" whose lives help us to round out some of the points we make.
>
> (Fiske & Chiriboga, 1990, p. 13)

other groups. In particular, findings from majority groups within the population – which may be the initial focus of attention – must not be unquestioningly applied to minority groups, or automatically taken as the definition of optimal development and held up as the standards to which other groups should aspire. The social and cultural context of the research must not be ignored.

An alternative to striving for a random or representative sample is to use purposive sampling, whereby the researcher seeks out as participants those likely to be "expert witnesses" (Pearsall, 1970), that is, people particularly qualified to contribute to the research study because of their relevant experience. This approach is sometimes called theoretical sampling because the "experts" are selected on the basis of their presumed ability to provide theoretical insights into the topic under investigation. It is a form of non-probability sampling in that not every individual in the general population has an equal chance of being included. It contrasts, however, with accidental or opportunity sampling, when the participants (sometimes referred to as a sample of convenience) are selected primarily because they happen to be around and are willing to take part in the research. Whilst purposive samples may be representative of the subsection of the population from which they are drawn, with accidental samples it is much harder (and perhaps impossible) to estimate the extent to which research findings would have been different with a different sample.

A purposive sample of "expert witnesses" can be expanded through the use of snowball techniques, whereby a small number of known contacts who meet the selection criteria are asked to suggest other possible participants. These participants are, in turn, asked to nominate others and, in this way, the sample "snowballs". As this happens the sample moves towards becoming an "accidental" sample in that it is determined by the social network of current participants. Not everyone who meets the criteria of being an expert witness in this instance has an equal chance of being included. However, with snowball techniques the sample does at least extend beyond the researcher's immediate contacts.

Evaluation

Researchers need to take trouble with the "how", "where," "what", "when", and "from whom" of research data collection if they are to maximise the likelihood of generating data that is meaningful and informative about the phenomenon under study. How can we judge whether or not they have succeeded? This question is frequently discussed in relation to the criterion of validity, with the term being used in a range of specific and technical ways. For research that is qualitative, exploratory, and/or collaborative, the concept of trustworthiness can be employed as a more appropriate alternative.

Validity

Validity is the cornerstone of assessments of positivist social science research. Such research rests on the assumption that there is an objective reality "out there" about which it is possible to discover value-free facts, providing the methods employed to do so are sufficiently rigorous. This assumption is frequently untenable in much research about the life course that explores the feasibility or reasonableness of a particular or world view. None the less, when research on human development is carried out within the hypothetico-deductive tradition, as, for example, when investigating stages of cognitive development in childhood, then it can be evaluated against the four criteria of internal validity, external validity, reliability, and objectivity:

- *Internal validity* is concerned with "the extent to which variations in an outcome (dependent) variable can be attributed to controlled variation in an independent variable" (Lincoln & Guba, 1985, p. 290). It is promoted by striving to reduce potential sources of variation other than the one being manipulated.
- *External validity* refers to generalisability – the degree to which research findings also hold for other groups and settings. To the extent that the research sample and research setting do not reflect the total population and all aspects of the environment, external validity (or generalisability) will be compromised. Internal and external validity are, therefore, "placed in a trade-off situation" (Lincoln & Guba, 1985) with each other: "If, for the sake of control (internal validity), strenuous laboratory conditions are imposed, then the results are not generalizable to any contexts except those that approximate the original laboratory" (Lincoln & Guba, 1985, p. 291).
- *Reliability* is concerned with the stability and replicability of research findings – would the research have produced the same results if conducted on a different occasion, and would a different researcher reach the same or different conclusions? Reliability is a precondition of validity. Measuring somebody's height with an elastic tape measure, for example, would produce unreliable results, thereby making it impossible to conclude whether manipulation of an independent variable (say, diet) was the cause of variation in the outcome (measured height) – the research would not have internal validity.
- *Objectivity* refers to the neutrality of the research – the detachment of the researcher from the data and its freedom from bias. It is established through the use of research instruments that minimise the need for the researcher to make judgements and interpretations (for example, using a maths test to assess mathematical ability, rather than asking teachers to make a rating). If totally "objective" research instruments are not available, then interobserver agreement can be used to check the objectivity of their observations.

It should be evident that these criteria rest on a number of assumptions. They assume, for example, that it is at least theoretically possible to control and manipulate all variables so as to establish internal validity, that all significant variables within a population and setting can be sampled in order to achieve external validity, that it is possible to develop sufficiently reliable research measures to allow for the conclusion that changes in the dependent variable are not the result of measurement error, and that there is one "objective" assessment on which researchers and research instruments can agree. These assumptions have increasingly been questioned and replaced with assumptions concerning the inevitably value-laden nature of both research "facts" and researchers' interpretations, the interactive nature of inquiry, the capacity of theory to provide alternative (but not necessarily mutually exclusive) accounts of these "facts", and the contextualised nature of knowledge.

All of these facets of research are important to the field of life-span development. Much research within this field is concerned with enhancing our understanding of phenomena rather than with their prediction and control (Datan et al., 1987). The question is not so much whether the research is valid in the technical, positivist sense of the word, but whether it is trustworthy.

Trustworthiness

Guba (1981; Lincoln & Guba, 1985) developed a set of criteria for evaluating the trustworthiness of naturalistic research – later to be re-named constructivist research (Guba & Lincoln, 1989), that parallel those listed in the previous section. The concepts of internal validity, external validity, reliability, and objectivity are replaced (or at least supplemented) by notions of credibility, transferability, dependability, and confirmability:

- With regard to *credibility*, which parallels the criterion of internal validity, we do not ask whether there is a perfect one-to-one relationship between the research findings and some ultimate, tangible reality (because the existence of such a reality is challenged). Instead, we ask whether there is agreement "between the constructed realities of respondents and the reconstructions attributed to them" (Guba & Lincoln, 1989, p. 237) by the researchers. That is, we ask about the extent to which the respondents and the researchers are seeing the world from a shared standpoint. We ask whether this worldview is understandable and credible to the respondents, researchers, the wider research audience and other interested parties. Lincoln and Guba (1985, 1986; Guba & Lincoln, 1989) suggest a number of techniques for promoting and checking research credibility, as summarised in Box 2.3.
- Guba and Lincoln's criterion of *transferability* is analogous to the positivist concept of external validity or generalisability. Claims for generalisability are researcher-led judgements grounded in the extent

Box 2.3 Strategies for promoting and checking the credibility of data (adapted from Lincoln & Guba, 1985, 1986; Guba & Lincoln, 1989)

1. *Prolonged engagement* – namely, the extended involvement of the researchers with the research participants in the settings where the research is located "in order to overcome the effects of misinformation, distortion, or presented 'fronts', to establish rapport and build the trust necessary to uncover constructions, and to facilitate immersing oneself in and understanding the context's culture" (Guba & Lincoln, 1989, p. 237).
2. *Persistent observation* – that is, the collection of sufficient material to enable the researchers to "identify those characteristics and elements in the situation that are most relevant to the problem or issue being pursued and [to focus] on them in detail" (Lincoln & Guba, 1986, p. 304). This adds depth to the breadth provided by prolonged engagement.
3. *Peer debriefing* – engaging in extended and extensive discussion of all aspects of the research with a disinterested peer who acts as a sounding board for ideas, challenges the researcher to make tacit knowledge and values explicit, and provides social and collegial support.
4. *Negative case analysis* – the process of revising working hypotheses in the light of hindsight until they account for all, or at least most, known cases.
5. *Progressive subjectivity* – this involves monitoring (or tracking) the development of the researcher's understanding of the research findings by recording his or her ideas as they develop. This renders the researcher's ideas open to scrutiny, in particular with regard to whether due attention is being given to the understandings and insights of the research participants.
6. *Member checks* – that is, an ongoing process of testing hypotheses, data, preliminary categories, and interpretations with the research participants who provided the initial data. Guba and Lincoln (1989) see this as the single most crucial technique for establishing credibility.
7. *Triangulation* or *crystallisation* – having, in their earlier publications (Lincoln & Guba, 1985, 1986) included triangulation (the use of multiple sources, investigators, theories, methods, and disciplinary frameworks) as a credibility check, Guba and Lincoln (1989) subsequently avoided it on the grounds that, "triangulation itself carries too positivist an implication, to wit, that there exist unchanging phenomena so that triangulation can logically *be* a check" (Guba & Lincoln, 1989, p. 240). Richardson (1994) addressed this issue by suggesting that the image of a crystal replace that of a rigid, fixed, two-dimensional triangle. Crystals, argues Richardson grow, change, and alter but are not amorphous. They combine, "symmetry and substance with an infinite variety of shapes, substances, transmutations, multidimensionalities, and angles of approach" (Richardson, 1994, p. 522).

to which the research data derives from the random sampling of a population identical to that to which the findings are to be generalised. In contrast, transferability is established by providing thick descriptions (Geertz, 1973) – extensive and careful descriptions of the time, the place, the context, and the culture in which the data were gathered in order to facilitate transferability judgements on the part of others who wish to apply the results of the study to another situation.
- *Dependability* is parallel to the conventional criterion of reliability in that it is concerned with the stability of the data over time. However, whereas reliability depends on the measurement conditions and instruments remaining consistent, dependability allows for the evolution and refinement of both research hypotheses and research methods. Indeed, "methodological changes and shifts in constructions are expected products of an emergent design dedicated to increasingly sophisticated constructions" (Guba & Lincoln, 1989, p. 242). As with transferability, sound judgements of dependability rest upon the availability of the relevant information for public scrutiny. Changes and shifts in the focus and methods of the research need to be both tracked and trackable so that outside reviewers, "can explore the process, judge the decisions that were made, and understand what salient factors in the context led . . . to the decisions and interpretations made" (Guba & Lincoln, 1989, p. 242).
- *Confirmability* is analogous to the conventional criterion of objectivity. Like objectivity, it is concerned with assuring that the data, interpretations, and outcomes of inquiries are rooted in contexts and persons other than the researcher. However, confirmability is achieved not by trying to remove all values, motives, and biases from the research method but, rather, by making the process of developing constructions explicit and trackable, so that their rationale can be inspected and confirmed by outside reviewers.

These four criteria of trustworthiness are relevant to much of the research conducted within the field of life-span development that does not conform to the traditional positivist, experimental paradigm. However, Guba and Lincoln go further and, along with theorists from other perspectives such as critical theory, advocate further criteria of research adequacy that do not mirror criteria developed within the conventional paradigm. Guba and Lincoln discuss these under the heading of authenticity.

Authenticity

The central focus of what Lincoln and Guba refer to as constructivist research is not, as is the case with conventional positivist research, the abstraction or the approximation of a single reality. Rather, it is concerned to present the multiple, holistic, competing, and often conflicting realities of all those with a stake in the research. Lincoln and Guba therefore introduced *fairness* as a criterion for evaluating this type of research – does it represent these different perspectives fairly? The first step in achieving fairness is to include as a permanent feature of the research the identification of all interested parties, the seeking out of their perspectives, and the incorporation of these perspectives into the research. The second step in achieving fairness is the involvement of all parties in negotiating the subsequent course of the research.

Research can be thought of as a process of learning, and Lincoln and Guba sought to establish criteria that evaluated the extent of learning that occurs within a project, and also the responsiveness of the project to that learning. These are reflected in the criteria of ontological, educative, catalytic, and tactical authenticity:

- *Ontological authenticity* is the extent to which the understandings (or constructions) of all parties, "are improved, matured, expanded, and elaborated, in that they now possess more information and have become more sophisticated in its use" (Guba & Lincoln, 1989, p. 248).
- *Educative authenticity* is the extent to which the individuals', "understanding of and appreciation for the construction of others outside their stakeholding group are enhanced" (Guba & Lincoln, 1989, p. 248).
- *Catalytic authenticity* is the extent to which the understandings generated by the research stimulate the various stakeholders to act – to alter the situation, to do things differently, to make changes.
- *Tactical authenticity* is the degree to which interested parties have the power to implement their action plans. To what extent does the research process empower them to act?

Lincoln and Guba suggest a range of specific strategies for demonstrating authenticity. In sum, these centre around, first, the gathering and using the testimonies of all interested parties, and, second, the careful documentation of all aspects of the research as it develops in the form of an "audit trail" that can be followed by both stakeholders in the research and outside parties.

Much research exploring life-span development is qualitative research designed to gain access to and then understand and interpret people's stories, making trustworthiness and authenticity highly relevant ways of construing the concept of validity.

Research ethics

Just as methodological issues permeate every psychological investigation, so, too, do questions of propriety and responsibility, that is, of ethics (Gross, 1996). The British Psychological Society (1998), in common with other professional associations such as the American Psychological Association (1990), publish guidelines that outline principles and procedures for both professional conduct in general and the conducting of ethical research in particular. Furthermore, many institutions (for example, hospitals and educational establishments) have Ethics Committees that must approve any research to be carried out under their auspices. The development of ethical guidelines is not a once-and-for-all activity. All positions need to be reviewed regularly and updated to reflect the changing social and political context in which research is conducted, and current debates about the nature of individual rights (Gross, 1996). The British Psychological Society (1998, p. 7) summarises its position as follows:

> The essential principle is that the investigation should be considered from the standpoint of all participants; foreseeable threats to their psychological well-being, health, values or dignity should be eliminated. Investigators should recognise that, in our multi-cultural and multi-ethnic society and where investigations involve individuals of different ages, gender and social background, the investigators may not have sufficient knowledge of the implications of any investigation for the participants. It should be borne in mind that the best judge of whether an investigation will cause offence may be members of the population from which the participants in the research are to be drawn.

Box 2.4 summarises in more concrete form strategies that will promote the attainment of these goals. In sum, they can be seen as addressing the two main issues of preventing risk (from stress, coercion, deception, or the invasion of privacy) and promoting informed consent (Malim & Birch, 1998).

Box 2.4 Ethical guidelines for research with human participants (adapted from British Psychological Society, 1998)

1. *Consent* – whenever possible, the investigator should obtain the informed consent of possible participants in an investigation. This requires the investigator to inform participants about all aspects of the investigation that might reasonably be expected to influence willingness to participate and to answer participants' questions about the investigation. Special safeguards are required for research with children, with participants who have impairments that may limit their capacity to give informed consent, and with participants over whom researchers are in a position of authority or influence.
2. *Deception* – intentional deception of the participants over the purpose and general nature of the investigation should be avoided whenever possible. The withholding of information or the misleading of participants is unacceptable if the participants are typically likely to object or show unease once debriefed.

3. *Debriefing* – in studies where the participants are aware that they have taken part in an investigation, when the data have been collected, the investigator should provide the participants with any necessary information to complete their understanding of the nature of the research. The investigator should discuss with the participants their experience of the research in order to monitor any unforeseen negative effects or misconceptions.
4. *Withdrawal from the investigation* – investigators should make plain to participants their right to withdraw from the research at any time, irrespective of whether or not payment or other inducement has been offered. In the light of their experience of the investigation, or as a result of debriefing, participants have the right to withdraw retrospectively any consent given, and to require that their own data, including recordings, be destroyed.
5. *Confidentiality* – subject to the requirements of legislation (including the Data Protection Act) information obtained about participants during an investigation is confidential unless otherwise agreed in advance. Participants have the right to expect that any information they provide will be treated confidentially and, if published, will not be identifiable as theirs. Participants must be warned in advance of their agreeing to participate if confidentiality and/or anonymity cannot be guaranteed.
6. *Protection of participants* – investigators have a primary responsibility to protect participants from physical and mental harm during an investigation. Risks greater than or additional to those encountered in the participants' ordinary lifestyles should be avoided. Participants should be asked about any factors, such as pre-existing medical conditions, that might put them at special risk, and be advised of any special action they should take to avoid risk. There should be mechanisms allowing participants to contact the investigators within a reasonable time period following their participation should stress, potential harm or related questions arise. When discussing results with participants care should be taken to ensure this does not produce undue anxiety.
7. *Observational research* – unless those observed give their consent to being observed, observational research is acceptable only in situations where those observed would expect to be observed by strangers. Account must be taken of local cultural values and of the possibility of intruding on the privacy of individuals who, even while in a normally public space, may believe they are unobserved.
8. *Giving advice* – if, during their research, investigators obtain evidence of psychological or physical problems of which a participant is seemingly unaware, there is an obligation to inform the participant if not to do so may endanger the participant's future wellbeing. Investigators should help participants obtain appropriate professional assistance if they so wish but should only proffer advice or other assistance themselves if they are suitably qualified to do so, if this forms an intrinsic part of the research, and if it has been agreed in advance.

9. *Colleagues* – investigators share responsibility for the ethical treatment of research participants with their collaborators, assistants, students, and employees. They should monitor their own work and that of colleagues. Investigators who believe that another psychologist or investigator might be conducting research that violates the above principles should encourage that investigator to re-evaluate the research.

Despite the detail and specificity of ethical codes they provide guidelines and principles, not sets of rigid rules. Researchers retain responsibility for thinking through the ethical implications of their work. The prominence of different ethical principles will vary depending on the nature of the investigation. Research in life-span developmental psychology is at times conducted by people in powerful positions with participants who are vulnerable and relatively powerless, for example, the very young, the impaired elderly, people who are developmentally delayed, or people who are coping with major psychological trauma. Such participants might not be able to give consent that is truly informed in any meaningful sense of the word. In such situations researchers need to be especially certain of the value and significance of their research. They need to discuss the research with those who have an interest in and are responsible for the potential participants, and obtain their consent as well as, or, if appropriate, instead of, that of the participants themselves. Monitoring of these (and, indeed, all) participants' experience of the research for evidence of possible risk is crucial and is addressed in guidelines 6 (protection of participants) and 8 (giving advice) in Box 2.4.

There are no short cuts to ensuring that research is ethical. It requires an ongoing ethical watchfulness (Pryor, 1989) that extends beyond familiarity with relevant codes and standards. Pryor suggests that researchers strive to anticipate ethical dilemmas before they actually happen, are alert to possible new dilemmas invoked by new research techniques, examine the legal and organisational constraints imposed on their research in relation to possibly conflicting professional and ethical allegiances, and take the time necessary to think through ethically ambiguous situations. In this way researchers can hope to achieve moral responsibleness (Tennyson & Strom, 1986) – a process involving not only rational thought and professional guidelines but also the personal values and morality of the researcher. All researchers need to develop their own principled position – resonating, perhaps, with the accounts of both cognitive development and moral reasoning outlined in Chapter 4 of this book.

3 Age stages and lifelines

> What is perhaps most obvious from our research is that no one set of attributes and no one theory of the life course can adequately explain the diversity of human lives, not even for a sample of Californians born in the first half of the twentieth century.
>
> (Clausen, 1993)

In weaving terminology, the warp is the thread that goes up and down a piece of cloth and the weft the thread that goes across. This image conveys metaphorically the two basic approaches to writing about life-span development. Analogous to the weft, and the main focus of the first section of this chapter, is the age-stage approach, which considers all aspects of development during particular phases of life. In contrast, the thematic approach, which is analogous to the warp, discusses a particular aspect of development through the entire life span. Many large introductory texts attempt to combine both (for example, Bee, 1994; Rice, 1995).

The age-stage approach to discussing the life course represents a cross-sectional, and the thematic a longitudinal, stance. Each has its strengths and weaknesses. The cross-sectional concentration on a particular age stage has the advantage of providing a more complete picture of the whole person at that point in time. It is less able to communicate the links between how the person is now and how they were, or what they will become. Like cross-sectional research, it is a snapshot of a particular moment. With longitudinal approaches, the advantages and disadvantages are reversed. It is easier to gain a sense of how a particular facet of development, for example cognitive, career, or motor development, typically progresses over time but this could be at the expense of a clear image of the whole person at a particular moment.

Age stages: the weft of development

An immediate question that confronts attempts to divide the life course into stages is that of how many stages to distinguish and where to place

Activity 3.1 How many life stages are there?

Using chronological age as the marker, divide the life course into what seem to you to be a logical series of stages.

- Where would you place the boundaries between the stages?
- What are the key characteristics of each stage in terms of:
  - key tasks and preoccupations for the individual?
  - societal expectations?
  - role occupancy?

In considering these questions, it might be useful to try and identify particular individuals who represent the different life stages, as well as thinking in generalities. Also, think back on your own life course.

Spend a few minutes thinking about these questions individually, and then, if possible, work in small groups to address them more systematically.

the boundaries between them. Activity 3.1 invites you to consider your own position on this, and on the characteristics of different age stages. It is suggested that you address this task before continuing with the text.

How many life stages did you distinguish in Activity 3.1? Perhaps it was only two – childhood and adulthood. Most people come up with between five and seven (Fry, 1976; Shannan & Kedar, 1979–80), for example, adding some or all of the following to the list: infancy, adolescence, middle age, old age. In the present chapter, eight stages are discussed: infancy (0–2 years), early childhood (age 2–6), middle childhood (6–12), adolescence (12–18), early adulthood (18–40), middle adulthood (40–60), the anomalous sounding early late-adulthood (60–75), and the tautologically sounding late late-adulthood (75+). The accuracy of both the number and age boundaries of these stages is open to debate and there has been a tendency for the number of recognised life stages to proliferate over time, for example adolescence and youth; early and late young adulthood (Levinson et al., 1978); early and later middle age (Chiriboga, 1989), and the young-old and the old-old (Neugarten, 1974).

The developmental threads identified earlier (in Chapter 1), namely, physical, cognitive, personal, and social development, provide a framework for the present review. In the discussion below, reference is also made to interaction between these domains and to the different levels of environmental influence as identified in Bronfenbrenner's (1977, 1979) model, also discussed earlier. It is necessary, however, to proceed cautiously with the task of identifying and describing age stages. The specificity with which we can stipulate a person's chronological age can lend it a distinctly spurious air of objectivity.

An overview of age stages

Despite the need for a degree of caution in identifying and describing life stages based on chronological age, because we undoubtedly live in an age-graded society, to ignore totally the use of chronological age as a marker would be tantamount to throwing the baby out with the bath water. In particular, chronological age provides a framework for considering a total life-span, total life-space (Super, 1980, 1990) overview of the life course. What follows, therefore, is a general but inevitably sketchy picture of the developing person at each of eight periods of life.

Infancy (0–2 years)

Even before birth there is interaction between the person and his or her environment. The mother's general health and nutritional intake influence the quality of the fetal environment, whilst alcohol, nicotine or other drugs can pass along the placenta and have a detrimental effect on the developing fetus. Despite the susceptibility of fetal development to negative environmental influences, in most instances prenatal development takes place in a relatively secure, stable, and facilitative environment. The birth process represents a sudden and perhaps traumatic entry into a world that immediately bombards almost every sense organ in the infant's body with a torrent of stimulation. Infancy, which extends through the initial neonatal period and on through approximately the first 2 years of life, witnesses a staggering rate and range of development.

In terms of physical development, infants acquire, in a relatively predictable manner, a range of sensory and motor skills. They progress from a neonate very much at the mercy of inborn reflexes through a series of identifiable stages to toddlers who can move about independently in their environment, discriminating between and responding to a range of visual, auditory, tactile, and other stimuli. Interactions with their environment are dominated by sensory (for example, seeing and hearing) and motor (such as sucking, touching, and grasping) actions. As infants explore their environment, striving both to perceive and influence it, they develop cognitively – learning, for example, that objects can continue to exist even when out of sight (object permanence) and also how to let one thing stand for another (symbolic capacity). They also develop the ability to understand and begin to use language. Socially, infants develop strong attachments to their primary caregivers and considerable ability to communicate their feelings and emotions. In the personal realm, they develop a distinct personality or temperament and a rudimentary sense of self, recognising their reflection in a mirror, for example, and knowing whether they are a girl or a boy.

Inevitably, these threads of development do not occur independently. There is interaction both between them, and between infants and their environment. Caregivers comprise the infant's main microsystem (Bronfenbrenner, 1977) and, through the nature and quality of their interactions with the infant, influence his or her perception and understanding of the world as either safe or fearful. Infants, through the expression of their temperament are experienced by caregivers as, for example, easy, difficult, placid, or excitable. This, in turn, influences how they are treated.

The wider environment in which infants are located also influences their development. At the mesosystem level, the different networks of which the infant is a part (home, extended family, clinic, community centre, for example) can interact to support the baby's development, or may conflict, as, for example, when home and clinic differ in their attitude to immunisation or diet. Forces at Bronfenbrenner's exosystem level, such as the society's economic system and its medical and childcare facilities will have a major impact of the infant's life experiences. Likewise, cultural values and traditions enshrined within the macrosystem will determine many aspects of childrearing practice.

Early childhood (2–6 years)

The early childhood or preschool period continues to see major developments in the physical, cognitive, personal, and social domains. Physically, the body proportions change and the child develops both gross and fine motor skills – growing from the 2-year-old toddler to the 6-year-old who can hop, skip, jump, catch a ball, and, possibly, ride a bicycle, and who has sufficient fine motor control to be able to use scissors and begin to write legible letters. In the cognitive realm, children learn to classify objects according to a range of criteria such as function, shape, size, or colour. Linguistically, they progress from using simple two-word sentences to much longer utterances employing a range of grammatical strategies such as plurals, tenses, and passive sentences. As their language develops children become able to use verbal representations and mental images to symbolise objects and events.

During early childhood, children's personal and social development frequently goes hand-in-hand. They exercise their developing ability to act independently, ideally under the care of adults who provide them with an appropriate balance of freedom and control. In this way they gradually learn to control their emotions and behaviour. During this stage their sense of self and their descriptions of other people expand beyond physical characteristics such as age, size, and gender, to include skills and activities.

Whilst the immediate family generally remains the most significant microsystem, the child's world typically expands to include peers, nurseries, play groups, and, at 4 or 5 years of age, primary school. Play and other interactions with peers stimulate developments within all domains.

Motor skills develop as children engage in physical play. Disagreements and conflicts between playmates teach them about the existence of different worldviews and help them to become more aware of other people's perspectives. Attempting to resolve disputes develops the skills of negotiation and compromise, and how to co-operate with others.

Middle childhood (6–12 years)

The beginning of the period of middle childhood is marked by a major cognitive development. From the age of about 6 years children start to develop the capacity to focus on more than one dimension of an object or situation at the same time. This enables them to begin to understand the laws of conservation and quantity, for example, that if water is poured from a small, wide glass into a tall, narrow glass, the amount of water remains the same. Applying these developing cognitive skills in the social and personal domains enables children to develop more complex understandings and relationships. Moral reasoning becomes more sophisticated, the capacity to understand the world from another's perspective begins to develop, and children start to describe themselves and others in terms of inner personality traits and motives, rather than only in terms of physical characteristics and activities.

The child's social network typically expands during middle childhood. The family remains important, but more time (see Super's [1980, 1990] life-career rainbow, Chapter 1) is spent with peers. Same-sex friendships predominate. Indeed, gender segregation by choice is more pronounced now than at any other stage of childhood. Also, children may increasingly become a part of microsystems involving adults beyond their immediate family, for example, through out-of-school activities such as Brownies, Cubs, football clubs, and dancing classes. Such cultural institutions represent influence emanating from the exosystem level of the environment, and clearly will vary across different cultural groups. Indeed, in cultures where formal education does not play a significant role, "middle childhood" may not be a very meaningful category. Instead, children may experience a gradual adoption of the roles they will fulfil as adults.

Physical development during middle childhood tends to be smooth and steady – a period of gradual, quantitative, cumulative growth before the qualitative and major developments of adolescence.

Adolescence (12–18 years)

The end of middle childhood and beginning of adolescence generally coincides with the physical changes that mark puberty, although for girls in particular these changes may have begun as early as 9 or 10 years of age. These developments herald a range of changes and developments in other domains – notably the personal and the social – indicating the multiplicity of interactions between different developmental arenas. Adolescence is a bridge between childhood and adulthood, and sexual maturation not only brings fertility and the possibility of adult sexual relations but also changed relationships with parents and other adults, and with both same-sex and opposite-sex peers. In preparation for the step into the adult world, generational relationships within the family must be renegotiated – sometimes a process fraught with pitfalls. Adolescents seek greater independence from, and/or more adult-like relationships with, their parents, with a corresponding increase in the significance of peer relationships. The function of friendship becomes less the provision of a setting for mutual play and more a vehicle for facilitating the slow transition from the protected life within the family to the independent life of adulthood (Bee, 1994). Friendships become a forum for the sharing of inner feelings and secrets. The needs of the adolescent for both security and independence are significant and often contradictory. Young people without a secure family base, for example those living in children's homes, can be especially vulnerable.

Unless cultural practice prohibits or strictly controls heterosexual contact, the structure of the peer group also typically changes during adolescence (Brown 1990; Brown, Mory, & Kinney, 1994; Dunphy, 1963). Same-sex "cliques" of between four and six young people give way to larger, mixed-sex "crowds" that provide a forum for developing skills and confidence to deal with heterosexual relationships. These crowds will frequently break down in late adolescence into mixed-sex cliques and are often a prelude to committed heterosexual pair relationships. Both peer pressure and the wish to conform to it can be intense, producing anxiety and confusion for many young people but perhaps particularly for homosexual adolescents, who can face high levels of prejudice and stereotyping, and the question of whether or not to "come out", and to whom.

The physical changes of adolescence are accompanied by equally significant cognitive developments. Beginning to emerge at about age 11 is a further stage of cognitive development, denoting the ability to distinguish the form of a problem from its specific content. Its main characteristics include the use of logical, abstract thinking in the solving of problems and the ability to apply concepts to different and hypothetical situations. These changes make possible the development of more abstract self-concepts that can embrace core values and philosophies. The combination of physical maturity, cognitive developments, and societal demands renders the formation of ego identity a central psychosocial task of adolescence.

Early adulthood (18–40 years)

"Achieving intimacy, making career choices, and attaining vocational success are important challenges of early adulthood" (Rice, 1995). Thus, some of the key preoccupations of this life stage are summarised – echoing Freud's reputed comments – in the words "lieben und arben" (love and work). Physically, the apex of the inverted-U-shaped, growth–maintenance–decline curve has been reached – strength, endurance, perceptual abilities, reaction time and sexual responsiveness are all at their peak. Socially and personally, however, the scene is very different. In these arenas early adulthood can be more stressful and more difficult than any other phase of adulthood (Bee, 1994). It is a period for making decisions that will have long-term or possibly life-long implications.

Marriage and parenthood demand and provoke major readjustments. Alternatively, rejecting these socially prescribed and sanctioned role changes brings its own challenges. Despite expectations to the contrary, a significant number of couple relationships fail, bringing the upheaval of separation, divorce, and/or the establishment of new relationships.

Along with expectations concerning marriage and parenthood, expectations regarding the work role serve to generate an anticipated future for the young adult. Becoming established in the world of work is generally a part of this set of expectations, although its precise nature will be influenced by factors such as educational level, family background, and social class (that is, by characteristics of the micro-, meso-, macro-, and exosystems in which the individual is embedded). Furthermore, for a significant minority of young adults, notably those living in economically deprived areas with parents who are amongst the long-term unemployed, the adult role of "worker" can seem irrelevant and/or unattainable. The forging of a satisfying alternative identity may be problematic. For most young adults, however, work is a time-consuming role that can make a significant contribution to their sense of identity and life satisfaction. The period of early adulthood can witness considerable career advancement, especially for those entering the professions. None the less, the expectation of a "career for life" is less realistic than before and most people can expect to make at least one significant career change during the course of their working life.

The tasks of this era may seem contradictory – in particular, competing and incompatible demands of work and family may need to be negotiated. Successful management of the challenges of this period, however, can lead to enhanced self-confidence and independence. Bee (1994, p. 365) summarises this process: "Having learned the key roles, we begin to free ourselves from their constraints; we figure out how to fulfil our various duties and still express our own individuality".

Middle adulthood (40–60 years)

During middle adulthood most cognitive skills are maintained on well-practised tasks. Indeed, experience may result in these skills being used more efficiently and effectively. There may be some deterioration on tasks that are highly dependent on speed of response or the use of unexercised skills. Memory, especially for unfamiliar material, may decline. However, these losses tend to be fairly minor.

Many physical signs of ageing begin to appear during middle adulthood – vision and hearing become less acute, hair begins to grey and thin, skin becomes less elastic and more wrinkled, and aerobic capacity declines. Such changes may, however, have little importance in everyday life. It may not be necessary to perform at peak levels outside the experimental laboratory. Spectacles can correct many difficulties of vision. Sport and physical activity can remain rewarding even if speed and agility begin to decline. Experience can compensate for youth.

Often it is the meaning attached to these changes both by the individual and by society that invests them with importance. Those whose personal identity is linked closely to a youthful appearance can find it hard to adjust. There might be gender differences. The cosmetic industry, the fashion industry and advertising in general tend to link beauty and physical attractiveness with youth. Women learn early that physical attractiveness is a valuable asset and the fact that they may appear to be losing this asset can negatively effect self-esteem.

Women's most major physical change during middle adulthood is the menopause, although its biological significance is overlaid with cultural meanings (Dan & Bernhard, 1989). Whilst women who have been through the experience see it mostly in positive or neutral terms (bringing freedom from the bother of menstruation, the risk of pregnancy, and the restrictions of childbearing), younger women (Neugarten, Wood, Kraines, & Loomis, 1963) and men (Kahana, Kiyak, & Liang, 1980; Perlmutter & Bart, 1982) report more negative attitudes – associating it with disease, deficiency, and/or decline (Dan & Bernhard, 1989).

If physical changes can have a significant impact on the sense of personal identity, then, so too, can events in the work and family domains. For many middle-aged workers careers will have reached a plateau, possibly without having fulfilled early hopes or promise. Expectations of future career prospects may need to be revised.

In the social or family realm, middle-aged parents need to renegotiate their relationship with their children and with each other. Parents have more time for each other as children reach adolescence (when peer relationships begin to take on some of the emotional importance previously invested predominantly in the relationship with parents) and subsequently move away physically and/or psychologically from the parental home. There tends to be an increase in marital satisfaction at this stage and a lessening of role segregation along gender lines. Men who have invested heavily in the role of bread winner might have more time to develop wider and more nurturing interests – serving the community perhaps – whilst women who have devoted much time and energy to child rearing could have more opportunity to develop their own independent interests. Whilst personality traits as measured on standardised inventories tend to remain fairly constant, researchers have found evidence of a turning of attention from the outer to the inner world – increasing interiority as Neugarten

(1977) described it. This can be manifested in a greater wish and determination to strive for what one really wants, rather than following societal dictates and norms.

The period of middle adulthood is not, however, without its stresses. Indeed, these have received considerable emphasis – encapsulated in the notion of the midlife crisis. This crisis is seen as being triggered by personal, family, and work pressures; for example, the need to come to terms with the reality of ageing (with its implication of mortality), the realisation that the next generation – both at home and at work – is snapping at one's heels, and possibly the need to care for ageing parents and come to terms with their death. However, whilst middle adulthood may often be a turning point, a crisis is, to quote Tamir (1989), optional. Evidence suggests that only a small minority – between 2 and 5 per cent of the population (Chiriboga, 1989; McCrae & Costa, 1984) – experience a midlife crisis.

Early late-adulthood (60–75 years)

Bee and Mitchell (1984) summarised the physical changes associated with ageing in five words: smaller, slower, weaker, lesser, fewer. The gradual declines that start to become apparent in middle adulthood tend to become more pronounced after the age of about 60. Increased attention to health care and exercise is needed to maintain physical vigour, and this accounts, at least partly, for the marked individual differences that exist in the physical capabilities of older adults. However, because sets of motor and perceptual tasks are generally undertaken in conjunction with one another, it is frequently possible to compensate for losses in any one particular area. Touch, smell, and sound may, for example, all be used to supplement vision in the identification of objects. Experience teaches us where steps, uneven pavements and the like are to be found, and we can learn where to proceed cautiously rather than assume we will see such hazards. Likewise, we can learn to listen carefully to conversations in noisy places.

Despite the increased incidence of "early retirement", most people relinquish the role of paid worker during their sixties. Whilst alternative roles may be forged within the community, late adulthood is, in general, a time both of fewer social roles and of fewer obligations within the roles that do remain. Thus, the role of parent, whilst still important, is likely to be less demanding. The role of grandparent might be added but, again in the main, its responsibilities and demands are less than when parenthood was added to the individual's role constellation. Relationships with partners must, again, be renegotiated as retirement throws couples more into each other's company. Questions of dependency must be addressed if one partner becomes sick or frail.

At the personal level, the way losses are perceived is important, in particular the degree of control the person feels he or she has. Thus, retirement that is voluntary is less likely to be a traumatic transition than retirement that is imposed on a reluctant retiree. In the personal as well as the physical domain there are adjustments to be made to the reality that one's life is drawing to an end. Late adulthood can be a time of significant spiritual growth. Self-acceptance may increase. An important element of the crisis of integrity versus despair (Erikson, 1959, 1980) revolves around the acceptance of one's life for what it has been and for what it will not now be.

Late late-adulthood (75 years and above)

The years beyond the age of 60 have often been placed together in the single category of late adulthood (for example, Rice, 1995). Increasing longevity and, in particular, the increasing health, wealth, and vigour of many older people makes this inappropriate. For many people it is not until their mid-seventies that physical and cognitive declines impinge significantly on their way of life. Neugarten (1974) made the distinction between the "young-old" and the "old-old", a distinction that has gradually become more widely adopted. Despite the continued existence of significant individual differences, by the time people have reached their mid-seventies they are likely to suffer from some degree of physical impairment. In the cognitive domain, the old-old will generally take longer to learn new things, will experience periodic memory lapses, and can have difficulty solving novel problems. Whilst fluid abilities tend to show gradual decline, well-practised linguistic and cognitive skills and crystallised knowledge may still be retained. There is some evidence that crystallised skills tends to undergo a rapid decline – known as terminal drop (Kleemeier, 1962; Riegel & Riegel, 1972) – some 5–7 years before death.

Social networks can become smaller as friends and peers become sick or disabled, move into sheltered accommodation or die. At the personal, level late late-adulthood is a period of adjustment to the changes already mentioned – the physical and cognitive decline and the altered, often more restricted, personal and social circumstances. It is also a period of review as people reinterpret their life experience as they continue to address the crisis of integrity versus despair, not only accepting one's own life but seeing its place amongst all human lives across all times.

Lifelines: the warp of development

The lifeline you were invited to draw at the beginning of Chapter 1 could have taken a variety of forms. Indeed, if you compared notes with friends or colleagues your discussion probably focused on the different ways in which you had each depicted your life. The present section is concerned with the different ways theorists of the life course have construed people's lifelines or, to use Bühler's (1933; Bühler & Massarik, 1968) term, "curves of life". Such constructions can be thought of as meta-models of the life course – overarching frameworks through which we can describe, understand, and possibly explain our own and other people's lives. Whilst there is no generally agreed set of criteria for comparing such meta-models, the present discussion is organised around three issues that recur repeatedly in the literature – change (and the extent to which it is ordered), consistency (or stability), and chaos (or chance). This echoes to a large extent Gergen's (1977) distinction between an ordered-change, a stability, and an aleatory-change orientation to development.

Change and the life course

Much developmental psychology has been concerned with looking for "patterned or orderly change across time" (Gergen, 1977, p. 38), and with presenting such change as a series of stages.

Stages

Like the concept of development, the concept of "stage" is used in a number of different ways (Kohlberg, 1973a). A strict use of the term confines it to a sequence of invariant, universal changes in cognitive structure that is consistent across generations and cultures. It has, however, also been used in relation to the stages of biological maturation that reflect the sequence of physical and physiological growth, maintenance, and decline. A further use of the term, this time as a sociocultural rather than cognitive or biological concept, concentrates on the sequence of social roles typically occupied by a person through their life, and/or the developmental tasks with which they are concerned at any particular point in time. These stages – both roles and tasks – arise from the range of environmental forces and person–environment interactions characteristic of a particular cultural and historical setting.

Whilst the biological conception of stage has least direct relevance to the present focus on the psychological and social, it should be remembered that the growth–maintenance–decline pattern that typifies biological stages is the model on which many taken-for-granted, lay understandings of the term are grounded. This can result in the growth–maintenance–decline model that characterises the biological life course being transferred unquestioningly to the psychological, personal, social, and/or spiritual domain. Similarly, theorists presenting a life-span account of sociocultural or cognitive development may draw to a greater or lesser degree on the biological model. Thus, Erikson's model of life-span psychosocial development is a maturational model incorporating the notion of sequential, cumulative, hierarchical stages that draws on both embryological and cognitive development. But more of Erikson's work later (in Chapter 4). For the moment, the aim is to summarise the key elements of these different uses of the term stage, examples of all of which are to be found in the account of age stages given earlier in the present chapter.

The structural conception of stage It has been argued, particularly by cognitive psychologists, that personal changes need to meet certain strict criteria in order to be defined as progression to a new "stage" of development. Such criteria include the requirement that the changes be universal, invariant, cumulative, hierarchical, and qualitative. Thus, only qualitative changes in competence are considered to reflect stages. Quantitative changes are not defined as stages, reflecting, as they do, changes in performance level rather than in underlying structural competence. To be defined as having moved to a new stage of development the person must do something qualitatively different, not just the same thing better. So, although there are decrements in, for example, the speed and efficiency of immediate memory and information processing with age, such quantitative changes are not taken to imply regression in the logical structure of the person's reasoning process.

Furthermore, stages do not occur randomly. They form an invariant sequence that can be speeded up, slowed down, or stopped by environmental factors, but not changed. In addition, such stages are hierarchical, that is, later (or higher) stages incorporate earlier (or lower) stages into their structure. In other words, later stages are more advanced, not merely different. Such stages could be represented on a lifeline as a series of rising steps, like a staircase. The uprights between the steps could be sloping rather than vertical because the transition between stages is likely to be gradual rather than sudden. Distinct stages can, however, be identified. They represent structured wholes, that is, they balance and unify interrelated behaviours, concepts, or skills. Stages can, therefore, be depicted on the lifeline as horizontal plateaux. Piaget's theory of cognitive development (see Chapter 4) incorporates this rigorous and rigid definition of stage.

The cognitive-structural (or cognitive-developmental) concept of stage has been highly controversial. In 1968, Bijou criticised the stage concept for being, in effect, an intellectual straitjacket that stunted divergent theorising and research. He complained that, instead of investigating all possible factors that may affect behaviour, researchers directed their energies at establishing, "whether certain behaviors do, in fact, occur at a particular stage as claimed and, if so, whether their onset can be modified" (Bijou, 1968, p. 422). Ten years later, Brainerd (1978) questioned the explanatory power of cognitive-structural stages on the ground that the argument is circular: "children do X because they are in stage two. We know they are in stage two because they do X". If, however, the conceptual-structural concept of stage does have validity, it is likely to be primarily in relation to the first 16 or so years of the life course. Despite evidence and debate concerning further cognitive developments during adulthood (see, for example, Commons, Sinnott, Richards, & Armon, 1989), the structural concept of stage is applied almost exclusively to child and adolescent development. Where adulthood is concerned, it is maturational and, in particular, sociocultural concepts of stage that predominate.

The maturational conception of stage The term "stage" can be used to denote some aspects of biological development. Here, the term refers to the maturational unfolding of a person's inbuilt potential according to a universal plan and timetable. The biological conception of stage reflects a growth–maintenance–decline model of development. Growth or maturation is seen as being complete by early adulthood, from whence the processes of maintenance and/or decline take over. A lifeline shaped like an inverted, splayed-out "U" would reflect this model of development. It is also implicit in arc-like metaphors of the life span. The gradient of the slopes could indicate the rates of growth or decline, with the length of the central plateau indicating the duration of the maintenance phase. Such a concept of development is controversial only if it is presented as the whole picture, ignoring, as it does, the possibility that at least in some domains new developmental stages can be reached throughout life.

Erikson's theory of psychosocial development (see Chapter 4) shares many similarities with the biological concept of stage outlined above, representing as it does a maturational model of psychological growth. Whilst recognising the interplay between personal and environmental factors, Erikson applied to psychosocial maturation a concept drawn from embryology – the epigenetic principle that, "everything that grows has a ground plan, and out of this ground plan the parts arise, each part having its time of special ascendancy, until all forms have arisen to form a functioning whole" (Erikson, 1980, p. 53). This is an organic perspective, in which the person is assumed to be inherently and spontaneously active and in which development proceeds in a specific way according to a timetable. It leads to the depiction of a series of universal, invariant stages, which may be correlated with, but not rigidly assigned to, particular age ranges. Erikson also sees development as cumulative but accepts that developmental crises can be returned to and reworked after their "time of special ascendancy" has passed. He also deviates from the biological model by not depicting the later stages of life as inevitably periods of decline.

The sociocultural conception of stage Whilst Erikson's theory has many characteristics of a maturational definition of stage, it also explicitly incorporates environmental factors, thus bringing it within the purview of a sociocultural understanding. The sociocultural conception of stage recognises that, "a culture (responding in part to maturational events) outlines a rough sequence of roles or tasks from birth to death, and adaptation to this task sequence leads to age-typical personality change" (Kohlberg, 1973a, p. 498). Kohlberg (1973a) distinguished two types of sociocultural stage – the age-linked social role concept (Kohli & Meyer, 1986) and the developmental task concept (Havighurst, 1972).

The social role definition of stage focuses on the part biological and part socially constructed roles the individual is called upon to fulfil at different points in the life course. It draws attention to how the life course is defined, constituted, and changed by external circumstances. It addresses the common markers we use to anticipate the form our life course will and, in our view, "should" perhaps take. Many of these markers or events correlate with age and together they comprise an age-grade system, "a prescriptive timetable for the ordering of life events" (Neugarten, 1977, p. 45). These social conventions, whilst they might help the wheels of society run smoothly, can inhibit rather than facilitate a particular individual's development and happiness. An alternative sociocultural perspective – the developmental task conception of stage – explicitly incorporates personal wishes and goals, recognising that these are influenced but not totally determined by social norms and expectations.

The developmental task notion of stage focuses on those things people need to learn at a particular point in the life cycle in order to be judged by themselves and others as being reasonably happy and successful. Thus, Havighurst (1972, p. 2), a key proponent of this perspective, described the developmental tasks of life as, "those things that constitute healthy and satisfactory growth in our society". Midway between "an individual need and a societal demand" (p. 2), the developmental task concept "assumes an active learner interacting with an active social environment" (Havighurst, 1972, p. 2). Havighurst saw developmental tasks as resulting from three interacting sources: physical maturation, the cultural pressures of a society, and personal goals, "the desires, aspirations, and values of the emerging personality" (p. 6). More often than not, developmental tasks arise, "from combinations of these factors acting together" (p. 6). Havighurst's work, along with other developmental task formulations (Newman & Newman, 1995; Oerter, 1986), are discussed in more detail in Chapter 5.

The social role conception of stage leaves unanswered the question of whether or which stage sequences constitute development. It describes the typical. The developmental task concept of stage, in passing judgement on what one "needs" or "ought" to do, offers an implicit definition of development as fulfilling the tasks that, within a particular society, result in the individual becoming reasonably happy and successful. Havighurst (1972) recognises that developmental tasks are culture-bound, thus acknowledging their value-laden basis.

Like the biological conception of stage, the concept of a socioculturally defined pattern of roles and tasks is readily accepted. Opinions vary, however, regarding the generalisability of the timing and content of such stages, and also regarding the relative importance of biological, social, and individual factors. It is not unusual for models to be presented as more rigid in their demarcation of the timing and ordering of their boundaries than their originators intended. This is the case, for example, for Erikson and for Levinson et al., whose work is discussed later. None the less, it is also the case that the same authors claim greater generality for their models than is warranted. One way to avoid getting bogged down in debates about the accuracy or otherwise of detailed stage descriptions is to group several stages into broad, overarching eras, and it is this term that is used here to describe the very general and encompassing sequence of phases that have sometimes been used to chronicle the life course.

Overarching eras

If we adopt a liberal rather than a restrictive definition of stage (that is, if we accept sociocultural as well as structural and maturational conceptions), then defining an account of the life course as a series of eras rather than a series of stages is largely a question of the breadth of view. Two main sequences of eras can be found in the literature. One has already been mentioned in the discussion of the stage concept, namely the growth–maintenance–decline pattern that characterises biological and physical developmental pathways and that has sometimes been transferred to the psychological domain. The main alternative proposition is a sequence that also begins with an era of growth – or acquisition (Kolb, 1984) – but is followed not by eras of maintenance and decline but by eras of specialisation (where some parts of the self are developed at the expense of others) and then, ideally, by an era of integration (where the unused or underused parts of the self return to the fore).

Growth, maintenance, and decline Before presenting his "total life-span, total life-space" life-career rainbow in the mid-1970s (Super, 1980), Super (1957) had proposed a theory of career development based on the individual's efforts to implement a self-concept in the workplace. Drawing on the even earlier work of Charlotte Bühler (1933), career development was depicted as proceeding through five stages: growth, exploration, establishment, maintenance, and decline.

Super's model is similar to that of Miller and Form (1951) who, several years earlier, had proposed a model of career stages that reflected the series of social adjustments imposed on individuals by the work culture: preparation for work through socialisation, initiation into work through part-time employment, trial period, stable period, and retirement period. From the outset, Miller and Form emphasised that not everyone experiences this stable, secure career path. They saw an individual's occupational attainment as being determined primarily by the accident of birth into a particular social class, with the individual's own efforts and aspirations being of more limited significance. This sociological perspective has echoed down the decades, being reflected, for example, in the work of Roberts (1977, 1997). Like Miller and Form, Super recognised that the smooth, linear model he depicted in his account of career development was not the whole story. His later work on the life-career rainbow sought to place career development in the context of the total life space and to incorporate the influence of both environmental and individual factors. None the less, he still included the five life stages as labels for different phases of the arc, an image that visually reflects the growth–maintenance–decline pattern.

Disengagement theory (Cumming & Henry, 1961) is likewise a model that identifies a period of decline in the later years of life. Disengagement theory advocates as "normal" (both statistically and in terms of what "ought" to happen) that older people "disengage" from many of the roles and activities in which they have participated. As was discussed in the opening chapter, this perspective has been challenged, first, by activity and continuity theories (which, in effect, argue in favour of continuing the "maintenance" phase as long as possible) and subsequently by the notion of selective optimisation with compensation (whereby people prioritise those areas in which they wish to concentrate their energies and seek to compensate for any personal limitations by developing additional psychological, social, and practical coping resources).

It is the first tenet of life-span developmental psychology that the potential for development exists throughout the life course. This challenges the assumption that adulthood is a developmental plateau and old age a period of decline. Kolb's (1984) three-phase overarching framework or metamodel of life-span development – acquisition, specialisation, and integration – represents a viable alternative to the growth–maintenance–decline series of eras.

Acquisition, specialisation, and integration Kolb (1984) divides the human developmental process into three broad developmental stages or, to use our current terminology, eras: acquisition, specialisation, and integration.

Developmental progress will vary depending on the individual and his or her particular cultural experience. Also, progression from one stage to the next rarely proceeds in a smooth linear fashion on all fronts simultaneously. Rather, such progression is likely to involve successive oscillations from one stage to the next, with individuals eventually either consolidating their position in the more advanced phase, or settling back into the earlier one.

The first era, acquisition, extends from birth to adolescence and involves the acquisition of basic learning abilities and cognitive structures. It is marked by the gradual emergence of internalised structures that allow the child to gain a sense of self that is separate and distinct from the surrounding environment. It ends with the delineation of the boundaries of self that characterise the adolescent search for identity.

The era of specialisation extends through formal education, career training, and the early experiences of adulthood in work and personal life. People – shaped by cultural, educational, and organisational socialisation forces – develop increased competence in a specialised mode of adaptation that enables them to master the particular tasks they encounter in their chosen life paths. Early experiences at home and school might have already encouraged children to begin to develop some interests and skills at the expense of others, but it is in secondary school and beyond that they begin to make choices that will significantly shape the course of their life and the nature of their development. These choices tend to encourage specialisation in that individuals tend to select environments (for example, careers and personal relationships) that they believe are compatible with their personal characteristics and adapt to the demands of the environments in which they find themselves. During this specialisation phase of development, a person's sense of self tends to be defined primarily in terms of content – things I can do, experiences I have had, goods and qualities I possess – and self-worth on the rewards and recognition thereby received.

The specialised developmental accomplishments of the second era can bring a sense of security and achievement, but sometimes at the expense of personal fulfilment. The demands of society will often, in the second era, conflict with, overwhelm and thwart personal aspirations and needs. The transition from the specialisation to the integration stage, that is, from the second to the third developmental era, is denoted by the individual's confrontation of this conflict. The recognition and facing of this conflict can develop as a gradual process of awakening or can occur dramatically as a result of a life crisis such as divorce or redundancy. In either case, the individual experiences a shift in the frame of reference used to experience life, evaluate activities and make choices. The non-dominant or underused parts of the self begin to find expression. A sense of greater integration and wholeness develops. There is an increasing sense of the self as process rather than content. Kolb likens the transition to Jung's process of individuation – the, "higher-level integration and expression of nondominant modes of dealing with the world" (Kolb, 1984, p. 144). Unlike the transition from the first to the second era, however, this transition to the era of integration is not inevitable: "Some may never have this experience, so immersed are they in the societal reward system for performing their differentiated specialized function" (Kolb, 1984, p. 145).

Comparing the growth–maintenance–decline and the acquisition–specialisation–integration frameworks shows that the acquisition and growth phases are synonymous and that the specialisation and maintenance phases share a number of characteristics, although the concept of "specialisation" suggests further progression rather than the more static imagery of the term "maintenance". The decline and integration phases, however, are very different constructions. Whilst decline may denote adaptation to many of the realities of ageing, integration implies the possibility of further growth.

This division of the life course into three broad eras is echoed in several other accounts of more specific threads, or themes, of development across the life course, for example, gender role development and models proposing new phases of cognitive development during adulthood. The broad sequences – be they growth, maintenance, decline, or acquisition, specialisation, integration – still, however, suggest a particular pattern to the life course. There is a concern with some particular end-point, namely, decline or integration. Perspectives that place more emphasis on the process of development than on some particular end-point present the life course not so much as a sequence of phases but more as a journey on which we may pause at various points for an indeterminate amount of time. The life course is seen as having direction (or order) but the model is non-normative in that there are no guidelines concerning how far a person might or should progress.

Non-normative progression

In Chapter 1 it was suggested that development might better be thought of as a process than as an end-state. This is consistent with a model of the life course as non-normative progression: a potential pathway is proposed but it is not assumed that we will all travel the same distance along it (Bee, 1994). This is an organic concept of development as the unfolding of inherent potential but, unlike the biological concept of stage, such unfolding is not seen as occurring in accordance with a fixed timetable. Thus, humanistic approaches to development (for example, Maslow, 1970; Rogers, 1961) assume a basic human drive to maintain oneself and move towards the constructive accomplishment of one's potential. "This tendency may become deeply buried under layer after layer of encrusted psychological defenses; it may be hidden behind elaborate facades which deny its existence; . . . however . . . it exists in every individual and awaits only the proper conditions to be released and expressed" (Rogers, 1961,

p. 351). Maslow (1970) talks of the process of self-actualisation and Rogers (1961) of the fully functioning person a concept summarized in Chapter 1 (Box 1.2).

Consistency and the life course

Until now, the discussion of meta-models of the life course has focused on life-span changes. There is, however, an alternative approach, also prevalent within developmental psychology, that focuses on invariance and stability rather than change. Following an initial period of growth and development, a person's personality is seen as firmly established and likely to be changed only by massive intervention and effort. This approach has shunned the transitory and attempted to identify the consistent (Gergen, 1977).

Among those advocating the stability argument most vehemently are the personality psychologists Costa and McCrae (1997; McCrae & Costa, 1990). They demonstrate considerable stability beyond the age of about 30 years in the "Big 5" personality traits of neuroticism, extraversion, openness to experience, agreeableness, and conscientiousness. They readily accept, however, that other aspects of a person's life do change during adulthood and that much of psychological importance occurs: "People live most of their lives in this period; they begin careers, raise children, fight wars, and make peace; they experience triumph and despair, boredom and love" (McCrae & Costa, 1990, pp. 5–6). Through all of this, however, personality – at least as measured by standardised personality inventories – remains remarkably consistent. The consistency orientation is also compatible with Berger's position, quoted in Chapter 1, that, in midlife, it may be continuities (or themes) rather than changes that are the more significant. Similarly, Atchley's (1989) continuity theory of ageing emphasises the extent to which we can retain a sense of internal continuity of identity even in the face of significant external or environmental discontinuity.

Consistency does not imply the total absence of change, however. In the same way as the ordered-change orientation to development includes different concepts of stage, so too does the consistency orientation include different forms of consistency. Thus, distinction can be made between level, structural, process, ipsative, and normative consistency.

Level consistency is a quantitative concept, referring to "persistence in the *magnitude* or quantity of a phenomenon over time" (Mortimer, Finch, & Kumka, 1982, p. 266; emphasis added). It is premised upon structural consistency, because consistency of score is meaningless if the nature of what is being measured has changed.

Structural consistency is a qualitative rather than quantitative concept, referring to, "continuity in the *nature* of the phenomenon under investigation" (Mortimer et al., 1982, p. 266; emphasis added). It concerns the extent to which a construct such as personality, intelligence, or personal values continues to comprise the same dimensions – demonstrated empirically by similarity in factor structure over time.

Process consistency is concerned with regularity in the form of change (Wohlwill, 1980), referring to the extent to which the course of development of an attribute is consistent across individuals. Thus, the development of mobility in infants demonstrates high process consistency, passing through the stages of sitting, crawling, standing, and walking. With such attributes it is possible to assess the extent to which an individual conforms to the typical pattern. So, a minority of infants may deviate from the typical mobility development pattern by, for example, substituting "bottom shuffling" for the more usual crawling stage.

Ipsative consistency is an intraindividual concept indicating stability in the relative strength of a person's attributes, that is, the, "persistence of a hierarchical relation between complementary dispositions within an individual" (Kagan, 1980, p. 32). Ipsative consistency would be shown, for example, in the similarity of an individual's pattern of occupational interests over time.

Whilst ipsative stability makes within-individual comparisons, normative consistency is an interindividual concept, referring to constancy of relative position amongst a group of people in relation to a particular attribute. Normative consistency implies the "preservation of a set of individual ranks on a quality within a constant cohort" (Kagan, 1980, p. 32). Thus, normative consistency is shown if children who are small relative to their peers at the age of 11 remain so at age 18, even though all have grown. Normative and ipsative change may be accorded different significance. Thus, a slight change in normative position, say from the 55th to the 58th percentile on a measure of personal warmth may be insignificant statistically (that is, be taken as indicative of normative consistency), but be experienced by the individual as an important and marked movement (and therefore be interpreted as ipsative change) (McCrae & Costa, 1990).

None of the above forms of consistency precludes all change. For example, structural consistency allows for changes in level. Level consistency could be accompanied by ipsative and/or normative instability. Process consistency actually implies some change, but in a prescribed way. With regard to ipsative and normative consistency, the absolute amount of an attribute may change (that is, level consistency is not required), but not the attribute's relative position with regard to, respectively, other attributes of the individual and the same attribute in other members of a consistent comparison group.

In sum, the polarising of the debate as a "change" versus a "consistency" issue is inappropriate. As McCrae and Costa (1990) note, much does change during adulthood – behaviours and habits, attitudes and opinions, and social roles, for example. What they argue is that personality – defined as enduring (albeit not necessarily totally immutable) traits – does not change significantly during adulthood and, furthermore, that these traits form an important part of our self-concept or identity. The self, is, however, composed of more than our personality traits, and elements such as social behaviour and roles can, and do, change. Part of the problem is one of terminology – Costa and McCrae restrict the use of the term personality to personality traits, whilst others (for example, Kimmel, 1974) use the term to include broader elements of a person's psychosocial system that Costa and McCrae would describe as part of the self. We can conclude, therefore, that whilst much changes, some things remain more or less the same. This "both/and" rather than "either/or" position is consistent with the tenets of the life-span perspective summarised in Chapter 1.

Whilst it is clear that some aspects of the life course are ordered and predictable in terms of the manner in which they do or do not change, there is much that is not preprogrammed. This brings us to the third orientation to looking at the life course, that is, one that takes as its starting point the recognition that significant parts of our life course are determined by chance and chaos.

Chaos and the life course

Rather than searching out ordered change across the life course, this third orientation focuses on how we cope with disorder. It assumes that we, "enter the world with a biological system that establishes the limit or range of our activities but not the precise character of the activities themselves" (Gergen, 1977, p. 148). This is consistent with the tenet of plasticity discussed in Chapter 1. The "precise character" of our life course is, from this perspective, highly dependent on a variety of environmental factors – economic, geographical, social, class, political, and so on.

Thus far the argument is congruent with the sociocultural concept of stage – an ordered-change orientation to development. However, concentrating on chaos and the life course diverts attention away from the regularity of role behaviour sequences emerging from person–environment interactions and towards the way in which specific environmental influences vary across time and culture. Your life course – your lifeline – will differ from that of your parents and grandparents simply by virtue of your having lived through different historical eras. The life courses of individuals are, in other words, neither universal nor invariant. For example, your experience of the nature and timing of the transition from education to the labour market will be different from earlier generations as a result of changes in the education system, with its gradual raising of the school leaving age, and in the occupational structure of society. Other outcomes of a societal change, such as improved medical care or the decreasing importance of the extended family, will also exert their influence.

Acceptance of the role of chaos or chance in determining the "precise character" of our life implies that life-span developmental psychology cannot hope to produce a definitive and everlasting picture of the life course.

It is concerned with a changing individual in a changing society. It must accept that any account can represent at best a temporary truth. It suggests that, rather than trying to identify stages or other forms of ordered change across the life course, we view the life course, or at least the adult years, as a, "continuing process of adjustment to external circumstances" (Pearlin, 1980, p. 180). A focus on chance leads to a search for basic processes for dealing with the chaotic and unpredictable that are valid for adults of any age. Two relevant bodies of work are considered here: first, the way in which we typically respond to stress or major upheaval in our lives (what can be termed psychosocial transitions) and, second, how we make sense of our experience (through the creation of a coherent personal narrative).

Transitions

A transitional perspective on life-span development focuses on life events entailing change (Schlossberg et al., 1995). It proposes a general structure for understanding people in transition that can accommodate both different individuals and different transitions. At its core is a model of people's changing reaction over time to major disruptions to their accustomed way of being. It is argued that such upheavals trigger a relatively predictable sequence of responses and feelings, known as the transition cycle (Hopson & Adams, 1976): shock, reaction, minimisation, self-doubt, accepting reality and letting go, testing the new reality, searching for meaning, integration. This, or a broadly similar, pattern of response, has been identified in studies covering a range of life events, for example, bereavement, job change, the birth of a first child. It is an approach considered in more detail in Chapter 6.

The work of Daniel Levinson (Levinson et al., 1978; Levinson, 1986) incorporates this concept of transition into a model of adult development. The stages, or "seasons", of adulthood identified by Levinson are reviewed in Chapter 5, but, for the moment, our interest is in his depiction of the life course as evolving through a sequence of alternating periods of change and consolidation. The pivotal concept in Levinson et al.'s work is that of the individual life structure: "the underlying pattern or design of a person's life at a given time" (Levinson et al., 1978, p. 41). It is, in effect, a unit comprising the individual and his or her immediate interpersonal, social and cultural environment – what Vygotsky (1994) refers to as the zone of proximal development. It is where learning and development occurs. The concept is used to explore "the interrelations of self and world – to see how the self is in the world and the world is in the self" (Levinson et al., 1978, p. 42). The life structure is considered from three perspectives: the individual's sociocultural world, the ways in which the person draws upon or ignores the self in everyday life, and the person's participation in the world, that is, the transactions between self and world.

Levinson et al. see the life structure as evolving through a series of alternating transitional (structure-changing) and more stable (structure-building) phases that give an overall shape to the course of adult development. During transitional phases, which will typically last about 5 years, individuals are faced with the need to make major life decisions and commitments concerning issues such as education, career, and intimate relationships. Levinson describes these phases as times when one life structure is terminated and another initiated. Having made some choices and commitments we then move into what Levinson calls a structure-building phase, where, in effect, we live with the consequences of our decisions. Thus, deciding what to study at college or university, and where, and then moving out of the parental home to student accommodation perhaps many hundreds of miles away, can be seen as a structure-changing or transitional phase of life. These decisions will, to a greater or lesser degree, set in motion the particular sequence of events or experiences that comprise the subsequent structure-building phase.

Although of major importance, the decisions made during any one transitional phase are not necessarily "for ever" decisions. Any one life structure has, according to Levinson et al.'s model, what might be described as built-in obsolescence. Both person and environment change, even during a structure-building phase, and, after a period of about 5 to 7 years, the "fit" between a person and his or her life structure is likely to have become so uncomfortable that a new transitional phases is initiated. Another period of stock taking, decision making and change begins. Even if the specifics of Levinson's description of particular life stages, with its claims of universality and limited variance, are criticised, we might still be able to recognise and accept this overall rhythm of alternating structure-changing and structure-building phases.

Salmon (1985) identifies three metaphors commonly used to describe the human life course: a natural cycle, a deck of cards, and a self-constructed narrative. When Levinson talks of the "seasons" of life, he is invoking the metaphor of the life course as a "natural" cycle. The focus on the alternating transitional and structure-building phases provides a framework within which to consider how individuals adapt to the "deck of cards" that life has, by chance, dealt them. It is, however, Salmon's third metaphor of the life course – as a process of narrative construction – that best accommodates the issue of how we deal with the inherently chaotic aspects of our lives (Cohler, 1982).

Narrative

If you were to write your autobiography, or tell someone about your own life-span development, the account would be more than a randomly selected list of your experiences. Instead, certain events would be selected (not necessarily consciously) because they illustrated something about "the sort of person you are", because of their particular significance and, in all probability, because they helped to communicate an account of your life that was consistent, coherent, believable, and acceptable. In other words, you would construct a story, or narrative, around the selected events. The term narrative is used to describe a number of events or experiences that are linked temporally, according to a theme, and in relation to an implicit or explicit endpoint. A narrative perspective on the life course focuses on the narratives that we construct about the events in our lives in order to make sense of them. These personal narratives (Cohler, 1982) or life stories (Linde, 1993) are distinct from other narratives in that they have as their primary purpose a point about the person telling the story, rather than a general point about the way the world is, and also are told and retold over a long period of time (Linde, 1993).

You have already been asked to construct a personal narrative in that the lifeline you have drawn can be thought of as a story of your life. Gergen and Gergen (1988; Gergen, 1988) use this linear, graphical representation of the life course as a basis for classifying different types of narratives or "story lines". They distinguish three simple story lines: progressive, regressive, and stability. A progressive narrative, where things get progressively better over time, is represented by an upwardly sloping graph; a regressive narrative, where events become increasingly negative, is represented by a downwards slope; and a stability narrative, where the story line is largely unchanging, by a flat, horizontal line. Compas, Hinden, and Gerhardt (1995) use these concepts to depict five different pathways through adolescence, as shown in Figure 3.1.

It is unlikely that the lifeline you drew earlier comprised just one story form. Progressive, regressive and stability elements represent what Gergen (1988) refers to as the "basic vocabulary" of possible narrative projections over time. In any one life story they will meld together into a more complex and convoluted pattern. Thus, the central trough in path 5 in Figure 3.1 reflects a regressive followed by a progressive narrative.

The lifeline not only reflects a combination of different basic narrative forms, it also reveals issues of dramatic tension. Some lifelines may characterise a life as flat and unexciting, others use an increase in the upward or downward incline of the slope to indicate significant or momentous experiences: "The steeper the incline of the story line, the more sharply events change in their evaluation. This shift is, in part, responsible for increased dramatic impact" (Gergen, 1988, p. 101). Story lines that incorporate a radical shift in their evaluation (that is, which suddenly slope steeply upwards or downwards) are likely to be seen as powerful and compelling. Stability narratives, on the other hand, will tend to be interpreted as undramatic and boring.

The concept of life-span development as a process of narrative construction acknowledges a person's individuality: "Each of us lives a story that is ours alone" (Salmon, 1985, p. 138). It allows us each an active role in authoring our own story. Whilst we may not control everything that happens to us, we can shape the meaning that we give to these events.

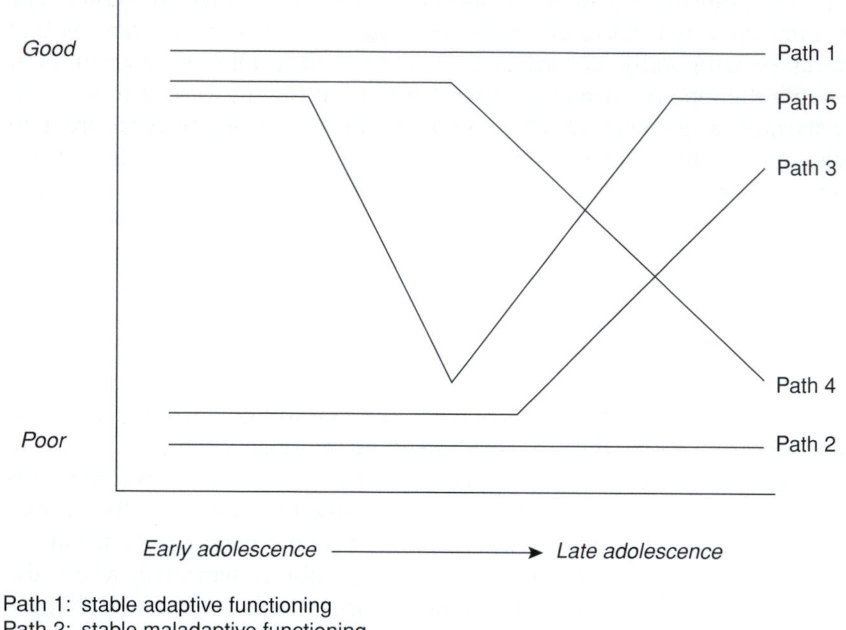

Path 1: stable adaptive functioning
Path 2: stable maladaptive functioning
Path 3: adolescent turnaround
Path 4: adolescent decline
Path 5: temporary deviation or maladaptation during adolescence

Figure 3.1 Different narrative pathways through adolescence (reproduced with permission from Compas, B.E. et al. (1995). Adolescent development: Pathways and processes of risk and resilience. *Annual Review of Psychology, 46,* 265–293. Copyright © 1995 by Annual Reviews: www.AnnualReviews.org).

We do not have total freedom, however. Our evaluation and interpretation is largely a social process, grounded in socially defined concepts of what constitutes success and failure. Even if we strive to "forge our own path" – write our own story – we are not totally immune to the environment in which we are embedded. The story lines we are able to think of, and our evaluations of them, cannot be divorced from our cultural, institutional, social, and interpersonal context, as represented by the bands in Bronfenbrenner's model of the environment (Chapter 1).

The narrative approach to life-span development has been developed in the work of Dan McAdams (1997), which is discussed in more detail in Chapter 7. Although the main focus is on how our identity is encapsulated in the personal narrative we create in order to make sense of our lives, there is a maturational element in McAdams' work in his adoption of the epigenetic principle. According to McAdams, the structural elements that form the bases of a person's personal narrative are developed in a fixed sequence according to a timetable. The acquisition is cumulative and, by adolescence or early adulthood, the person has sufficient "tools" to begin constructing his or her personal narrative. This combination of different perspectives on the life course within one account again points to the inclusive tolerance that comprises the life-span perspective. The next four chapters consider in more detail different ways of construing the life course.

4 Cumulative sequences

> We cannot live the afternoon of life according to the program of life's morning, for what in the morning was true will at evening be a lie. Whoever carries into the afternoon the law of the morning . . . must pay with damage to his soul.
>
> (Jung, 1972)

Research in life-span developmental psychology has consistently addressed the question of the extent to which the shape and/or content of the life course is ordered and predictable. As discussed in earlier chapters, such order as is found is frequently described as a sequence of stages or phases that represent the maturational unfolding of an individual's potential. The psychoanalytic theory of Freud and the cognitive theory of Piaget probably represent the most widely known stage theories in developmental psychology and are reviewed and discussed in virtually all texts on child development. For this reason alone it seems superfluous to consider them here, but, in addition, the priority they give to the pre-adult years makes them less than ideal candidates for a book focused on the whole of the life span. None the less, to ignore Freud and Piaget completely would seem so odd in a text on developmental psychology that I have succumbed to a brief overview of each. Kohlberg's stages of moral development, also fairly ubiquitous, is covered partly for the same reason, but also in order to contrast it with the Gilligan's competing model. The alternative perspectives offered by Kohlberg and Gilligan serve to demonstrate how any particular theory is but one way of telling the development tale.

Most of the chapter, however, is taken up with a more detailed review of two accounts of development as a cumulative sequence of stages spanning the whole life course. The first is Erikson's (1980) theory of eight developmental crises extending from infancy to old age and the second is McAdams' (1997) more recent, but none the less important, account of the life course as a process of narrative construction.

Freud's stages of psychosexual development

One of Freud's most fundamental ideas is the notion that human behaviour is largely governed by instinctual, unconscious, and irrational forces within the individual. He saw the human organism as selfish, aggressive, beset by internal and external conflicts, and motivated by an instinctual sexual drive – the libido. Throughout his career, Freud developed and revised his model of the mind, eventually proposing three interacting personality structures:

- the *id* – entirely unconscious and comprising all the instinctual urges (notably the libido) present at birth
- the *ego* – a more rational, intellectual, and conscious personality structure that strives to satisfy the needs of the id in a way that takes account of the demands and restrictions of external reality
- the *superego* – the centre of conscience and morality that sets itself up in opposition to the id and the ego, incorporating prevailing cultural norms and standards.

Freud proposed that the three structures develop in sequence, with the id being present from birth, the ego beginning to develop between the ages of 2 and 4–5 years, as the infant learns strategies that allow for the deferment of gratification, and the superego beginning to develop just before school age as the child starts adopting parental and cultural values and mores. Freud's account of the development of these three levels of personality incorporates what is one of the most familiar aspects of his work – the fixed, five stages of psychosexual development through which the child passes, as summarised in Table 4.1.

Each stage of psychosexual development is distinguished by the zone of the body in which the libido is invested at that time. The *oral* stage, which lasts through infancy until the age of approximately 12–18 months, can be subdivided into two phases – the first, "sucking" phase, during which the baby sucks, and the later "oral-sadistic" phase of biting.

Towards the end of the first year of life the area of sexual gratification begins to shift from the oral to the anal region, marking the onset of the anal stage. Early in this stage the child is assumed to derive pleasure from bowel movements, but later, when control over the sphincter muscles has been acquired, equal pleasure may be derived from withholding bowel movements. An important aspect of this stage is toilet training, which involves children and parents in issues of social interaction, conflict, and control.

The third stage of infantile sexuality is the phallic stage, lasting roughly between the ages of 3 and 6 years. During this stage, the zone of sexuality shifts from the anal to the genital region, with satisfaction being gained primarily by stimulation of the penis or clitoris through masturbation. This stage is marked by the so-called Oedipus complex. A boy's increasing

Table 4.1 Freud's stages of psychosexual development

Stage	*Approximate age (years)*	*Erogenous zone*	*Major developmental task*	*Characteristics*
Oral	0–1	Mouth, lips	Weaning	Sources of pleasure include sucking, biting, playing with lips Preoccupation with immediate gratification of impulses Id is dominant
Anal	2–3	Anus	Toilet training	Sources of pleasure include urination and expelling faeces, as well as retaining faeces Personality comprises id and ego
Phallic	4–5	Genitals	Oedipus/ Electra complex	Source of sexual pleasure involves manipulation of genitals Personality comprises id, ego, and superego
Latency	6–11	No specific area	Development of defence mechanisms	Loss of interest in sexual gratification Identification with same-sex parent
Genital	12 +	Genitals	Mature sexual intimacy	Concern with adult modes of sexual pleasure, unless fixated or regressed

awareness of the sexual meaning of his genital area leads him to desire his mother and unconsciously to wish to replace his father. For girls there is the Electra complex, in which a girl's sexual feelings for her father lead her to become jealous of her mother.

The Oedipus and Electra complexes are resolved through the process of identification, whereby the image of the same-sex parent is incorporated into the child's self-image and the child tries to become as much like the same-sex parent as possible. At the same time, development of the superego is initiated as the child begins to form an inner moral code based on the introjection of the values and rules of the same-sex parent. Freud labels this stage the latency period because it is characterised by a loss of interest in sexual gratification. It is followed at puberty by the onset of the genital stage of psychosexual development – the stage of mature sexual love directed towards another person. This final stage in Freud's theory is also characterised by the previously rigid superego becoming more flexible with increased maturity.

Freud's writings make scant reference to later life (Biggs, 1998). Because he saw the years beyond adolescence as a site for the reworking of childhood conflicts, rather than a time for the emergence of new developmental tasks, Freud prioritised the experiences of childhood. Problems were traced to certain key events of childhood, regardless of the age of the client. None the less, two other psychodynamic theorists, Erikson and Jung, broke away from this perspective and sought to explore the distinctive developmental tasks across the whole life span. Erikson, whose theory is considered in more detail below, focused on the interaction between the individual and the social demands characterising different life stages. Jung identified individuation – the process whereby we increasingly become who we really are – as a primary task for midlife and beyond. Having contributed to the collective sphere through social conformity, the task of the middle years is to become a whole person, through activating or resuscitating underused aspects of the self. This precedes old age, which, Jung argued, involves a return to submersion in the unconscious, especially as manifested in religious symbols such as the idea of life coming full circle and of life after death.

Criticisms of Freud's work have been manifold, and include the weak scientific basis of his theories, the selective data base from which they were developed, his neglect of social factors, the inadequate treatment of women in his theories, and his dark and somewhat pessimistic view of human nature. None the less, all reviewers would concur in the view that his theoretical ideas have had a major impact in the fields of psychiatry, social work, psychology, literature, and history. Furthermore, his ideas have had a direct impact on all of us through increasing our awareness of childhood influences on adult behaviour and our understanding how the unconscious and irrational are expressed.

Piaget's stages of cognitive development

Cognitive development (that is, the development of thinking processes) has long been a core feature of developmental psychology. With regard to childhood, Piaget's work (for example, Inhelder & Piaget, 1958) is ubiquitous. His theory of cognitive development comprises four main stages, with the final stage beginning to emerge at around the age of 11 years (see Table 4.2).

The first, or sensorimotor, stage extends through approximately the first two years of life, during which interactions with the environment are dominated by sensory (for example, seeing and hearing) and motor (such as sucking, touching, and grasping) actions. In sum, learning at this stage is concerned with the concrete rather than the abstract, and is active ("learning by doing") rather than reflective ("learning by thinking"). Piaget divides the sensorimotor stage into six substages, with the most significant transition occurring between the fifth and sixth substages.

At the sixth and final substage of the sensorimotor period the child starts manipulating internal representations of objects. This lays the foundations

Table 4.2 Piaget's stages of cognitive development

Stage	*Approximate age (years)*	*Characteristics*
Sensorimotor	0–2	Learning is concrete and active, dominated by sensory and motor interactions with the environment
Pre-operational	2–6 or 7	Learning becomes more reflective as the child develops the ability to use symbols and verbal representations of objects and events
Concrete operational	6 or 7–12	A developing understanding of the logic of classification and of relations enables the child to grasp the laws of conservation, provided the objects can be seen and manipulated
Formal operational	12+	The young person gradually develops the ability to apply abstract reasoning to real and hypothetical situations

for Piaget's second, pre-operational or representational stage of cognitive development, which lasts from about the age of 2 to the age of 6 or 7. During this time the child develops the ability to use symbols (for example, mental images of objects) and, as language develops, verbal representations of objects and events. The appearance of these processes denotes the development of a more reflective approach to learning. The child collects different images of the world and brings them together, in fantasy play for example, in inconsistent ways that do not have to comply with any laws of logic or reality.

Another feature of the pre-operational stage is centration – the focusing on only one dimension of an object or situation at a time. A perceptual manifestation of this would be when a sausage of plasticine is rolled thinner and longer, and the child, attending only to the length, thinks it has become bigger. Another form of centration is egocentricism – having difficulty or being unable (opinions differ) to see objects or situations from other than a personal perspective. The ability to focus on even one dimension is, however, a significant achievement and enables the child to perform simple classifications of objects according to a single dimension such as shape, colour, or size.

Piaget's third stage, that of concrete operations, lasts from about 6 to 11 or 12 years of age. It is characterised by the development of an understanding of the law of conservation, by decentration, and by seriation. These processes reflect the developing understanding of the logic of classification and of relations between dimensions. Thus, comprehension of the law of conservation involves the realisation that the mass, weight, and volume of an object remain the same (are conserved) despite changes in their shape or physical arrangement. Decentration is the ability to focus on more than one of an object's dimensions at the same time. This enables, for example, objects to be classified hierarchically. That is, objects of the same shape can be classified by size and colour, and different objects by, let us say, shape and size. Seriation is the increasing ability to order objects according to some quantified or perceptual appearance such as relative size or relative brightness.

This third stage is termed the stage of concrete operations because the child can perform these tasks only when the objects can be seen and manipulated. Beginning to emerge at about the age of 11 is Piaget's fourth and final stage of cognitive development – the stage of formal operations. It is indicated when the young person begins to employ abstract reasoning, denoting the ability to distinguish the form of a problem from its specific content. Its main characteristics include the use of logical, abstract thinking in the solving of problems and the ability to apply concepts to different and hypothetical situations.

Post-formal thought

Piaget acknowledged that formal reasoning continues to develop during adulthood but formulated no distinct fifth stage of cognitive development. However, several suggestions for an additional, post-formal way of reasoning have been proposed. Thus, Arlin (1975, 1977, 1989) suggests a problem-finding stage; Riegel (1973) and Basseches (1984) a stage of dialectical operations; Kitchener (1986; Kitchener & King, 1981, 1990) a stage of reflective judgement, and Labouvie-Vief (1980; Labouvie-Vief & Hakim-Larson, 1989; Labouvie-Vief & Lawrence, 1985) the emergence of pragmatic wisdom.

Kramer (1989) summarises three general features of these different characterisations of post-formal thought as involving:

- an awareness of the relativistic nature of knowledge – that is, rather than being seen as comprising value-free "facts", information is recognised as value-based material that has been mediated through a person's world view
- an acceptance of contradiction – of "both/and" rather than "either/or" – between, for example, thoughts and feelings or different self-perceptions
- the integration of contradictions into a dialectic whole.

Thus, Riegel (1973) characterised Piaget's theory as emphasising the removal of conceptual contradictions – the child, initially content with making contradictory judgements about, for example, the relative mass of two balls of plasticine, develops during the stages of concrete and formal operations increasingly non-contradictory thought. The child's thinking becomes logically consistent. However:

> The mature person needs to achieve a new apprehension and an effective use of contradictions in operations and thoughts. Contradictions should no longer be regarded as deficiencies that have to be straightened out by formal thinking but, in a confirmative manner, as the very basis of all activities. In particular, they form the basis for any innovative and creative work. Adulthood and maturity represent the period in life during which the individual knowingly reappraises the role of formal, i.e. noncontradictory, thought and during which he may succeed again (as the young child has unknowingly achieved in his "primitive dialectic") to accept contradictions in his actions and thought ("scientific dialectic").
>
> (Riegel, 1975, pp. 100–1)

The developmental task of being an adult does not, in Riegel's view, demand or require the exorcism of contradictions, merely their temporary resolutions. It requires the ability to live with complexity and tolerate a high level of ambiguity. This is achieved, Riegel argues, not through a higher or more advanced form of logical reasoning but through a different form of cognition, which facilitates a new understanding and effective use of contradictions in operations and thought. The dialectical-operations stage of cognitive development is achieved through intuitive thought, that is, through insight and understanding based on hunch, sensing, and immediate apprehension rather than reasoning, which Riegel sees, like logical thought, as making a significant contribution to intellectual growth.

Basseches (1984) also argues for the importance of dialectical thinking as a way of analysing and interpreting the real world situations faced during adulthood – situations that might have to do with personal relations, artistic activities, business transactions, and so forth. The constraining rules of logic that govern formal reasoning could be of less importance in such situations than the intuition and value judgements that characterise dialectical thinking. Labouvie-Vief (1980; Labouvie-Vief & Hakim-Larson, 1989; Labouvie-Vief & Lawrence, 1985), similarly points to the inadequacies of formal reasoning in the many situations with which adults must deal that impose, for example, practical, social, and ethical constraints. Adult thinking, like politics, is, "the art of the possible" and requires subjective value judgements as well as objective rational logic. As a result, adults develop a pragmatic wisdom that enables them to take account in their thinking of more factors than are allowed for by formal operations.

In sum, adult thinking in the "real world" requires the ability to transcend the rules of logic and rationality to incorporate values, ethics and pragmatics – a process that requires the recognition and tolerance of complexity, ambiguity and contradictions. As a result, adult thinking needs to be flexible and open. It is not that formal reasoning is obsolete, rather that it is not the whole story (Stevens-Long, 1990).

Moral reasoning

Moral reasoning is concerned with the types of thinking employed by older children and adults in the face of moral and ethical dilemmas. The distinction, on the one hand, between the development of logically coherent, rational, and abstract principles by which to resolve such dilemmas, and, on the other, the incorporation of the contextual realities of a particular situation, is reflected clearly in the contrasting theories of moral development proposed by Lawrence Kohlberg and Carol Gilligan. It is to these that our attention now turns.

Kohlberg's stages of moral development

In his work on the development of cognitive structures, Piaget investigated the development of moral reasoning as well as the development of reasoning about concrete, physical objects. It is, however, Kohlberg's research and writing on the topic (for example, Kohlberg, 1969, 1980) that has been most widely discussed. Like Piaget, Kohlberg was concerned with *how* rather than *what* people think. In particular, he focused on the reasons people gave for their moral judgements. Subjects were presented with a series of stories in which one or more individuals are faced with a moral dilemma. From respondents' answers Kohlberg identified three distinct levels of moral reasoning, labelled pre-conventional, conventional, and post-conventional. Each level comprises two stages. Like Piaget, Kohlberg proposed that all individuals pass through these levels in invariant order, irrespective of their social and cultural environment.

- *Pre-conventional thought.* External criteria, such as whether or not the behaviour is going to be punished, form the basis or moral judgements at this earliest level. In the first stage, the punishment and obedience orientation, the child acts so as to avoid punishment. In the second, instrumental-relativist, stage the child acts to gain personal rewards as well as to avoid punishment. The child might engage in an exchange of favours – "I'll scratch your back if you scratch mine", one might say.
- *Conventional thought.* As the name suggests, the touchstone of the child's moral reasoning at this level shifts from the personal consequences of behaviour to the definitions of what is "right", as evidenced by key reference groups such as the family, the peer group, or the nation. The child places prime importance on conformity and loyalty. During the first stage – the "good boy–nice girl" orientation – the

child's reference group is the people in contact with the child who have the power to reward or punish behaviour. Good behaviour is defined as that which pleases other people. In judging an act, intention is considered for the first time; that is, a misdeed is seen as worse if committed on purpose than if committed accidentally or with good intentions. During the second stage – the law-and-order orientation – the frame of reference shifts from emotionally significant others to societal institutions such as the school, the church, or the law. Duty and respect for authority are primary concerns, and good behaviour is that which obeys authority and maintains social order.

- Between the second stage of the conventional-level reasoning and the first stage of the post-conventional level the individual may pass through an intermediary phase of moral development. This is characterised by a questioning of the societal definitions of right and wrong that had previously been unreservedly accepted. Originally, Kohlberg saw this challenging of conventional moral norms, which may, unlike the other stages, be omitted, as regression to the instrumental-relativist orientation. Subsequently, however (Kohlberg, 1973b; Kohlberg & Turiel, 1973) he reinterpreted it as representing self-realising rather than selfish functioning on the grounds that it involves a general rather than a self-centred questioning of morality.
- *Post-conventional thought.* Recognising the discretionary nature of social conventions and laws, the individual develops during the post-conventional level personal standards of behaviour that are independent of the views of other people and external authority, and which may or may not conform to conventional standards. Its two stages comprise the social-contract orientation and the conscience, or universal ethical principle orientation. The first of these is marked by a strong social conscience, with the welfare of the majority being the key criterion by which actions are judged. Commitment and obligation are felt towards freely agreed contracts. Social orders and rules that are imposed and that disadvantage large sections of society are challenged.

  At the level of the universal ethical principle, actions are judged on the basis of personally chosen, but universal, ethical principles. People assume personal responsibility for their actions. Justice and reciprocity retain great significance but it is accepted that deviation from conventional ideas of goodness can be justified in the face of violations of the individual's sense of morality. Originally Kohlberg believed that this level was reached by the end of adolescence. Later he was to relax his views, seeing moral development as potentially continuing during adulthood, and this level as, "a theoretical construction suggested by the writings of 'elite' figures like Martin Luther King, and not an empirically confirmed developmental concept" (Kohlberg, 1978, p. 86). Indeed, he questions (Colby & Kohlberg,

1984) whether the post-conventional level should even be included as a stage in moral development.

Gilligan's (1982) different voice

Carol Gilligan challenges Kohlberg's definition of the highest level of morality as being based on an ethic of justice. The origin of Gilligan's thesis lies in her experience of listening to men and women, but particularly women, talk about both real and hypothetical moral dilemmas. She was particularly concerned with people's response to moral dilemmas they were actually facing, for example, deciding whether or not to have an abortion, rather than the hypothetical situations with which Kohlberg's subjects were presented, for example, what you would do if you had to choose between letting your partner die or spending the rest of your life in jail. She observed a way of talking about the relationship between the self and others that was different from that described and defined as development in the studies of people like Levinson et al. (1978), Vaillant (1977), and, in particular, Kohlberg. Gilligan described this alternative way of talking as a different voice – identified by theme, but found empirically to be strongly, although not absolutely, associated with women rather than men.

The essence of the different theme articulated by Gilligan lies in the centrality accorded to questions of relationships, responsibilities, and care in situations of choice and moral dilemma. The sequential elaboration of these concepts forms a developmental trajectory distinct from that depicted in models based on studies of men. It centres on the development of attachment rather than separation, its polar opposite. Gilligan found that women tended to see the world in terms of connectedness, and, may therefore, find isolation frightening, whereas men, who tended to see the world in terms of autonomy, may be threatened by intimacy. Recognition of the significance of intimacy and relationships with others, which Levinson and others observe as dawning on men during midlife, "is something women have known from the beginning" (Gilligan, 1982, p. 17). Gilligan describes the elaboration of this knowledge as the development of the ethic of care. She identifies three distinct stages, each separated by a transitional period.

- *Care for one's own survival.* The initial focus in Gilligan's developmental sequence is on caring for oneself in order to survive. The individual feels isolated and not connected to others. The self is, therefore, of sole concern. There is no conflict between one's own needs and those of others because only the former is recognised. Dilemmas exist only when one's own needs or wants are in conflict. Development is denoted when this perspective comes to be viewed as selfish. This marks the transition to stage 2, with the transitional issue centring on a developing awareness of the inevitable connection or attachment between the self and others, and the responsibilities that this implies.

- *Care for others*. Recognising the earlier perspective as selfish expresses a new insight into the connection between self and other, which is evidenced by the concept of responsibility. It is, however, a self-sacrificing definition of responsibility in which good is equated with caring for others. It is a caring that takes as its touchstone the avoidance of hurting others. In such a situation the needs of the other are met but the needs of the self are excluded, or else are recognised only at the cost of guilt. Another developmental transition is triggered when, and if, such denial to the self of that care that is extended to others comes to be perceived as an inappropriate imbalance.
- *Care for integrity*. The concept of care, having previously been equated with not hurting others is complicated at this stage by recognising the legitimacy of care for oneself. The tension between selfishness and responsibility (or between responsibility to self and responsibility to others) is addressed through attending to the dynamics of relationships. Thus, care remains the principle on which judgements are made, but now it is a principle that extends to the self, based on the insight that self and other are interdependent. To deny legitimacy to the needs of the self is, because of this interdependence, eventually to harm others as well as the self. It would thus be inconsistent even within a principle of care directed solely at others. Concepts of selfishness and responsibility to others are mediated through an understanding of the dynamics of social interaction. General notions of rights and justice are tempered by contextual factors – by the details of a particular situation.

Gilligan contrasts the theme of morality based on the ethic of care with the theme of morality based on the ethic of justice, as exemplified by Kohlberg's work. She sees it as a morality concerned with relationships rather than rights. "While an ethic of justice proceeds from the premise of equality – that everyone should be treated the same – an ethic of care rests on the premise of non-violence – that no one should be hurt" (Gilligan, 1982, p. 174). The principled conception of human rights that Kohlberg sees as the pinnacle of moral development rests on the, "human being's right to do as he pleases without interfering with somebody else's rights" (Kohlberg, 1973b, pp. 29–30). It is orientated towards individual autonomy, impartial judgement, and behaving in an objectively fair and rational way. From a moral perspective that rests on the concept of care and mutual responsibilities, such a stance can appear unsatisfactory, potentially justifying indifference and unconcern. On the other hand, the alternative – which looks to what is left out in a supposedly objectively fair assertion of rights, and to who is hurt by such a resolution – can appear inconclusive and diffuse from a moral perspective based on rights. Gilligan construed maturity as a combination of both, a dialogue between fairness and care premised on "the realization that just as inequality adversely affects both parties in an unequal relationship, so too violence is destructive for everyone involved" (Gilligan, 1982, p. 174). Thus, Gilligan identifies two developmental routes. One, typically followed by men and well articulated by theorists of the life cycle, has separation as its organising principle and rights as its yardstick. The other, typically followed by women and accorded only a secondary role in many accounts of development, centres on attachment and responsibility. Maturity combines both.

The question remains of why the definitions of morality and the routes to maturity should be differentially associated with men and women. Gilligan, following Chodrow (1978), see this as originating in women's virtually universal responsibility for early childcare. There is greater similarity and continuity between mother and daughter than between mother and son. The boundary between self and other is thus more blurred for girls and more distinct for boys. That is, attachment is a more prevalent aspect of the relationship for girls whilst separation is for boys. This sets the stage for a continuing female development around the theme of connection and relationship, and a continuing male development based on separation and individuation. However, men's and women's development and world views are not inevitably different. Gilligan and Attanucci (1988) found, for example, that when asked to describe a moral problem or conflict they had faced recently, more than two-thirds of their educationally advantaged sample of American adolescents and adults described considerations involving both justice and care. None the less, Gilligan's argument is that men's and women's experience tends to place them in closer proximity to one of these moral discourses than to the other. Moreover, it is often the man's rather than the woman's voice that is heard at full volume. Both need to be heard and placed alongside each other if a mature morality based on integration of justice and care is to be attained.

Erik Erikson: the sequential resolution of psychosocial crises

Whilst Freud and Piaget may be the authors most widely cited when child development is the focus of psychologist's attention, Erik Erikson holds pride of place when the whole life span is considered. Erikson's work, beginning with the publication of *Childhood and society* (1950), spanned over 30 years, with some of his earlier writings (Erikson, 1959) being reissued more than 20 years after their original publication (Erikson, 1980). His eight-stage theory of psychosocial development remains one of the most widely known and widely quoted account of the life cycle in the social science literature.

Erikson's model is of a changing individual operating in a changing society. As the individual develops, society places new demands on him or her; demands to which the ego must adapt. Each new demand provokes an emotional crisis, the successful resolution of which leads to the development of a new "virtue" or "vital strength". Erikson sees this development as ordered rather than random; specifically, as a cumulative process occurring in accordance with a timetable. He presents this timetable as a series of eight psychosocial tasks or crises, as summarised in Table 4.3. Although the crises are represented as a series of polar opposites, they in fact represent dimensions rather than alternatives. Thus, the outcome of the first stage can range from basic trust to basic mistrust; the outcome of the second stage from a strong sense of autonomy to a profound sense of shame and doubt, and so on. Whilst each task has a period of ascendancy, they all exist in some form throughout life and, may, therefore, be addressed at other times as well. Thus, whilst failure to deal adequately with a task during its period of ascendancy is damaging to the ego's development, this damage is not entirely irrevocable. As development proceeds it becomes more complex. As each new task is addressed, earlier resolutions are questioned. The struggles of yesteryear may, for better or worse, be fought again.

Erikson sees the struggles of both previous and present generations as being enshrined in a culture's social institutions. In other words, there is a cultural manifestation of each stage of individual development. These institutions impinge on the individual, thereby influencing both the specific form and the outcome of the crises. Development is a function of both individual and cultural factors – hence Erikson's description of his theory as a theory of psychosocial development and of his tasks as psychosocial tasks. The cultural manifestations of the psychosocial tasks are indicated on the right-hand side of Table 4.3. Erikson did not explicate this aspect of his theory as fully as he did the stages of individual development. It is, however, summarised in the appendix to *Identity and the life cycle* (1980) and can be gleaned from his discussions of the psychosocial stages.

Erikson's stages of psychosocial development

1. Basic trust versus basic mistrust. During the first year of life infants learn to trust or mistrust the predictability of their environment. Through the experience provided by their major caregivers they learn whether they can depend on their needs for food, warmth, and other forms of comfort being met. It is during this time as well that the beginnings of trust in oneself are learned as the infant comes to trust his or her body to cope with its necessary functions – breathing, feeding, digestion, elimination. Thus, in addition to a reasonable trustfulness of others, a sense of basic trust also implies a reasonable trust and confidence in oneself. Erikson sees this as manifested in the willingness and ability to allow the major caregivers out of sight without suffering undue anxiety or rage – an achievement that is dependent on a sense of inner certainty as well as

Table 4.3 Erikson's stages of psychosocial development

Approximate age (years)	*Stage*	*Crisis*	*Potential new virtue*	*Societal manifestation*
0–1	Infancy	Basic trust versus basic mistrust	Hope	Religion and faith
1–6	Early childhood	Autonomy versus shame and doubt	Will	Law and order
6–10	Play age	Initiative versus guilt	Purpose	Economics
10–14	School age	Industry versus inferiority	Competence	Technology
14–20	Adolescence	Identity versus role confusion	Fidelity	Ideology
20–35	Young adulthood	Intimacy versus isolation	Love	Ethics
30–39		*Career consolidation**		
35–65	Maturity	Generativity versus stagnation	Care	Education, art and science
50–59		*Keeping the meaning versus rigidity**		
65+	Old age	Ego integrity versus despair and disgust	Wisdom	All major cultural institutions

* These additional stages were suggested by Vaillant (1977), see text for further details.

outer predictability. In other words, it is dependent on a rudimentary sense of ego identity.

The cultural institution that Erikson sees as deeply related to the issue of trust is that of religion or, more generally, of faith. Individual trust becomes, at this level, a common faith, and individual mistrust a commonly formulated evil. If not derived from religion, basic faith can be derived from some other source – fellowship, productive work, social action, scientific pursuit, or artistic creation, for example. Erikson's theory links generations when he argues that without such faith an adult is unable to nurture and support the infant's developing sense of trust.

2. Autonomy versus shame and doubt. During the second and third year of life children become more mobile and, thereby, more independent. They need no longer be content with what others bring to them but can move about the world and choose how and with what they interact. This development of motor skills can facilitate psychosocial development, demonstrating the interconnections between different arenas or strands of development. However, at this age, children's sense of discrimination is as yet untrained. They do not know what is possible and what impossible; what is safe and what is dangerous. Without protection and guidance the child will experience repeated failure and ridicule, which foster feelings of doubt and shame rather than bolster the child's sense of autonomy, promoting instead a sense of inadequacy.

The goal of this stage is to attain self-control without loss of self-esteem. Being made to see oneself as inadequate makes one ashamed. Too much can lead either to defiant shamelessness or to a determination to get away with things unseen. Thus, to develop a healthy sense of autonomy, the child must be given both choice and protection, and must experience a reasonable balance between freedom and control. At the societal level, concerns about the balance between freedom and control are to be found in debates concerning law and order and the relationship between obligations and rights. Likewise, a society's resolution of these issues is to be found in its system of laws, rules and regulations, and its mechanisms for the disciplining of transgressors. As with the crisis of trust versus mistrust, the question of autonomy can be revisited in adulthood. If adults experience relationships with individuals and institutions that undermine their sense of autonomy this also undermines their ability to provide their children with an appropriate balance between freedom and control.

3. Initiative versus guilt. A sense of autonomy gives the child the sense of him or herself as a person. Through the crisis of initiative versus guilt children begin to explore the question of the kind of person they are going to be. Being able now to move around independently and vigorously in almost the same way as adults, children can begin to imagine themselves being as large as adults and fulfilling adult roles. Largely through imitative play with other children, they begin to explore possible future roles for themselves. In particular, they play with the idea of what it would be like to be like their parents.

Erikson defines initiative as a truly free sense of enterprise, manifested at the societal level in a society's economic structure and endeavour. Initiative is largely governed by conscience – a self-dependence that in turn makes the individual dependable. With the development of conscience also develops the potential for guilt. "The child now feels not only ashamed when found out but also afraid of being found out . . ., (and) guilty even for mere thoughts and for deeds which nobody has watched" (Erikson, 1980, p. 84).

Whilst being a cornerstone of individual morality, a child's conscience can be overburdened by adults. When this happens, initiative may be thwarted. Instead of developing a sense of purpose – the new virtue that results from successful resolution of this crisis – the child may learn to constrict him or herself to point of general inhibition, or may become excessively good and obedient, or may develop "deep regressions and lasting resentments because the parents themselves do not seem to live up to the new conscience which they have fostered in the child" (Erikson, 1980, p. 84).

4. Industry versus inferiority. Erikson (1980) summarises the convictions around which personality crystallises during the early part of the life cycle. At stage 1 (trust versus mistrust), there is the belief that "I am what I am given". At stage 2 (autonomy versus shame and doubt), this becomes "I am what I will". At stage three (initiative versus guilt), the child comes to believe that "I am what I imagine I can be". At the fourth stage (industry versus inferiority), this becomes transformed into "I am what I learn". At this stage, the child is involved in learning to use the physical and intellectual tools of his or her society. In other words, the society's technology (the societal manifestation of this crisis) is now imparted to the child. Through this process the child, ideally, learns industry, that is, he or she becomes competent in managing "the inorganic laws of the tool world" (Erikson, 1980, p. 91).

The risk at this stage is the development of a sense of inadequacy and inferiority rather than industry. This may result from the insufficient resolution of preceding conflicts. Perhaps the child still wishes or needs to remain tied to the apron strings of home, or else is comparing him or herself with parents and feeling guilty about personal shortfalls. Alternatively, or as well, feelings of inferiority can result from the child being unable to learn or being prevented from learning the set of specific skills needed for effective functioning in that society. Another danger is that of over-exaggerating the role and importance of technology and technological competence. In accepting work (or industry) as more or less the only obligation, and "what works" as the only criterion of value, a person or society becomes a slave rather than a ruler of technology.

5. Identity versus role confusion. Erikson is best known for his theory of the adolescent identity crisis. Rapid physical growth and hormonal changes (described by Erikson as a physiological revolution) marking the attainment of genital maturity combine with awareness of tangible adult tasks ahead to produce a questioning of "all samenesses and continuities relied on earlier" (Erikson, 1963, pp. 252–3). In the struggle, the crises of earlier years might need to be fought again. The search is for a new sense of continuity and sameness. Questions of sexual and, for most people in our society, occupational, identity are paramount. Particularly for members of ethnic minorities, the development of a sense of ethnic or racial identity is also central (Phinney, 1990; Phinney & Rosenthal, 1992).

Successful resolution of this crisis leads to a sense of ego identity: "a conviction that one is learning effective steps toward a tangible future, that one is developing a defined personality within a social reality which one understands" (Erikson, 1980, p. 95). Ego identity is premised upon, but is more than, the virtues marking successful resolution of earlier stages – hope, will, purpose, and competence. The identity crisis involves a reworking of such attributes into a more coherent set of values and beliefs to which the individual feels commitment and loyalty. It is a state of flux between the morality of childhood and the ethically principled adult. The resulting new virtue or vital strength is fidelity, and its cultural manifestation is in a society's ideology.

The danger of this stage is identity diffusion or role confusion – uncertainty about who one is and what one is to become. To counteract such uncertainty, or to bolster a still fragile sense of identity, the young person might temporarily over-identify with a clannish subgroup of peers and/or particular cults or individuals. The development of a self-destructive or socially unacceptable identity might be preferable to no identity. Thus, the young person might cling to an identity of addict, delinquent or hooligan if more attractive and socially acceptable alternatives seem unavailable.

6. Intimacy versus isolation (distantiation and self-absorption). Having achieved and developed some confidence in his or her separate identity, the young adult is now able to risk destroying this individuality by fusing it with another's. This fusing is achieved through intimacy – the capacity to commit oneself to "concrete affiliations and partnerships and to develop the ethical strength to abide by such commitments, even though they may call for significant sacrifices and compromises" (Erikson, 1950, p. 255). Love is the potential new strength to be developed at this stage. At the wider level the resolution of this crisis is to be found in a society's explicit or, more often, implicit ethical standards.

Intimacy calls for self-abandonment. The often painfully acquired sense of identity is thereby put at risk. To take such a risk, the individual must have some confidence that his or her ego will remain intact. If the threat of ego loss is too great, the individual will avoid potentially intimate relationships, leading to a deep sense of isolation. Intimacy involves rising above and beyond oneself. Without it, the risk of prolonging the self-absorption characteristic of the adolescent is high. For some, intimacy may be seen as a solution to the crisis of identity, harnessing one's identity to that of another rather than struggling to fashion an independent identity of one's own. Such a strategy is likely to lead to an unbalanced partnership, with one partner being relegated to a subordinate role and the other partner bearing the burden of providing a sense of identity for two people.

At this point in Erikson's sequence of crises the age boundaries dividing the different stages start to become extremely unclear. For example, Havighurst (1973) sets the end of the intimacy versus isolation stage at the age of 40, Turner and Helms (1979) place it at age 34, and Bee (1994) as early as 25 years. Sheehy (1996), writing about the two decades between the early 1970s and the early 1990s, noted many changes in the age norms of adulthood, and so this variation in the suggested timing of the crises of adulthood is, perhaps, unsurprising.

The variation in the age identified as marking the end of the crisis of intimacy also reflects individual variations in the timing of the stages of adulthood, as well as, perhaps, Erikson's general reticence about the tasks of the thirties. Vaillant (1977) describes Erikson as leaving an uncharted period of development between the 20s and the 40s. In his own contribution to a longitudinal study of high-achieving students at Harvard University, Vaillant identified an intermediate stage of career consolidation occurring between Erikson's crisis of intimacy and the one that follows, namely, that between generativity and stagnation. He also points to the sequence of identity, intimacy, career consolidation, and generativity found by other American studies of adult development (for example, Block & Haan, 1971; Levinson et al., 1978; Oden & Terman, 1968). During their early thirties, Vaillant (1977, p. 202) found his subjects to be, "too busy becoming; too busy mastering crafts; too busy ascending prescribed ladders to reflect upon their own vicissitudes of living". By their mid-thirties they were pressing "to step into the driver's seat" (Vaillant, 1977, p. 202). Such a self-centred preoccupation tended, however, by the age of 50, to be replaced with a much greater concern for those working with and for them – in other words, a generative concern, the focus of Erikson's next psychosocial stage.

7. Generativity versus stagnation. Erikson's seventh crisis is between generativity and stagnation. Finding expression most usually through the experience of parenthood, Erikson defines generativity as, "primarily the interest in establishing and guiding the next generation" (Erikson, 1980, p. 103). It is not, however, synonymous with parenthood. Indeed, difficulties with the parenting role could stem from the inability to achieve generativity, and its consequent virtue of care. Parenthood is not the only mechanism for achieving generativity. It can also be expressed through other forms of creativity and altruistic concern. At the societal level generativity is evidenced most clearly through education, although, "all institutions codify ethics of generative succession" (Erikson, 1950/1963, p. 259).

More than any other of his psychosocial stages, Erikson's crisis of generativity serves to demonstrate the interdependence of generations:

> The fashionable insistence on dramatizing the dependence of children on adults often blinds us to the dependence of the older generation on the younger one. Mature man needs to be needed, and maturity needs guidance as well as encouragement from what has been produced and must be taken care of.
>
> (Erikson, 1950/1963, p. 258)

Failure to attain generativity will lead, Erikson argues, to stagnation and personal impoverishment. The care that, to be growthful, needs to be directed towards one's child or other creation, could instead be turned inwards. The individual becomes (or remains) self-centred; in effect being like his or her own child, and possibly succumbing to early physical or psychological invalidism.

Vaillant (1977), in addition to pinpointing a stage of career consolidation between the crisis of intimacy and generativity, also found evidence in his study of another phase, this time occurring between the crisis of generativity and the final struggle identified by Erikson between integrity on the one hand, and despair or disgust on the other. Vaillant describes this intermediary phase as a tension between "keeping the meaning" and rigidity. He sees it as characterising the decade of the fifties, a time during which a new generation is beginning to take over: "as this happens, rigidity interferes with generativity" (Vaillant, 1977, p. 231). Vaillant found rigidity to be denoted by efforts on the part of his subjects to ensure the perpetuation rather than the replacement of their own culture and values, and by their experiencing of mild regret about aspects of the direction in which they saw society heading. The positive side of this rigidity was shown in his subjects' concern with "keeping the meaning" – their efforts to teach what they themselves have learned to others who can perpetuate that which is of worth in society and continue the attempt to accomplish goals that will not be attained in the lifetime of those now into middle age. "Passing on the torch" and exposing his children to "civilized values" was how one of Vaillant's subjects described this stage. Another positive aspect of the rigidity of this phase was denoted by the men's clearer and seemingly enduring sense of their own identity – they believed they knew who they were, and the best adjusted felt, correctly or otherwise, that they had found their niche in society. In narrative terminology this can be seen as a tension between, on the one hand, using personal, organisational, or cultural stories to guide the younger generations and ensure continuity through the transmission of value-laden narratives and, on the other hand, the dynamic pressure towards revision and reworking of narrative plots. Vaillant saw this stage of keeping the meaning versus rigidity as a precursor of Erikson's final stage of development – the struggle of ego integrity versus despair and disgust.

8. Ego integrity versus despair and disgust. Erikson describes an integrated ego as the ripe fruit of the seven earlier stages. It is attained through resolution of the crisis of integrity versus despair. Lacking a clear definition, Erikson points to several indicators of ego integrity, many of which echo Maslow's (1970) description of the self-actualising person, and Ryff's (1989) characteristics of successful ageing. Integrity is denoted by an acceptance of one's life for what it has been and a freedom from the burden of excessive regret that it has not been different. It involves a willingness to defend the dignity of one's own lifestyle whilst at the same time experiencing a sense of comradeship with people of other times, cultures, and walks of life. There is recognition of the value of other ways of expressing integrity, but this is not seen as threatening or incompatible with one's own version. There is also a recognition of the smallness of one's own place in the universe – the realisation that, "an individual life is the accidental coincidence of but one life cycle with but one segment of history" (Erikson, 1980, p. 104). Successful resolution of this final psychosocial crisis leads to the emergent virtue of wisdom. Rather than being embodied in any one cultural organisation, integrity permeates, or not, all of a society's institutions and mores.

Lack or loss of accrued ego integration leads to despair. This is often revealed in a fear of death and expresses the feeling that life is too short to alter anything. One cannot start a new life or plan to do things differently next time. Despair may be hidden behind a show of disgust – a contemptuous displeasure with particular institutions and people. This in turn signifies the individual's disgust with him or herself.

Although remaining firmly within the psychoanalytic tradition, Erikson's focus of attention differs from Freud's in a number of significant ways. First, Erikson focuses on the conscious self (the ego) whereas Freud's attention is directed primarily at the unconscious drives or instincts (the id). Second, Erikson sees the personality as developing throughout life, whereas Freud viewed the course of adulthood as having been largely set by the events of early childhood. Third, and in contrast to Freud's emphasis on the biologically based components of psychosexual development, Erikson concerned himself with the social, cultural, and historical determinants of personality development. He recognised that both his and Freud's theories were the outcome of the historical era and social milieu in which each worked. Thus, Freud worked in a society that needed liberation from sexual repression, whereas Erikson operated in an environment (namely North America in the middle years of the twentieth century) where questions of identity – of "who am I and what am I to become?" – were of central concern. The integrating theme in Erikson's work is the transformation of ego identity. This in turn pointed to a concern with issues of the ego rather than the id. The goal of the ego is survival in the real world, adapting to reality. As this reality is largely socially constructed, concern with the ego also implies concern with the role of society in individual development.

Erikson's theory has not, however, been without its critics. The comprehensiveness of both the number and content of his stages have been questioned. Vaillant's (1977) elaboration of additional stages in the thirties and fifties has already been discussed. Levinson et al. (1978) and Gould (1978) refined the stages around midlife. Peck (1968) subdivides the final stage into two phases.

Other criticisms centre on Erikson's value assumptions. At times he overemphasises the symbiotic relationship between individual development and societal progress and, as a consequence, has been criticised for promulgating a conformist theory that is excessively supportive of the status quo (Roazen, 1976). Objection has been made (Buss, 1979) to Erikson's sometimes naive and accepting attitude towards the family.

In fact, Erikson's attitude to the role of social institutions in general and the family in particular is ambivalent rather than uncritically laudatory, although as Buss (1979) points out, he does tend to defuse critiques as soon as he makes them.

Buss (1979, p. 328) also points to a major value assumption in Erikson's work, namely that, "psychological growth and health is possible only to the extent that the individual is not out of step with society". This demands an unduly benign view of society, denying that the social reality may be psychologically and/or physically repressive, alienating, or constricting. Under such conditions, argues Buss, the valid and healthy response could be shame and doubt rather than autonomy, guilt rather than initiative, and so on. Buss thus disagrees with Erikson's view of integrity as the culmination of development when it includes the acceptance of the inevitability of one's life as it has been. "Integration of the individual into society is not an absolute to be unquestioningly sought after . . . Unqualified acceptance of one's total life history, and by implication of the external forces that have helped to shape that life, is too heavy a price to pay for the comfort of integration" (Buss, 1979, p. 320). Similarly, identity diffusion or confusion may be the most reality-based resolution, at least temporarily, of the identity crisis for gay and lesbian youth in a society whose definition of an acceptable identity includes the development of intimate heterosexual relationships. Contravention rather than acceptance of societal norms could pave the way to a stronger and more positive sense of identity or self. These criticisms of Erikson's perspective highlight in a concrete fashion the value-laden nature of definitions of development.

Dan McAdams: Creating a life story

McAdams (1985, 1997), like Erikson, is concerned with identity. However, rather than seeing identity as the outcome of resolving sequential psychosocial crises, McAdams' basic thesis is that, in the modern world, identity is a person's life story, "a personal myth that an individual begins working on in late adolescence and young adulthood in order to provide his or her life with unity or purpose and in order to articulate a meaningful niche in the psychosocial world" (McAdams, 1997, p. 5). In developing his thesis out of Erikson's work, McAdams also draws on a tradition incorporating anthropology, theology, ancient mythology, and aesthetics, thereby exemplifying Baltes's (1987) central tenet of life-span developmental psychology as an interdisciplinary and contextual field of study.

The concept of the life course as a narrative construction is developed later in Chapter 7. For the present, attention is focused on how the key features of our life story develop through infancy, childhood, and adolescence, so that by the time we reach early adulthood we have available to us the tools needed to enable us to fashion our life experiences into a coherent, purposeful and meaningful story. In keeping with the epigenetic principle, McAdams sees the key structural elements of a person's life story developing in a cumulative sequence across the life cycle. Thus, important raw material for our personal narrative – and, therefore, for our identity – is generated before the adolescent or young adult begins to think of his or her own life in storied terms, and, indeed, even before the child has a clear idea of what a story is. McAdams' seven key features of a life story, and the timetable of their emergence, are summarised in Table 4.4.

McAdams' theory of life story development

1. Narrative tone. McAdams argues that the pervasive tone of a person's narrative is laid down during infancy, influenced largely by the nature of the infant's relationship with his or her primary caregivers. Secure attachments lead the infant towards a confident and coherent childhood self, reflected in an optimistic narrative that implicitly proclaims the world to be basically trustworthy, predictable, knowable, and good. There are echoes here of Erikson's crisis of basic trust versus mistrust. Insecure attachments, by contrast, lead towards a more pessimistic narrative tone, where it is accepted that wishes and intentions are generally thwarted by a capricious and unpredictable world, so that stories do not have happy endings. The mythic forms of comedy and romance reflect an optimistic narrative tone, whilst tragedy and irony reflect an underlying pessimism.

Table 4.4 The emergence of key structural elements of a life story (adapted from McAdams, 1997)

Life stage	*Emerging narrative element*
Infancy	Narrative tone – a general sense of optimism or pessimism that pervades a person's narrative
Pre-school years	Personal imagery – memorable images of a particular episode, combining feelings, knowledge, and inner sensations
Childhood	Thematic lines – recurrent patterns reflecting what the characters in a narrative want and how they pursue their objectives over time
Late adolescence	Ideological settings – a set of beliefs about what is right and true
Young adulthood	Characters (or imagoes) – internalised complexes of actual or imagined persons
Middle adulthood	Generative denouement – an envisioned ending to one's personal narrative that allows some aspect of the self to live on
Late adulthood	Narrative evaluation – the review, evaluation, reconciliation to, and acceptance of, our life story

2. Imagery. Complete stories are too big, complex, and ordered for pre-school children to grasp and manipulate, but "arresting images" serve to make the stories memorable. Such images are, "a synthesis of feeling, knowledge, and inner sensation, captured in an episode in time" (McAdams, 1997, p. 65). Images are unwittingly collected and reworked into the child's daily make-believe play such that, in the child's mind, fictitious characters from different stories interact with each other, with the child, and with significant people in the child's life. These emotionally charged images help children to make sense of their experiences and, whilst many will be transient, some images will survive into adulthood to animate the personal narrative.

The images that the pre-school child draws upon can emanate from all levels within Bronfenbrenner's model of the environment. The family – an immediate personal setting, in Bronfenbrenner's language – is a significant conveyor of images. Emotionally laden images such as the good mother, the frustrated mother, the strong father, and the helpless father are unconsciously appropriated. They become incorporated into the child's self and can continue to influence behaviour and experience throughout life. Other important sources of significant images include religion, the media (especially television), and traditional stories and customs. Although children are not in a position to determine the quality of the imagery to which they are exposed, it exerts, argues McAdams, "as much long-term influence on the quality of their lives and identities as narrative tone receives from infancy" (McAdams, 1997, p. 65).

3. Thematic lines. As children progress through formal schooling, their developing cognitive skills enable them to appreciate story themes, that is, recurrent patterns of human intention. Story themes – or thematic lines – reflect what the characters in a narrative want and how they pursue their objectives over time. Understanding stories as organised wholes in this way develops between the ages of about 6 and 12 years. From appreciation of the motivations and intentions of story characters, and from other sources, school-age children begin to establish their own motivational patterns that, over time, become consolidated into stable dispositions. Ultimately, these traits will be reflected thematically in personal narratives.

The content of thematic lines centres on the needs for power and love, corresponding, asserts McAdams, to the two central psychological motivations in human lives. Characters in stories, "desire, as we do, to expand, preserve, and enhance the self as a powerful and autonomous agent in the world, and to relate, merge, and surrender the self to other selves within a loving and intimate community" (McAdams, 1997, p. 68). Since Freud's delineation of two fundamental, but contradictory, human motives – the "life instincts" (that motivate human beings to seek each other out in sexual, pleasurable, and loving unions) and the "death instincts" (that propel human beings toward masterful and destructive sorts of behaviour, through aggression and bold displays of personal power) – there have been many other formulations of human motivations that set two general tendencies against each other. Levinson et al. (1978) often refer to the tension between attachment and separation. McAdams draws on Bakan's (1966) distinction between agency and communion as an especially clear analysis of this motivational duality. Agency is, "the individual's striving to separate from others, to master the environment, to assert, protect and expand the self" (McAdams, 1997, p. 71) in an attempt to become an influential autonomous "agent". The desire for power is a highly agentic motive. Communion, on the other hand, is, "the individual's striving to lose his or her own individuality by merging with others, participating in something that is larger than the self, and relating to others in warm, close, intimate, and loving ways" (McAdams, 1997, p. 72). The desire for love is a highly communal motive.

If our motives change – if the motivational strength of our wish for power and/or love either increases or decreases – then so too will the significance of that theme in our personal narrative. Motives, proposes McAdams, exist within the person, themes within the story. Theme is an aspect of the personal narrative that first emerges during the school years. It is not, however, until young adulthood that these themes coalesce into complete characters or imagoes who occupy our narratives.

4. Ideological settings. With adolescence comes, as Erikson expressed it, the challenging of all our previous certainties. Biological, cognitive and social changes bring awareness of the incongruities between who we were and who we are now. But to know who we are now, we must know who we were. This sets the scene for the adolescent identity crisis and also for what may be somewhat clumsy attempts at constructing an ultimately transient personal narrative.

By the time we reach adolescence, several key components of our personal narrative are in place. The tendency towards a particular narrative tone has been established, emotionally charged images have been gathered, and motives have been given shape in the themes of agency and communion. In adolescence an ideological setting – a set of beliefs about what is right and true – is defined. This task is an issue that the adolescent mind, with its newly developed facility for formal reasoning, is able and frequently hankering to address. Whilst people can and do make important changes in their belief systems during middle and late adulthood, late adolescence and young adulthood is frequently a formative period for the establishment of a personal ideology concerning the meaning of the world. It is necessary to address this issue if the future personal narrative is to be founded on a base of perceived truth and anchored in, "a particular ethical, religious, epistemological 'time and place'" (McAdams, 1997, p. 81). It is perhaps more necessary amongst contemporary, Western societies than in other times and places. Identity and ideology are no longer passed smoothly from generation to generation but, instead, must be fashioned by individuals themselves, through the exploration of viable alternatives.

Although the ideological setting in which each person grounds his or her identity is unique, McAdams does distinguish some common types. He suggests two key ways to comprehend and categorise ideological setting – by content and by structure.

With regard to content, McAdams proposes that the two superordinate themes of narratives, namely, agency and communion, also reflect two sets of fundamental beliefs and values characterising distinct ideological settings. An ideological setting centred on the theme of agency would place supreme value on the autonomy and wellbeing of the individual. Individual freedom would be prized, with an emphasis on individual rights rather than social responsibility. Because in this situation each person has his or her own view of the world, there is a need for general principles of ethics and justice that transcend personal biases and provide for the universal good. Otherwise, "an agentic world deteriorates into chaos, with each individual bent on maximizing his or her gain at the expense of others" (McAdams, 1997, p. 87).

A highly communal ideological setting would, by contrast, value the group and interpersonal relations most highly. Social responsibility would take precedence over individual freedoms and rights. Whilst fairness would be seen as important, it would be of greater importance to care for others and be connected to others in bonds of friendship or kinship. The goodness of an action could be evaluated only by taking into consideration its ramifications in a social context. Rather than relying on universal imperatives and abstract principles of justice, what is good and what is true is likely to depend on the specific situation – who is involved and what is at stake. McAdams' distinction between agentic and communal ideological settings mirrors Gilligan's distinction between a moral system based on the ethic of justice and one based on the ethic of care.

The structure, as opposed to the content, of an ideological setting refers to the complexity of an individual's belief system. A complex system is high differentiated (that is, has many parts or distinctions) and highly integrated (that is, the parts are connected to each other in many ways). In a simple system few distinctions are made and few connections discerned. As children mature into adolescence, their belief systems concerning, for example, morality, justice, interpersonal responsibility, politics, and religion, become more complex. There may be a temporary lessening of the perceived attractiveness of stories. To the adolescent, stories may appear to contain much that is irrelevant or superfluous. Their concrete details, conflicting motives, complicated plots, and contradictory messages may confuse rather than enlighten and fail to provide reliable and valid ideological answers. Systematic systems of philosophy or belief may provide a clearer set of guidelines and standards around which to construct a personal ideology. Creeds that provide unambiguous statements about what is "true", and clear rules about how to behave can be highly appealing, seeming to answer for the adolescents the questions with which they are grappling.

Although perhaps finding stories less appealing than previously, adolescents might begin to make initial attempts at constructing their own personal narrative. McAdams draws here on Elkind's (1967; Elkind & Bowen, 1979) evidence for what he terms "personal fables" in teenagers' diaries and letters. These personal fables reflect young people's striving to separate psychologically from childhood and will often emphasise their perceived uniqueness and, perhaps, greatness. They comprise, "a very rough draft of an integrative and self-defining life story" (McAdams, 1997, p. 80). Whilst significant elements of the personal fable are likely to be unrealistic and highly egocentric, it can be reworked and revised as experience makes the young person more knowledgeable about the opportunities and limitations for defining the self in his or her particular society.

The process of constructing a personal fable provides adolescents with a vehicle for exploring, clarifying, and testing their developing ideological beliefs. Despite individual differences with respect to the complexity of ideological settings, simplistic and stereotypical patterns of reasoning tend to be replaced by more sophisticated and subtle conceptions of what is good and true. Sometime during late adolescence or young adulthood most of us reach a point when we feel fairly confident about what we believe to be right and true. The kind of ideological belief system established in adolescence – its structure and its content – will probably stay with us through our adult years, with, in most cases, but minor changes and variations.

After the consolidation of an ideological setting in late adolescence or young adulthood, the person's interest in stories revives. Having attained the building blocks of stories we now, however, become a story maker. We become both the architect and the master mason of our own personal myth.

5. Imagoes. Having established the ideological scene in which the personal narrative is to be set, the main task of story construction (or "mythmaking", as McAdams calls it) during young adulthood – the twenties and thirties – concerns the creation and refinement of its main characters or imagoes. Imagoes are internalised complexes of actual or imagined people. They pull together social roles and other divergent aspects of the self (including, for example, some of the significant images collected during the pre-school years) into complete, albeit exaggerated and one-dimensional, characters. Our life stories might have one dominant imago or many, with the existence of two central and often conflicting imagoes being relatively common.

From his own research, McAdams developed a taxonomy for classifying imagoes according to the properties of agency and communion, thereby reflecting the central narrative themes of power and love laid down during the school years. Some imago types are highly powerful and some are highly loving. Others blend both power and love, whilst still others emphasise neither. This gives a four-fold taxonomy, as shown in Box 4.1, which also includes examples of different imagoes (many of which can be found in world mythologies such as those of ancient Greece) representing each category. Thus, under the heading of agency are characters such as the warrior, the traveller, the sage, and the maker. Communal imagoes include the lover, the caregiver, the friend, and the ritualist. The healer, the teacher, the counsellor, the humanist and the arbiter are amongst the imagoes high in both agency and communion, whilst the escapist and the survivor draw on neither of these themes. McAdams stresses that his taxonomy does not incorporate all possible imagoes, and also that any one imago can be manifested in many ways within a life story. Thus, the courageous battle in which a warrior engages could take a physical, verbal, mental, or spiritual form.

Box 4.1 Imagoes in people's life stories (adapted from McAdams, 1997)

		Communion	
		High	Low
Agency	High	The healer The teacher The counsellor The humanist The arbiter	The warrior The traveller The sage The maker
	Low	The lover The caregiver The friend The ritualist	The escapist The survivor

The label given to a particular imago is not the central issue. McAdams' key point is that during early adulthood most of the effort we expend on creating our identities is concerned with fashioning main characters for our life story. Generally these characters are fashioned around the themes of agency and communion and, whilst it is possible to identify general "types" of imago, there also exists a good deal of individuality. Each imago, like each personal narrative, is both common and unique.

6. Generative denouement. The fashioning and refinement of the imagoes that people our life stories continues into the years of middle adulthood. As our personal myths mature, we cast and recast our central imagoes in more specific and expansive roles, striving for greater harmony, balance, and reconciliation between them. Also increasingly emerging during this time is a concern with our myth's denouement or ending. Whilst few of us are eager to die, "Mature identity requires that we leave a legacy that will, in some sense, survive us. Many individuals, at this stage in their lives, refashion their myths to ensure that something of personal importance is passed on" (McAdams, 1997, p. 37). The concern here is Erikson's theme of generativity. We seek, in McAdams' (1997, p. 224) words, "to fashion personal myths that defy the most basic convention of stories – that an ending is really the end. We seek endings that furnish new beginnings through which the self may live on. In our endings, we seek to defy the end, like the genes that replicate themselves from one generation to the next. As hopelessly narcissistic as it may seem, we are all looking, in one way or another, for immortality".

The main narrative task of middle adulthood is, therefore, to fashion a generativity script – a plan for what we hope to do in the future in order to leave a heroic gift for the next generation. In this way, although our own life will eventually end, some aspect of our self will live on.

7. Narrative evaluation. McAdams' work is concerned with the "pre-mythic" days of childhood and adolescence, and the "mythic" days of adulthood. He comments briefly, however, on the final, possibly "post-mythic", period of life. Narrative construction does not cease at the end of the middle years. We continue to revise and reconstruct our life story in order to make sense of changing life circumstances and new concerns. Nothing is ever final. None the less, for older people there may come a time when story "review" replaces story "making" as the central concern. We begin to look back and evaluate the life story we have created. Erikson's notion of ego integrity involves the eventual acceptance, valuing, and cherishing of our own life story, despite its shortcomings and limitations. To reject our story as unworthy is to experience despair.

For McAdams, personal identity in the modern world is a life story: "If you want to know me, then you must know my story, for my story defines who I am. If *I* want to know *myself*, to gain insight into the meaning of my own life, then I, too, must come to know my own story" (McAdams, 1997, p. 11). He offers a theory of how we create identities through narrative. In childhood we develop the raw materials or building blocks that we will later use to construct our narrative. During early and middle adulthood we create imagoes that express and enact our most cherished, but often conflicting, goals and desires. Through the middle years we become increasingly concerned with crafting a satisfying ending to our story, a generative script whereby our own death is, in some way, not final. In later years, the balance may shift from story creation towards evaluation, and we come to judge and, ideally, accept, the self we have created in our life story.

The work of Erikson and McAdams epitomises a view of the life course as a cumulative sequence of experiences and tasks. In the next chapter the theories of Havighurst, Levinson, and Gould are reviewed. There are elements of the "cumulative sequence" perspective in each of their contributions in that previous experiences and tasks impact on subsequent ones. However, they also have a strong proclivity to characterise life stages by a number of age-related developmental tasks.

5 Developmental tasks

> To every thing there is a season, and a time to every purpose under the heaven.
>
> (Ecclesiastes, 3, 1)

Also based on the epigenetic principle and related to, although both more optimistic and more concrete than Erikson's psychosocial crises, is the idea of developmental tasks. Elaborated most fully by Robert J. Havighurst, an educational psychologist, the idea has also been utilised by several others, including Daniel Levinson and his colleagues (1978), whose work is considered later. Gould's theory of adult development, also considered in this chapter, reflects a cumulative sequence of tasks and could equally well have been included in the previous chapter along with Erikson and McAdams. It is included here because, being a theory developed at the same time as Levinson et al.'s, the two theories are often spoken of together. In addition, the work of both Gould and Levinson was drawn on extensively by Sheehy (1974) in her best seller, *Passages: predictable crises of adult life*.

First, however, we turn to the work of Havighurst, whose publications (for example Havighurst, 1953, 1982) span an even longer period than Erikson's. His most comprehensive exposition of the concept of developmental tasks is to be found in *Developmental tasks and education*. Originally published in 1948, this book was reprinted several times and revised in 1971 (Havighurst, 1972).

Robert Havighurst: concrete developmental tasks

A developmental task is defined as, "a task which arises at or about a certain period in the life of the individual, successful achievement of which leads to . . . happiness and to success with later tasks, while failure leads to unhappiness in the individual, disapproval by the society, and difficulty with later tasks" (Havighurst, 1972, p. 2). As was stated in Chapter 3, Havighurst saw developmental tasks as being midway between, "an individual need and a societal demand" (p. 2) and proposed that the developmental task concept, "assumes an active learner interacting with an active social environment" (p. 2). He distinguished three sources of developmental tasks: biological maturation; cultural pressures (the expectations of society); and individual desires, aspirations, and values. Some tasks will arise primarily from one source, although in most instances developmental tasks arise, "from combinations of these factors acting together" (Havighurst, 1972, p. 6).

Learning to walk, for example, is a developmental task whose timing derives primarily from physical maturation, although child rearing practices in different societies may vary in the extent to which they encourage the infant's development of independent mobility. Learning to read, however, whilst obviously dependent on cognitive development, occurs primarily in response to the cultural pressure of a society. Because the timing and degree of this pressure can vary across societies, there will be a corresponding variation in the timing and importance of the developmental task of learning to read.

Havighurst sees the personality, or self, as emerging initially from the interaction of organic and environmental forces. However, as it evolves, the self becomes a force in its own right, capable of directing the individual's subsequent development. Thus, Havighurst sees both choosing and preparing for an occupation, and achieving a scale of values and philosophy of life, as developmental tasks arising primarily from the personal motives and values of the individual. Given his definition of the self, however, there are inevitably some cultural (that is, environmental) implications in such tasks. He suggests (Chickering & Havighurst, 1981) that during early and middle adulthood social demands and personal aspirations dominate in setting and defining developmental tasks, but that from later middle age onwards biological changes become, as they were during childhood, increasingly significant considerations. It has also been suggested (Featherman, Smith, & Peterson, 1990) that there is an increase throughout the life course in the proportion of developmental tasks that are ill-structured as opposed to well-structured.

Activity 5.1 Developmental tasks

Make a list of seven to nine important tasks you are currently working at, or goals you are currently striving towards.

Do they fulfil the criteria of developmental tasks? (i.e. are they tasks that arise at or about a certain period in the life of the individual, successful achievement of which leads to happiness and to success with later tasks, while failure leads to unhappiness in the individual, disapproval by the society, and difficulty with later tasks?)

Havighurst (1972) identified three sources of developmental tasks:

- biological maturation
- social pressures and norms
- personal choice.

Draw a pie chart to indicate your estimate of the relative importance of these three sources of developmental tasks for each of those you have identified.

To what extent are the tasks you identified peculiar to people of your age, gender, social, cohort and ethnic group?

To what extent do the characteristics you identified in the "stages" exercise (Activity 3.1) reflect developmental tasks?

The identification of developmental tasks is seen largely as an empirical issue. Havighurst (1956) distinguishes three procedures for discovering and defining them: observation, questioning, and introspection. Activity 5.1 encourages you to use the third of these methods to identify tasks you are currently "working at" (to use Havighurst's phrase), and the extent to which they are specific to your age, gender, social, cohort, and ethnic group. Havighurst employed all these methods, plus a scouring of the social science literature, to pinpoint six to nine developmental tasks for each of six age periods ranging from "infancy and early childhood" to "later maturity". Being both empirically defined and relatively concrete, and especially because of the acknowledged influence of cultural factors in the definition of developmental tasks, it is inevitable that such lists will be socially, culturally, and historically specific. This can be seen clearly, for example, in the list of developmental tasks for "middle age" shown in Box 5.1 and compiled by Havighurst in 1972 to replace earlier versions.

Somewhat less specific, and therefore somewhat less culture-bound, lists of developmental tasks for different life stages have been devised by Newman and Newman (1995), who identified what they believed to be the major issues that, "dominate a person's problem-solving efforts and learning during a given stage" (Newman & Newman, 1995, p. 46) – a total of 42 tasks, as listed in Table 5.1. They still recognise the cultural specificity of their list, however, seeing it as representing the tasks central to successful adaptation in a Western, post-industrial society, and not

Box 5.1 Havighurst's (1972) developmental tasks of middle age

- Assisting teenage children to become responsible and happy adults.
- Achieving adult social and civic responsibility.
- Reaching and maintaining satisfactory performance in one's occupational career.
- Developing adult leisuretime activities.
- Relating to one's spouse in a less role-dependent fashion.
- Accepting and adjusting to the physiological changes of middle age.
- Adjusting to ageing parents.

As is evident from the above list, the developmental tasks of middle age are strongly influenced by social demands and norms (Chickering & Havighurst, 1981). Decisions to delay parenthood until the late thirties or forties, plus the preponderance of "second" families means, for example, that many adults in middle age, rather than being concerned with launching their offspring into independent adulthood, are involved in tasks that in 1972 Havighurst located within "Early adulthood":

- selecting a mate
- learning to live with a partner
- starting a family
- rearing children.

With regard to the second of the above tasks, Havighurst had, in 1972, explicitly said "Learning to live with a marriage partner", something that now sounds outdated in view of both the increasing trend for couples to cohabit prior to marriage and also the increasing recognition of same-sex relationships as an acceptable lifestyle.

The third in Havighurst's 1972 list of developmental tasks for the middle years, "Reaching and maintaining satisfactory performance in one's occupational career", with its implicit assumption of a single, "career-ladder" type of occupational path, also reflects an outdated view of the labour market. Today, more people experience "portfolio" (Handy, 1989) and "boundaryless" (Arthur, 1994) careers, with a significant emphasis on the continual need for people to make sense of their careers and to monitor and review their career skills, attitudes and beliefs (Arnold & Jackson, 1997).

necessarily appropriate for a person living in a developing country or a more traditional tribal culture.

Similarly, Gail Sheehy (1974, 1996) found in her research on the crises of adulthood that, when she was updating her 1974 book some 20 years later, there had been what she describes as "a revolution" in the life cycle: "In the space of one short generation the whole shape of the life cycle had been fundamentally altered. People today are leaving childhood sooner,

Table 5.1 Life stages and associated developmental tasks (adapted from Newman & Newman, 1995)

Life stage	*Developmental tasks*
Infancy (0–2 years)	Social attachment Maturation of sensory, perceptual and motor functions Sensorimotor intelligence and primitive causality Understanding the nature of objects and the creation of categories Emotional development
Early childhood	
Toddlerhood (2–4 years)	Elaboration of locomotion Fantasy play Language development Self-control
Early school age (4–6 years)	Sex-role identification Early moral development Self-theory Group play
Middle childhood (6–12 years)	Friendship Concrete operations Skill learning Self-evaluation Team play
Adolescence (12–18 years)	Physical maturation Formal operations Emotional development Membership in the peer group Sexual relationships
Early adulthood	
Youth (18–22 years)	Autonomy from parents Gender identity Internalised morality Career choice
Young adulthood (22–40 years)	Exploring intimate relationships Child-bearing Work Lifestyle
Middle adulthood (40–60 years)	Management of career Nurturing the couple relationship Expanding caring relationships Management of the household
Early late-adulthood (60–75 years)	Promotion of intellectual vigour Redirection of energy toward new roles and activities Acceptance of one's life Development of a point of view about death
Late late-adulthood (75 years onwards)	Coping with physical changes of ageing Development of a psychohistorical perspective Travel through uncharted terrain

(Reproduced with permission from Newman, B. and Newman, P. (1995) *Development Through Life: A Psychosocial Approach*, 6th edition. Brooks/Cole.)

but they are taking longer to grow up and much longer to grow old. That shifts all the stages of adulthood ahead – by up to ten years" (Sheehy, 1996, p. 4). See Box 5.2 for further discussion of this. Despite these shifts, if you accept the social, cultural, and historical specificity of Havighurst's notion of developmental tasks, they do provide a coherent framework for portraying the specifics of a life course. There is a risk, however, of conflating the "is" with the "ought", that is, assuming that what is typical is also preferable. Thus, Reinert (1980, p. 17) described such lists of tasks as "a kind of culturally specific guidance system" pointing to their normative role as a series of goals to which individuals in a society are motivated or persuaded to pursue, and against which they are evaluated, as well as their role as a description of the "typical". Possible advantages of deviating from the norm are not explored. It is assumed that all tasks are appropriate for all – marriage is mentioned, but not remarriage or other forms of intimate couple relationships. Finding a social and civic role is included, but ethnic identity receives no mention.

Box 5.2 The case of the moving tasks

Sheehy (1996) argues that since the publication in 1974 of *Passages: predictable crises of adult life*, age norms prevalent at that time have shifted. She cites several examples (Sheehy, 1996, p. 4):

> Puberty arrives earlier by several years than it did at the turn of the century. Adolescence is now prolonged for the middle class until the end of the twenties, as young adults delay marrying and having children later and later. True adulthood begins only around 30. Most people born after World War II do not feel fully "grown up" until they are into their forties, and even then they resist. Unlike members of the previous generation, who almost universally had their children launched by that stage of life, many late-baby couples or stepfamily parents will still be battling with rebellious children who are on the "catastrophic brink of adolescence" while they themselves wrestle with the pronounced hormonal and psychic changes that come with the passage into middle life.
>
> When our parents turned fifty, we thought they were old. But today, women and men I have interviewed for *New Passages* routinely believe they are five to ten years younger than the age on their birth certificates. "Everything seems to be moved off by a decade," comedian–director David Steinberg observed in our interview. His instinct was right on target.
>
> Fifty is now what forty used to be.
>
> Sixty is what fifty used to be.

Despite these problems, however, the concept of developmental tasks, like the concept of the evolving life structure (discussed in the following section) can be used in a content-free way as a framework for describing the life course. Its greatest strength lies in its potential as a device for emplotting the life story (see Chapter 7). In her Growth Task Model, Weick (1989) employs the developmental task concept in this "meta-model" fashion, conceptualising growth as a cluster of developmental tasks that form cyclical themes in individuals' lives. The environment – both physical and social – provides the context for the enactment of growth tasks, which cluster around five domains: intimacy, nurturance, work and productivity, creativity, and transcendence (i.e. the communal and the spiritual rather than the personal).

Daniel Levinson: an evolving life structure

Aspects of the work conducted by Daniel Levinson and his colleagues at Yale University (Levinson et al., 1978) – notably his diagrammatic representation of the developmental periods of early and middle adulthood (Figure 5.1) – are now referred to widely in discussions of adulthood. Directed at the general question, "What does it mean to be an adult?", the research comprised a multidisciplinary, in-depth study of 40 men drawn from four different occupational groups (business executives, university biologists, industrial workers, and novelists). When the sample was selected in 1969 the age range of the subjects was from 35 to 45 years. Data was collected primarily through in-depth interviewing over a period of several weeks (see Box 2.1, page 34 for more details of their method, which they termed "biographical interviewing").

Chapter 3 outlined Levinson's overall view of the life course as a sequence of alternating phases of change and consolidation, each lasting several years. Whilst Levinson recognises that each structure-changing period has features in common with all other transitional periods (and similarly with regard to the periods of consolidation or structure-building), he also argues that each has specific tasks reflecting its place in the life cycle and distinguishing it from the other transitional and stable phases. That Levinson's diagrammatic representation of the "seasons of a man's life" is the most widely known aspect of his work. This is unfortunate. It does little more than indicate the demarcations of the various seasons that, as Levinson and his colleagues are at pains to point out, are merely averages. However, whilst acknowledging the existence of individual differences with regard to the timing of the different stages, the researchers do also maintain that the variation is contained within fairly narrow limits, "probably not more than five or six years" (Levinson et al., 1978, p. 19). These life stages, or periods, are reviewed in the following section, and then there is consideration of the characteristics of the different eras, or seasons, into which these periods are grouped.

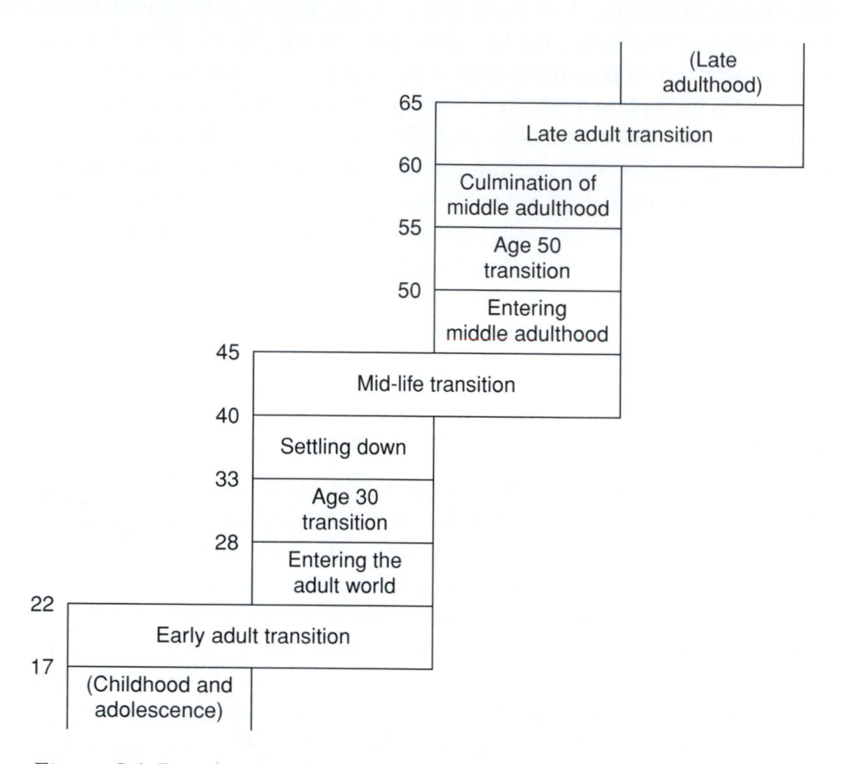

Figure 5.1 Developmental periods in early and middle adulthood (reproduced with permission from Levinson, D.J. et al. (1978). *The seasons of a man's life*. New York: A.A. Knopff, a division of Random House, Inc. Copyright © 1978 by Daniel J. Levinson).

The developmental periods of adulthood

Levinson describes the early adult transition (EAT) as a developmental bridge between childhood and adolescence on the one hand, and adulthood on the other. The pre-adulthood sense of self must be reappraised and modified. The key theme is separation from our pre-adult world, especially from our family of origin. Outwardly denoted by such things as increasing financial independence, moving out of the family home, and adopting more autonomous, responsible roles, internally it involves increasing differentiation between self and parents, greater psychological distance from the family, and less dependency on parental support and authority. A second theme is the forging of initial attachments to the adult world – exploring its possibilities, imagining oneself as a participant in it, and making and testing some preliminary identities and choices for living.

The next phase, entering the adult world (EAW) is a structure-building phase. The tentative basis for adult life established during the EAT is tested, refined, and consolidated in an attempt, "to fashion a provisional structure that provides a workable link between the valued self and the adult society" (Levinson et al., 1978, p. 57). It involves two primary yet antithetical tasks. The first task is to explore possibilities by keeping options open, avoiding strong commitments, and maximising the alternatives. In contrast to the first task, the second task addresses our desire for stability, order, and roots. It involves creating a stable life structure through making choices and commitments – most typically through choice of occupation and/or intimate partner (see also Havighurst, 1972), the development of life goals (see also Bühler & Massarik, 1968), and the establishment of a more organised life. Levinson et al. found that, whilst work on one of the two EAW tasks may predominate, the other was never totally absent. If the emphasis was very strongly on the first task, the young person's life had a transient, rootless quality. If the second task predominated, there was the risk of making major commitments on the basis of insufficient exploration of alternatives.

The age 30 transition (ATT) provides an opportunity to change the first adult life structure. It is heralded by the sensation that life is losing its provisional quality and is becoming more serious. There is a feeling of time pressure – that if we want to change our life we must do so now, for soon it will be too late. Whilst some of Levinson et al.'s subjects had a fairly smooth ATT, most experienced some degree of crisis at this time. It tended to be a period of moderate or high stress.

During the settling down phase (SD) the second life structure that began to take shape at the end of the ATT is consolidated and built on. The major goal, "is to 'settle for' a few key choices, to create a broader structure around them, to invest oneself as fully as possible in the various components of the structure (such as work, family, community, solitary interests, friendships) and to pursue long-range plans and goals within it" (Levinson et al., 1978, p. 139). This period of settling down is characterised by two potentially contradictory tasks, albeit that the conflict is less marked than during the EAW phase. The first task concerns consolidation – establishing one's niche in society. It entails a deepening of roots, an anchoring of oneself more firmly in one's family, occupation, and/or community. The second task concerns advancement – progression within the stable structure resulting from work on the first task. Levinson et al. use the imagery of the ladder (see also Vaillant's [1977] stage of career consolidation reviewed in Chapter 4) to describe this process, despite also emphasising that they use the term "advancement" in its broadest sense: "building a better life, improving and using one's skills, becoming more creative, contributing to society and being affirmed by it, according to one's values" (Levinson et al., 1978, p. 140).

Distinction is made between the earlier and later parts of the SD phase. The latter is described as the time of "becoming one's own man", which reduces to the evocative acronym BOOM. It marks a period of special emphasis on the struggle to be more fully one's own person than is found at many ages. It concerns our desires and efforts to be more independent and self-sufficient, and less subject to the control of others. Levinson et al. also, however, see contradiction here, as the man (and remember that all the subjects in their original study were male) seeks affirmation in society as well as freedom from its pressures and blandishments. It may become a time of severe conflict and difficulties. External circumstances, particularly in the workplace, can be restrictive and damaging to self-esteem, whilst, at the same time, the wish for advancement and affirmation may generate susceptibility to social pressure. Individual distress will often take the form of feeling held back and may be confounded, Levinson et al. believe, by the resurgence of unresolved pre-adult conflicts triggered by the attempts to "become one's own man". This boy–man conflict is, however, seen as a step forward, providing an opportunity to resolve the conflict more completely. There are echoes here of Gould's (1978, 1980) analysis of adult development as the substitution of a childish with a more adult view of reality.

Levinson et al. (1978) identified the onset of a new period at around the age of 40. Concerns about not advancing sufficiently, or gaining too little affirmation, independence, and seniority give way to a different type of issue, marking the onset of the midlife transition (MLT). The unique characteristic of this period is a continuation of the process of individuation began during the BOOM phase. As this occurs:

> . . . the person forms a clearer boundary between self and world. He forms a stronger sense of who he is and what he wants, and a more realistic, sophisticated view of the world: what it is like, what it offers him and demands from him. Greater individuation allows him to be more separate from the world, to be more independent and self-generating. But it also gives him the confidence and understanding to have more intense attachments in the world and to feel more fully a part of it.
>
> (Levinson et al., 1978, p. 193)

As Levinson et al. acknowledge, this description resonates with the last two of Erikson's psychosocial crises. They also refer to Jaques' (1965, 1980) emphasis on confronting mortality as a midlife issue and to Neugarten's (1965) discussion of increasing interiority as a basic process of this period. Also acknowledged is Jung (1972), who placed the age of 40 at the meridian of his arc of life and saw the midlife as marking the onset of a new effort at individuation.

The evidence in support of Levinson et al.'s next stage – that of entering middle adulthood (EMA) – is more sketchy than for earlier stages because it is based on information from only fifteen of their subjects who, by 2 years after the initial contact, had reached the end of the MLT. None the less, the researchers pinpointed several distinguishing features of the EMA phase.

The distinction between MLT and EMA is, again, the distinction between a structure-changing and a structure-building period. Thus, the MLT ends when, between 2 years either side of age 45, the person reduces the amount of energy devoted to reappraising the past and attempting to integrate the polarities of the midlife period. Instead, the main tasks centre on making and implementing choices around which a new life structure can be built. Levinson et al. found that the making of choices was generally most problematic, and that the research participants needed most of the EMA period to establish the choices on which to build the new life structure.

Detachment from the previous life structure during EMA might involve such personal upheavals as marital separation, job resignation, termination of significant relationships, or home relocation. Such choices "create a space" within which the individual, "may succeed in improving his life, but he may find himself temporarily – and unhappily – suspended within this space until he can go on to make some positive choices and start the restructuring" (Levinson et al., 1978, p. 279). The restructuring process comprises many steps and might, likewise, be beset with difficulties. Options must be determined and explored. Choices must be made, implemented, evaluated, and, if necessary, abandoned – thus requiring the cycle to be repeated over again.

The EMA period continues so long as the individual's predominant task remains the attempt to build a satisfactory life structure. Irrespective of the degree of success, the phase ends when attention shifts from structure-building to a new transition. Levinson et al. label this next phase the "age fifty transition", but, as with their later periods entitled the "culmination of middle adulthood" and the "late adult transition", they lack empirical data on which to base any detailed discussion of their characteristics. None the less, they are confident that whilst each of these periods will have its distinguishing features, it will also demonstrate, as appropriate, the general characteristics of a structure-building or a structure-changing phase.

The eras of early and middle adulthood

Superimposed on their concept of alternating structure-changing and structure-building phases is Levinson et al.'s concept of "eras" – contour maps "within which to examine the terrain" of the "seasons" that make up the human life cycle. They distinguish five eras:

- pre-adulthood, extending from conception to roughly age 22 years and representing the "formative years"
- early adulthood, which lasts from about 17 to 45 years
- middle adulthood, roughly between 45 and 65 years
- late adulthood, which starts at about age 60
- late late-adulthood, the final era, which incorporates the final years of the life course.

Levinson's own work concentrates on early and middle adulthood and it is these eras that are reviewed in the following section. For the early, or novice, phase of adulthood – the period from the onset of the EAT to the end of the ATT – five over-riding developmental tasks are identified, and for middle adulthood attention focuses on four components of the overall task of developing greater individuation.

The developmental tasks of the era of early adulthood

The four main tasks Levinson et al. (1978) identify as distinguishing the novice phase of adulthood are: forming a "Dream" and giving it a place in the life structure; forming mentor relationships; forming an occupation; and forming love relationships, a marriage and a family. In addition, Levinson et al. identified a fifth task – forming mutual friendships – which was notable for its absence from the life work of their participants. Each of these five tasks is summarised below.

1. Forming and living out "the Dream". An individual's life course is strongly influenced by factors such as family, class, subculture, and social institutions. It is also affected by attributes of the individual – such things as values, abilities, efforts, anxieties, and goals. Levinson et al. identified another factor that was crucial in early adulthood – "the Dream". A key developmental task of early adulthood was to give the Dream a clearer definition and find ways of living it out:

> In its primordial form, the Dream is a vague sense of self-in-adult-world. It has the quality of a vision, an imagined possibility that generates excitement and vitality. At the start it is poorly articulated and only tenuously connected to reality, although it may contain concrete images such as winning the Nobel Prize or making the all-star team. It may take a dramatic form as in the myth of the hero; the great artist, business tycoon, athletic or intellectual superstar performing magnificent feats and receiving special honors. It may take mundane forms that are yet inspiring and sustaining: the excellent craftsman, the husband–father in a certain kind of family, the highly respected member of one's community.
>
> (Levinson et al., 1978, p. 91)

If the Dream cannot be incorporated into the initial adult life structure to at least some extent then it may fade and die, and with it the person's sense of vitality and purpose. Many of Levinson et al.'s subjects experienced a conflict between a life direction in which their Dream could find expression and one that was quite different. Thus, factors ranging through parental pressure, lack of money or opportunities, or personal characteristics, might hinder the implementation of the Dream. Building an initial life structure around the Dream increases the chances of the person attaining personal fulfilment, whilst those whose life structure is a betrayal of the Dream "will have to deal later with the consequences" (p. 92).

2. Forming mentor relationships. Levinson et al. describe an effective mentoring relationship as one of the most complex and developmentally important relationships of early adulthood. They also conclude that most men receive inadequate mentoring and that the situation for women is probably worse still. Ideally, a mentor is half a generation (8–15 years) older than the protégé. With a greater age gap the older person may represent a parental rather than a mentoring figure. Someone closer to the same age as the protégé will be less likely to be perceived as someone of greater relevant experience and seniority, or as a responsible and admired older sibling – all key features of a mentor.

When available, a mentor can perform a range of functions for a protégé. These include being a teacher and, thereby enhancing the young person's skills and intellectual development; serving as a sponsor who, through the use of influence, facilitates the young person's entry and advancement; welcoming, as host and guide, the initiate into a new occupational and social world, and providing an entreé to its values, customs, resources, and members. A mentor can also be a role model and might offer direct assistance in the form of counsel and moral support. The most important function of the mentor is to support and facilitate the protégé's Dream.

By its very nature, a good mentoring relationship is a temporary phenomenon. A mentor who was a permanent figure would be confirming the younger person to a position of immaturity rather than facilitating the protégé's move towards maturity. A relationship between mentor and protégé might remain, but it must change if it is to continue to facilitate the development of both parties. A peer relationship is "the ultimate (though never fully realized) goal of the relationship" (p. 99).

3. Forming an occupation. Levinson et al. make a useful and important distinction between "forming" and simply "choosing" an occupation. Rather than being a single once-and-for all decision, career choice is seen as "a complex, social–psychological process that extends over the entire novice period and often beyond" (p. 101). Initial career choices, no matter how definite they seemed at the time, generally turn out to represent only a preliminary definition of interests and values. Whilst occupational formation is frequently not the steady, single-track progression that it is often assumed to be, if no firm commitment is ever made, the person is deprived of what Levinson et al. describe as the satisfaction of engaging in enduring work that is suitable for the self and valuable for society.

4. Forming a love relationship, marriage, and family. As with the task of forming an occupation, work on the fourth of Levinson et al.'s tasks can extend throughout the novice period and beyond. It begins long before and continues long after the marker events of marriage and the birth of a first child. The cultural and historical relativity of Levinson et al.'s model is vividly revealed in their comments about marriage. They concluded that the ideal marital relationship for fostering the man's development is one where the women is able to support and animate his Dream, with the man's Dream often serving as a vehicle for defining the woman's pursuits as well. "The big challenge for her comes in the thirties and forties: her husband and children need her less and offer her less, and she must then form a more distinctive identity of her own" (p. 110). Changes in social attitudes since Levinson et al. first put forward their model, and the shift in the timing of the birth of children such that many women now have children in their late thirties and forties, make such pronouncements outmoded. Further, Levinson et al. give scant attention to childless marriages, cohabitation, or remaining single, and none to homosexual partnerships. They do, however, make the point that a couple can form a lasting relationship only if it furthers the woman's development as well as the man's, but then go on to argue that if the woman's Dream involves an identity more distinct than one based on the roles of wife and mother, then to build a life structure that contains both persons' Dream is a heroic task, "and one for which evolution and history have ill prepared us" (p. 110).

5. Forming mutual friendships. Levinson et al.'s subjects had, in adulthood, few intimate male friends of the kind they recalled fondly from their childhood and youth. Nor did they seem to develop intimate non-sexual relationships with women. The researchers considered the forming of mutual friendships to be a valuable, but often poorly addressed, developmental task of adulthood. They wondered as to the reasons for its rarity and expressed concern as to the consequences of its absence from adult life.

The tasks associated with different elements of the life structure continue to demand and receive attention during the middle years. However, they become, argue Levinson et al., subordinate to concerns associated with the process of individuation.

THE COMPONENT PARTS OF MIDLIFE INDIVIDUATION

Levinson et al. present midlife individuation as being addressed through the confrontation and reintegration of four polarities within the person: young/old; destruction/creation; masculine/feminine; and attachment/separateness. These are each considered below.

1. Young/old – the major polarity. We think of children as young and of the elderly as old. And yet these concepts are only tangentially related to chronological age. At every point in our life we are both young and old.

The 3-year-old is "too old" to have a dummy. The 59-year-old is "too young" to have a Senior Citizen's travel pass. Levinson et al. describe the separation and reintegration of the young and old within us as the major polarity to be resolved during human development. It is an inherent part of every transitional period. And yet, during the midlife period there is an added dimension because then this recurring dynamic coincides with the chronological middle of the life course. The young/old polarity is experienced with special force. The man feels that "the Young – variously represented as the child, the adolescent and the youthful adult in himself – is dying. The imagery of old age and death hangs over him like a pall" (p. 213). The beginning of physical decline intensifies this sense of losing touch with one's youth. Responsibility for ageing and dying parents adds further force, for, when they are gone, it is our turn next. At work we are no longer "up and coming" – that term is now applied to those who joined after us. These indicators of mortality are so painful, maintain Levinson et al., because of our wish for immortality, "one of the strongest and least malleable of human motives" (p. 215).

Levinson et al. (1978) see resolution of the young/old polarity during midlife as involving acceptance of "the symbolic death of the youthful hero within himself" (p. 215) and discovery of "how he might be a hero of a different kind in the context of middle adulthood" (p. 215). This requires relinquishing the illusion of immortality, with awareness of personal mortality being seen in the context of generational continuity. The challenge is to develop a wiser and more mature middle-aged self that is "still connected to the youthful sources of energy, imagination, and daring" (p. 217). From this greater sense of individuality, concern can turn outward from the self towards the generations that will follow: "Slowly the omnipotent Young hero recedes, and in his place emerges a middle-aged man with more knowledge of his limitations as well as greater real power and authority" (p. 218).

2. The destruction/creation polarity. Growing realisation of our own mortality heightens our awareness of destruction as a universal process. This recognition intensifies the wish to be creative, "to bring something into being, to give birth, to generate life" (p. 222). One aspect of the midlife task is to find an appropriate outlet for this creative urge. As with the young/old polarity, both sides of the destruction/creation polarity are particularly salient and evident during the midlife period. We become aware of what has been sacrificed or destroyed as we strove to create the life structures of early adulthood – what we ourselves have hurt or destroyed and, in turn, what, or who, has been destructive of us. Another component of the midlife task is, therefore, to come to terms with our guilt concerning our destructiveness towards others and our rage concerning their destructiveness towards us.

3. The masculine/feminine polarity. To the extent that during early adulthood we develop only one side of the masculine/feminine polarity, Levinson et al. see the midlife period as offering an opportunity to redress this imbalance. Whilst they describe the struggles to resolve this imbalance as typically meeting with mixed success, they also present the self-acceptance that both results from and is instrumental in promoting this confrontation of the contradictions within oneself as a sound basis for developing a more highly integrated personality or life structure.

4. The attachment/separateness polarity. Levinson et al. use the term "attachment" to include all the forces that connect a person to his or her environment. These may be positive forces – interest, love, excitement – or negative forces – hate, confusion, fear. "Separateness", which must be clearly distinguished from isolation or aloneness, prevails when we are primarily in our inner world of imagination and fantasy. Attachment is the mechanism through which we meet our needs to be engaged, involved and rooted. Separateness fosters creativity and individual growth.

During childhood the forces of attachment need to be channelled in a way that enables the individual to operate in society. The forces of imagination and fantasy – of separateness – must also, however, be allowed a place because they are the routes through which creativity is nourished, individuality is sustained, and the Dream is formulated. During early adulthood Levinson et al. see separateness as normally being sacrificed in the interests of attachment. Forming a family and an occupation, struggling with external pressures and demands, fulfilling the wish to establish a niche in society, all serve to push separateness into second place. The midlife period offers an opportunity to find a new balance between attachment and separateness, which provides for a better balance between the needs of the self and the needs of society.

Levinson et al.'s data fade at this point. Their subjects tended to be embarking on rather than established in the era of middle adulthood. We might speculate about developmental tasks but empirical evidence, at least from Levinson et al.'s study, is sparse.

Levinson (1986, p. 5) concluded that the "idea of age-linked eras and periods now has the status of an empirically grounded hypothesis that needs further testing in various cultures". However, although Levinson et al.'s model has been widely cited since it was first expounded, it has also been contested and challenged on the grounds of gender, racial, cultural, and/or historical parochialism (Schlossberg et al., 1995). It can also be criticised for the lack of attention it gives to sexual orientation. From the data cited it would appear that none of Levinson et al.'s research participants either adopted or even considered a homosexual or bisexual life style.

Roberts and Newton (1987) reviewed four doctoral studies that used Levinson et al.'s theory to study women's adult development. The women's life structures followed to some extent the developmental pattern of alternating transitional and stable phases, although the stable phases were less marked than those of their male counterparts. A number of factors contributed to this finding. The women's Dreams tended to be more complex, multi-faceted and nebulous than were the men's. They generally had vague images of themselves in a particular kind of environment or community rather than specific images of themselves in particular occupational roles. They tended to take longer to form an occupation and had fewer mentors. Their propensity to give greater priority than did the men to relational concerns contributed to the development of "split dreams" that incorporated – not always very successfully, clearly, or harmoniously – both relational and individual elements. These findings concurred with Levinson's own conclusions from his subsequent study of the early and middle adulthood of 45 women (Levinson, 1996).

In a study of major personal upheavals in the lives of middle-class American women (Reinke, Holmes, & Harris, et al., 1985), over three-quarters of the participants indicated starting a period of major psychosocial transition between the ages of 27 and 30: "Although the manifestations of the transition were idiosyncratic, it was generally characterized initially by personal disruption, followed by reassessment and a search for personal growth, and finally by a spurt in self-concept and psychological well-being" (Reinke et al., 1985, p. 1361). The studies reviewed by Roberts and Newton (1987) also revealed the "age thirty transition" to be particularly significant for many of the women studied, and to involve a reassessment and possible realignment of the nature and relative significance of the career and relational components. In an extension of Reinke et al.'s (1985) study, it was found that the major psychosocial transitions in the lives of women aged between the ages of 36 and 60 years were more likely to be associated with phases of the family cycle than with chronological age (Harris, Ellicott, & Holmes, 1986). Within the family cycle transitions were more likely to occur during the "pre-school", "launching", and "post-parental" phases than during the "no children", "school-age", or "adolescent" phases.

Studies examining the adult development of minority ethnic groups have emphasised the strong influence of racial identity on developmental phases (Gooden, 1989; Ross, 1984; Ruffin, 1989). Mentoring functions were often fulfilled by family members rather than work associates. Occupational goals frequently focused on security and independence (Ross, 1984) or on becoming successful in a White world (Ruffin, 1989). Social class has been found to interact with race. Thus Gooden (1989) found the school teachers in his study of African-American men fitted Levinson et al.'s theory better than did the "street men".

The attempt to incorporate factors associated with cohort, gender, race and class into Levinson et al.'s theory leads to the conclusion that the specific content of stages such as those proposed by Levinson et al.

lack the universality that the authors suggest. None the less, the basic rhythm or pattern of alternating transitional (structure-changing) and consolidating (structure-building) phases is found consistently and provides a useful backdrop against which the life course of particular individuals can be considered.

Roger Gould's evolution of adult consciousness

Whilst Levinson and his colleagues at Yale were developing their account of adult development, another researcher, Roger Gould, was doing likewise on the other side of America – at the University of California, Los Angeles. Gould and his associates initially observed patterns emerging from the life stories of psychiatric patients and subsequently tested their hypotheses in a questionnaire study of more than 500 "non-patients" between the ages of 16 and 50 years (Gould, 1978).

Gould (1980) indexes adult development against the individual's changing sense of time. Until we leave our family of origin at around the age of 18 we are protected by our parents. However, we are also constrained by them, never quite believing that we will escape from our family world. Gould (1980, p. 35) describes this experience as like being in a timeless capsule: "The future is a fantasy space that may possibly not exist". During the process described by Levinson as separation from parents, Gould argues that we begin to glimpse an endless future. We see an infinite amount of time ahead of us provided – and this is our fear – that we are not suddenly snatched back into the restricted world of our childhood. Once into our twenties we are more confident that we have separated from our family of origin but, to incorporate Levinson's terminology again, we have not yet formed a coherent early-adult life structure.

> Because of all the new decisions and novel experiences that come with setting up new adult enterprises, our time sense, when we're being successful, is one of movement along a chosen path that leads linearly to some obscure prize decades in the future. There is plenty of time, but we're still in a hurry once we've developed a clearer, often stereotyped, picture of where we want to be by then.
>
> (Gould, 1980, p. 56)

By the end of our twenties our sense of time incorporates our adult past as well as our future. We begin to become aware that our future is not infinite and our pathway is not linear – we must choose between different branches because there is not time to take them all. The sense of urgency that time is running out, which Levinson attributes to the age thirty transition, is ascribed by Gould to the decade between the mid-thirties and the mid-forties. It is combined with an emotional awareness of our own mortality – a regularly cited characteristic of the midlife transition (Jaques,

1965, 1980; Levinson et al., 1978). Once attained, this awareness of our own death is never far from consciousness, "How time is spent becomes a matter of great importance" (Gould, 1980, p. 56).

For Gould, the thrust of adult development is towards a realisation and acceptance of ourselves as creators of our own lives and away from the assumption that the rules and standards of childhood determine our destiny. Thus, whilst Levinson talks of the evolving life structure, Gould (1978, p. 15) talks about "the evolution of adult consciousness as we release ourselves from the constraints and ties of childhood consciousness". He envisages our childhood consciousness existing alongside our rational, adult view of reality. On the one hand, this link with our past supports and stabilises us, but on the other hand it also interferes with and constrains our life. Adulthood is a dynamic and changing time during which we can and must release ourselves from arbitrary internal constraints if we are to have an unfolding, creative life. These internal constraints originated as the internal standards of childhood that were instilled in us at home and school. They represent the values and assumptions of our parents and their contemporaries and must be replaced by values and assumptions more truly our own.

This process of growth or transformation occurs as we correct the false assumptions we have lived by until then and which have restricted and restrained us unnecessarily. These false assumptions bolster the individual's illusion of safety, "a fixture of childhood encompassing belief in omnipotent thought, omnipotent protective parents, the absoluteness of parental rules and world view, and a whole system of defenses as controlling structures against a rage reaction to separation" (Gould, 1980, p. 65).

Between the ages of 15 and 50 years the four major false assumptions that maintain this illusion surface are challenged and found wanting. This process can, like Levinson's model of adult development, be presented as a series of age-related developmental tasks. This time the tasks are associated with the challenging of one particular false assumption, as outlined and summarised in Table 5.2.

Assumption 1: "I will always belong to my parents and believe in their world." (late teens, early twenties). This assumption is challenged when we leave home to go to college, to go to work, or to move in with friends or partner. As with Levinson's developmental tasks, the experience is profoundly contradictory. It mirrors the dynamics of Erikson's psychosocial crises – on the one hand the wish to advance and progress, and on the other hand the desire to remain in or retreat to an earlier, less threatening mode of living.

Gould identified five components of this first major false assumption around which the characteristic conflicts of late adolescence coalesce:

Table 5.2 False assumptions challenged during adulthood (adapted from Gould, 1978, 1980)

Age	*False assumption and component parts*
Late teens, early twenties	*I will always belong to my parents and believe in their world.* • If I get any more independent it'll be a disaster. • I can only see the world through my parents' assumptions. • Only they can guarantee my safety. • They must be my only family. • I don't own my body.
Twenties	*Doing it their way with will power and perseverance will probably bring results. But when I become too frustrated, confused, or tired, or am simply unable to cope, they will step in and show me the way.* • Rewards will come automatically if we do what we are supposed to do. • There is only one right way to do things. • My loved ones are able to do for me what I haven't been able to do for myself. • Rationality, commitment and effort will always prevail over all other forces.
Late twenties, early thirties	*Life is simple and controllable. There are no significant coexisting contradictory forces within me.* • What I know intellectually, I know emotionally. • I am not like my parents in ways I don't want to be. • I can see the reality of those close to me quite clearly. • Threats to my security aren't real.
35–50	*There is no evil in me or death in the world. The sinister has been expelled.* • My work (for men) or my relationship with men (for women) grants me immunity from death and danger. • There is no life beyond the family. • I am innocent.

- *"If I get any more independent, it'll be a disaster."* This component encapsulates the fear of being unable to cope with the new-found separation from parents, the anxiety lest our newly independent selves will not be loved by misunderstanding parents and envious friends, and/or the concern lest our parents' relationship will not survive the loss of their special child.
- *"I can only see the world through my parents' assumptions."* This component reflects the fear of risking being different from one's primary reference group – the family. The myth of family one-mindedness must be challenged if the young person is to escape its powerful and constraining dynamics.

- *"Only they can guarantee my safety."* Whilst wishing to become independent the young person is either concerned lest he or she is unable to match the ostensibly absolute safety provided in childhood by parents, or else takes excessive risks in the seeming assumption of absolute invulnerability. In either case, the lesson to be learned is that the impression we gained as children of our parents being able to provide absolute safety was an illusion.
- *"They must be my only family."* To challenge this myth we must cope with the conflicts of loyalty experienced when friends become as important or more important to us than our parents.
- *"I don't own my body."* It is mainly in choosing to engage in sexual relations that this component of the false assumption is contradicted. Allowing ourselves physical pleasure is a statement of our ownership of our own body.

Assumption 2: "Doing it their way with will power and perseverance will probably bring results. But when I become too frustrated, confused, or tired, or am simply unable to cope, they will step in and show me the way" (the twenties). During this period, which Gould calls the apprenticeship period of life, we experience some confirmation of this false assumption. We are often required to do things in the socially accepted way, even if we disagree with it, in order to be accepted at our workplace. However, the important choices that must be made in order to establish our own life structure during our twenties do none the less provide us with experiences sufficiently powerful to challenge its validity. Gould (1980, p. 68) identifies four component parts of this major false assumption, "each causing a specific warp in our thinking and relating":

- *"Rewards will come automatically if we do what we are supposed to do."* At the centre of this assumption is the belief that life is just and fair and that it operates an automatic payoff system. It engenders excessive expectations about life that are bound to be disappointed. Amongst those likely to hold to this false assumption most forcibly are those who have had a particularly successful, privileged and easy childhood, and also those who have always kept to the rules, "over-conforming in order to receive rewards" (Gould, 1980, p. 69).
- *"There is only one right way to do things."* This assumption is challenged as the infallibility of our parents' way is questioned. We are reluctant to relinquish our attachment to it, however, because in so doing we relinquish the childish hope that, even though it can also be a prison, if we find their one right way "we've found a magic key to the complex processes of reality and can guarantee our future against the terror of the unknown" (Gould, 1980, p. 69). Between what Gould calls the grinding wheels of current social expectations that we be a different kind of person and an internal imperative to be exactly like

our parents we must forge a self-definition that is nobody else's "only right way". In so doing we can be unreasonably hard on ourselves and intolerant of others.

- *"My loved ones are able to do for me what I haven't been able to do for myself."* Termed by Gould the "cure by love" fallacy, this assumption leads to dependency on others (for those competencies we feel to be lacking in ourselves) and to perceived power over others (with regard to those competencies we see ourselves as providing for them). To the degree that the cure by love myth is shared by both partners in an intimate relationship they will construct mutual conspiracies, feeling (and being seen as) superior to their partner on some issues, and inferior on others.
- *"Rationality, commitment, and effort will always prevail over all other forces."* Gould sees this final component assumption as a very cherished belief because, if it were true, we would be totally in control of our destiny. It must, however, be challenged if we are not to ignore the role of that which is irrational. This assumption is contradicted most forcibly in the experiences of intimacy and of power relationships such as those between employer and employee or parent and child. Dynamics set in motion largely by the invocation of the cure by love myth, "are unrelated to the rationally committed partnership tasks of the relationship and can't be totally understood on a conscious level" (Gould, 1980, p. 71).

During the twenties certain false assumptions must remain unchallenged if we are to fulfil the basic task of that era: becoming sufficiently independent of our parents to set up our own self-determined life structure. It is only when we reach what Gould describes as a new platform of strength at the threshold of the thirties that we are ready to handle the negation of the third major false assumption.

Assumption 3: "Life is simple and controllable. There are no significant coexisting, contradictory forces within me." (late twenties, early thirties). The tasks of the twenties require us to look outwards. They are concerned with developing competency in roles beyond those defined by our family of origin. Having succeeded in this, to at least some extent, we can return to our inner selves and confront aspects of ourselves that were suppressed or shelved. It is a confrontation that "is ushered in with disillusion, confusion about what life is all about, or a depression" (Gould, 1980, p. 72). Gould identifies four subcomponents in the major false assumption that is challenged by this self-confrontation. The reward for working through them is a new, more direct way of dealing with reality:

- *"What I know intellectually, I know emotionally."* In the return to our inner selves at this time emotions that may have been held at bay during the twenties are allowed to surface. We extend our emotional knowledge and learn how it is different from intellectual knowledge. To the extent that we can face our emotions we need no longer fear them – we, "come to see that a bit of sadness today is not the same as the endless pool of childhood sadness" (Gould, 1980, p. 72). Awareness and knowledge of our own inner complexity leaves us more self-tolerant and tolerant of others. This opening up phase draws to our attention the limits and disadvantages of our career and family situation to date – what has been missing and what sacrifices we have made.

- *"I am not like my parents in ways I don't want to be."* Whilst struggling to maintain the illusion during our twenties of the possibility of complete independence from parental influence it was too threatening to admit to being like them in ways we did not want to be. During the thirties we must acknowledge these similarities if we are to avoid, "blind repetition of their patterns" (Gould, 1980, p. 73). Most frequently, this false assumption is contradicted by our experiences of child rearing. We find ourselves reproducing in our own parental behaviour aspects of our own parents' treatment of us that we most disliked. Unless this can be faced, we "pass on the problem to our children who have to live with our conscious repudiation and our unconscious repetition" (Gould, 1980, p. 73).
- *"I can see the reality of those close to me quite clearly."* Gould sees this component of the third major false assumption being challenged primarily through the questioning of marital conspiracies formed during the twenties. Such questioning is essential for the occurrence and confirmation of a significant change in self-definition. We must recognise that what was a "true" picture of us and our partner is no longer the whole truth. The process of confrontation and acceptance of our own and our partner's new selves can be accompanied by high levels of marital tension.
- *"Threats to my security aren't real."* Gould lists a number of very real threats to our security that can occur during this opening-up period: career change, seeking either more intimacy or more space, returning to school, seeking more fun or bodily pleasure, settling down, having a baby, ceasing to be a baby, ceasing unnecessary fights with our parents, or starting to fight parents when we must. Gould suggests that the most profound threat to our security is if we consider breaking up our marriage, especially if there are children. "The critical issue to decide is whether the apparent enemy, the spouse, is really an enemy to our growth or a projection of our internal inhibitor" (Gould, 1980, p. 74).

Assumption 4: "There is no evil in me or death in the world. The sinister has been expelled." (35–50 years). Gould described the midlife period as ending the illusion of absolute safety and as marked by three central "subjective shifts". First, we discover that we are no longer young. As children begin to leave home and the relationship with our parents, if they are still alive, begins to undergo a subtle role reversal (with them depending on us rather than vice versa), we can no longer sustain a self-image based on the conception of ourselves as young. Second, we question again the values, life style, and life structures that we had been pursuing with full commitment. We return with the benefit of "a ripe and mature mind" (Gould, 1980, p. 77) to the questions that we first addressed during late adolescence. The third subjective shift is a sense of time urgency, "a vague but implacable sense that it is becoming time to act in some definitive and important, and, therefore dangerous way" (Gould, 1980, p. 77).

As with previous major false assumptions Gould identified a number of component parts. He saw them as applicable to those currently in the midlife period, but raised the question of historical and generational change when he suggested that the specific pillars propping up this assumption may possibly change for subsequent cohorts:

- *"My work (for men) or my relationship with men (for women) grants me immunity from death and danger."* Gould suggested that for men this false idea tends to take the form, "Death can't happen to me", and for women the form, "I can't live without a protector in life". He described the immunity pact many men seem to have with their work – a delusion that, "if we are successful we will never feel like small helpless little boys again, and the prospect of our death is banished" (Gould, 1980, p. 77). It is the delusion that success will solve all problems. Awareness of mortality seems to weaken this pact, and as this happens the costs of our illusion of immunity become apparent. The costs are in terms of constrictions to our humanity and authenticity. This awareness can either be denied by working harder than ever, or else it can be accepted and the challenge of finding a new balance between self and work can be undertaken. Gould described the issue as one of deadness versus aliveness, embodying a drive towards authenticity: "The dams we've erected against the feared reentry of a vital passion come crumbling down, not because there's a new biological surge of instincts, but because the deterred imperative of wholeness and deep self-knowledge can wait no longer" (Gould, 1980, p. 125).

  Women in the midlife period are, like men, seeking an authenticity and wholeness that has been lacking in their lives to date. Gould suggests that whilst women's biological role as child-bearers keeps them in touch with their own mortality, the awareness of its relevance to their own lives operates as a spur to act each on her own behalf. Whereas men's immunity pact is traditionally with work, women's has traditionally concerned their relationships with men. Whereas men's immunity pact provides them with the illusion that they can be protected from death, women's false assumption is that they cannot expand themselves beyond that which their protector (normally their husband) supports and condones. To do so would be to risk losing the protection that they falsely believe they need to live. Whilst the life choices and circumstances of many women demonstrate the falsity of this assumption, Gould (1980, p. 82) maintained that, "each woman must carry out her own transformation on the deeply embedded and often cleverly disguised version of this false idea".

For both men and women, the rewards of dispelling their respective versions of this component of the false assumption is the acknowledged coexistence within the same individual of both positive masculine-stereotyped and positive feminine-stereotyped attributes.

- *"There is no life beyond this family."* In our teens and twenties we have to dispel the myth that we must always belong to our family or origin. In midlife we must challenge the assumption that separation and divorce are not possible, that is, "that there is no life beyond our current husband or wife" (Gould, 1980, p. 83). If we do not challenge this belief then there is no room for the marital relationship to develop and change. Change is achieved under this false assumption not by negotiation, but by one partner, "leading the way and dragging the other" (Gould, 1980, p. 83). When the assumption is challenged there is an injection of energy into the marriage. An opportunity is created for a more satisfactory resolution of issues relating to such matters as the couple's sexual relationship, their roles within the family, and the degree of difference and aloneness that is acceptable. The risk is that irreconcilable differences and incompatibilities will emerge and the marriage will end in divorce, or will continue but be characterised by chronic hostility.
- *"I am innocent."* This component of the false assumption is a defence against, "our deep demonic childhood badness" (Gould, 1980, p. 84) that we came to believe in through the experiences of infancy. To be expunged, these experiences must be relabelled from the perspective of adult rather than childhood consciousness. This is often achieved by reanalysing feelings of inadequacy and finding them to reflect an overly moral labelling of what Gould refers to as vital passions, rather than inadequacy *per se*. We must relabel our inner processes so that, "we no longer interpret dissatisfaction as greed, self-concern as selfishness, sensuality as lasciviousness, pleasure as irresponsibility, curiosity as something forbidden, anger as something destructive, love as weakness, imperfection as a fault, change as danger, or wicked thoughts the same as wicked actions" (Gould, 1980, p. 85). This process frees us to be vital and alive, living our life freely and joyfully. It is a process of working through negative self-images.

Life after 50. Gould argues that through our negation of the four major false assumptions of our childhood consciousness we make the transition from the belief that "I am theirs" to the recognition that "I am myself". With this awareness we are finally able to escape from the struggle for status. We are free to acknowledge what Gould called our mysterious, indelible "me" as the core of the rest of our life. This does not mean there is no more disappointment, ill health, or pain to bear. It does, however, mean that those who have made contact with this inner core can face such experiences with greater strength. Their sense of meaning resides within them and it cannot be removed by misfortune. This does not happen to everyone. Older people who have not made this contact with their inner core have no recourse against the feeling that they are losing the battle with life. Finding no meaning in their own life, they attack life itself as meaningless. They have lost Erikson's struggle between integrity and despair.

This chapter has explored the notion of age- or life-stage-related developmental tasks. Such tasks have a range of specificity – from highly specific to so general as to perhaps best be thought of as themes rather than tasks. Perhaps thinking of a hierarchy of such preoccupations is in order – specific tasks, broader goals, and missions. The concept of developmental tasks is a useful, albeit a culturally and cohort-specific way of construing the life course, and one to which many people respond with elements of both recognition and rejection.

6 Life events and transitions

> "How old are you?" people sometimes ask me. "I am seventeen battle scars old," I say. Usually people don't flinch, and rather happily begin to count up their battle scar ages accordingly.
>
> (Estes, 1993)

Life events are benchmarks in the human life cycle. They are the milestones or transition points that give "shape and direction to the various aspects of a person's life" (Danish, Smyer, & Nowak, 1980, p. 342). However, life events are more than markers. They are also processes having, "antecedents, durations, contexts and outcomes" (Reese & Smyer, 1983, p. 2). It is likely that the lifeline you drew earlier was punctuated by a number of such experiences – indeed the exercise, with its invitation to plot "peaks and troughs", draws attention to what have been termed turning points (Rutter, 1996; Wethington et al., 1997) in the life course. By their mid-thirties, most adults can list more than 30 or 40 transitions or significant life events that they have experienced to date (Hopson, 1981).

Types of life events

Baltes et al. (1980) distinguish between normative age-graded, normative history-graded, and non-normative life events or influences. Normative age-graded influences are biological and environmental determinants of development, such as many aspects of physical development and of a society's age-graded socialisation practices that have (in terms of onset and duration) a fairly strong relationship with chronological age. Thus, we all tend to go to school or reach our peak of physical strength at about the same age. In terms of the earlier discussion of stability and consistency (Chapter 1), such phenomena can be said to show high process stability. As stated in Chapter 1 in relation to the tenets of life-span developmental psychology, normative history-graded influences on life-span development are biological and environmental determinants that have a strong relationship with historical time rather than chronological age. They are cohort specific, being shared by members of a society at a particular point in time but not, or not in the same way, by members of preceding or subsequent generations. Finally, non-normative influences or systems of change are biological or environmental influences that do not, for most individuals, occur in any normative age-graded or history-graded manner. Adaptation to non-normative events is a hallmark of the "life course as chaos" perspective identified in Chapter 3 as a distinctive orientation to life-span development.

Baltes (1979; Baltes et al., 1980) suggests that the relative impact of age-graded, history-graded, and non-normative influences varies across the life course. He is on fairly firm ground in suggesting that normative age-graded influences might predominate during childhood and show a second, but lesser, peak in old age. In childhood there are significant age-graded influences stemming from both biological maturation and educational/socialisation events. In advanced old age, whilst there are still significant individual differences, both biological declines and social role restrictions are likely to become increasingly influential. With regard to normative history-graded influences, Baltes et al. suggest a peak during the adolescence/early-adult period on the grounds that the transition to adulthood is one particularly susceptible to sociocultural factors. The greater heterogeneity in the life courses of adults in comparison with children – stemming at least in part from an overall weakening of age-graded and history-graded influences – leads Baltes et al. to suggest a steadily increasing relative impact from non-normative influences throughout life. The suggested relative impact across the life course of the three types of influence is shown graphically in Figure 6.1. It implies that whereas for researchers of child development it may be appropriate to look for age-graded patterns of development, researchers of adulthood would be better employed in examining the impact of major life events.

The normative/non-normative distinction is, however, a dimension rather than a dichotomy. Thus, whilst we all experience bereavement, accident, or illness at any point in the life course (making them non-normative life events), both the absolute incidence and the type of these events will have some, albeit imperfect, correlation with chronological age. Furthermore, a society's age-grade system constantly evolves, such that events that were once rare can, over time, become normative (or vice versa). The incidence of married women in the work force is a case in point. At one time most women gave up paid employment on marriage. Now this is highly unusual. Datan (1983, p. 41) details such progressions: "the exceptional becomes the scarce, the scarce becomes the infrequent, the infrequent becomes the acceptable, and finally the acceptable becomes the norm". Note how this is not merely a numerical progression. Accompanying the constantly increasing statistical likelihood of, in this example, married women retaining their job on marriage, is a change in social attitudes. A point is reached where what might have been frowned on or thought odd becomes not

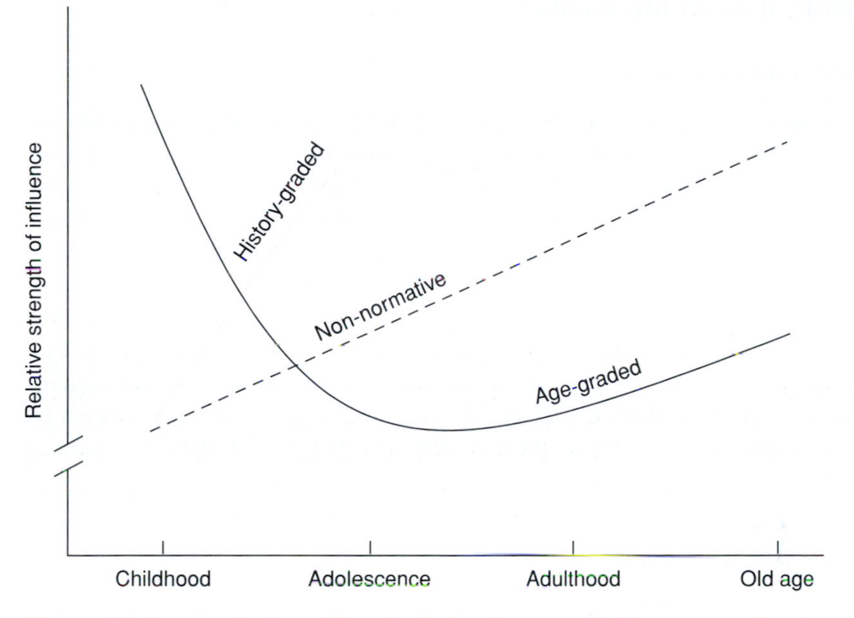

Figure 6.1 Prototypical profiles of relative impact of influences on development across the life course (reproduced with permission from Baltes, P.B. et al. (1980). Life-span developmental psychology. *Annual Review of Psychology, 31,* 65–110. Copyright © 1980 by Annual Reviews: www.AnnualReviews.org).

only statistically more likely but also socially acceptable. Now many people would consider it wrong, or at least "not right" for women to relinquish paid employment on marriage.

The sheer number of life events can be thought of as a history-graded influence because it is also likely that your lifeline is punctuated by more events than the lifelines of your grandparents or great-grandparents would have been. Technological change, greater geographic mobility, more frequent and more drastic job moves, more frequent divorce and remarriage – all this and more has contributed to a climate of social instability and a dramatic increase in the amount of change with which most people must cope during their lives. It is perhaps not surprising, therefore, that the study of significant life events and of our response to these upheavals has emerged as a field of study in its own right. In the present chapter the two concepts of life events – as markers and as processes – are discussed.

Life-events as markers: the description and classification of life events

Life event dimensions

Life events have been described using at least 35 variables (Reese & Smyer, 1983) that can be grouped into event, perception or effect dimensions (Brim & Ryff, 1980), as shown in Table 6.1. Event dimensions describe objective characteristics of the events themselves. Perception dimensions concern the affected person's subjective impression or evaluation of the events. Effect dimensions refer to the outcomes or consequences of events. To manipulate 35 dimensions conceptually, let alone practically, would be more than a little unwieldy and most discussions of transitions and life events focus a more restricted number and type – selected on theoretical, empirical, and/or pragmatic grounds. Box 6.1 (page 149) shows the dimensions identified by Schlossberg et al. (1995) as particularly pertinent to the way we manage and experience transitions.

Life-event taxonomies

Life-event taxonomies classify life events according to one or more dimensions such as those listed in Table 6.1, with theoretical and pragmatic considerations, along with what Reese and Smyer (1983) term "informed conjecture", determining which dimensions are chosen. Selecting more than one dimension offers the possibility of defining categories by the intersection of dimensions, thus leading to more sophisticated analyses.

A three-dimensional taxonomy of life events was compiled by Brim and Ryff (1980) on the basis of: (1) the probability (or likelihood) that an event will take place; (2) the correlation of the event with chronological age (age-relatedness); and (3) whether the event will occur for many people or just a few (prevalence). Distinguishing between a "high" and "low" category for each dimension produces an eight-cell taxonomy as shown in Table 6.2, along with illustrative life events. It is worth noting how several of the events in the "Experienced by many/High probability of occurrence/Strong correlation with age" category probably have a weaker correlation with age now than when the taxonomy was first produced. The dimensions were selected to help people contemplating their future address three key questions with regard to life events: "How likely is it that a particular event will happen to me? If it does happen, when will it happen? Will I be the only person it happens to, or will there be others?"

A two-dimensional taxonomy comprising 4 event "types" and 14 event "contexts" was proposed by Reese and Smyer (1983), making a total of 56 cells. The event types were social–cultural, personal–sociological, biological and physical–environmental, and the event contexts (listed in

Table 6.1 Life-event dimensions (Reese & Smyer, 1983)

Dimension	*Definition*
"Effect" dimensions	
Contextual purity	Extent to which one event influences the resolution or outcome of concurrent events
Direction of impact	Enhancement or debilitation of the life course in response to the event
Direction of movement	Entering or leaving a role or social field as a result of the event
Domain	Type of functioning affected, for example biological or social (also called "context" or "life area")
Focus	Person directly affected by the event (self or others)
Impact	Amount of behavioural change in response to the event; or amount of stress engendered by the event (also called "severity" or "stressfulness")
"Perception" dimensions	
Control	Belief that the event was chosen versus imposed, or under personal control versus uncontrolled
Desirability	Perception of the event as desirable versus undesirable, or good versus bad
Expectation	Extent to which the event was expected or anticipated
Familiarity	Familiarity with an event through prior experience versus novelty of the event
Long-range threat	Perceived severity of the negative impact over a long period
Meaning	The person's interpretation of the event (for example, as an "accident" or as "the will of God")
Perceived gain or loss	Perceived amount of gain or loss resulting from the event
Social desirability	Perceived evaluation of the event by society at large or by a smaller reference group
Stress	Perceived stressfulness of the event
Timeliness	Belief that the event occurred "on time" or "off time"
"Event" dimensions	
Adequacy of functioning	Extent to which the event reflects inferior or superior functioning of the individual (e.g. the failure of a relationship might reflect inferior functioning)
Age congruity	Typical amount of overlap in the spread of two or more specified events
Age relatedness	Strength of correlation with age (also called "age grading" or "temporal predictability")
Breadth of setting	Extent to which the event is limited to or is independent of particular settings
Cohort specificity	Extent to which the nature of an event depends on the individual's cohort or generation
Context	Area of the life space in which the event occurs, for example, "family", "work" (also called "domain")
Duration	Amount of time required for the event to transpire (also called "chronicity" or "chronic" versus "acute")
Integration	Extent to which the occurrence of one event depends on the occurrence of another

Table 6.1 (cont.)

Dimension	*Definition*
Likelihood of occurrence	The probability that the event will occur for a given person
Onset	The suddenness or gradualness of the onset of the event
Order	The sequence in which events typically occur
Prevalence	The proportion of individuals in a particular population who experience a given event (also called "extensiveness of occurrence", "generality", or "social distribution")
Recency	The amount of time passed since the occurrence of the event
Reversibility	The degree to which a transition is reversible
Sequencing	The sequence in which events occur in an individual case
Source	The cause of an event, or the domain of the cause, for example, "heredity", "physical environment" (also called "domain")
Spread	The age range within which an event typically occurs.
Timing	The average age at which the event occurs (also called "age grading")
Type	The nature of domain of an event, for example "biological processes", "physical-environmental events" (also called "domain")

Reproduced with permission from Reese, H.W., & Smyer, M.A. (1983). The dimensionalization of life-events. In E.J. Callahan & K.A. McKluskey (Eds.) *Life-span developmental psychology: Nonnormative events*. Copyright © 1983 by Academic Press.

Table 6.3) were grouped into 5 superordinate sets – family, self, social relations, work, and miscellaneous. Whilst such a taxonomy does make life events data somewhat more manageable, it can still produce a rather untidy ragbag of categories. When they classified 355 life events according to the context by type taxonomy, Reese and Smyer found wide variation in the frequency with which categories were used. Although the miscellaneous category was used for only 3.7 per cent of the events (suggesting that their list of contexts was reasonably comprehensive), two of the contexts – friendships and community – were used even less often. At the other extreme, almost half of the events (48.8 per cent) fell within the four categories of family, work, health, and love and marriage.

Whilst uneven distribution of events across categories could reflect real differences in the frequency of occurrence of events in different contexts, Reese and Smyer suggest that the heavily used categories might have been too broadly, and the underused categories too finely, drawn. Alternatively, or in addition, the disproportionate distribution of events in the some contexts could merely be a reflection of the interests of the investigators sampled. The former is a theoretical and the latter an empirical question. Reese and Smyer also found a varied distribution of events among the types, with sociocultural events accounting for 48 per cent of the total,

Table 6.2 Life-event taxonomy based on probability of occurrence, correlation with age and numbers affected (Brim & Ryff, 1980)

	Experienced by many		*Experienced by few*	
Correlation with age	*High probability of occurrence*	*Low probability of occurrence*	*High probability of occurrence*	*Low probability of occurrence*
Strong	Learning to walk Marriage Starting to work Woman giving birth to first child	Military service draft Polio epidemic	Coming into a large estate at 18 years old	Spina bifida School drop-out
Weak	Father's death Husband's death "Topping out" in work career Children's marriages Moving home	War Great depression Plague Earthquake	Succeeding father in family business	Loss of limb in car accident Accident at work Death of daughter Adult children returning home to live Cured of alcoholism

Reproduced with permission from Brim, O.G., & Ryff, C.D. (1980). On the properties of life events. In P.B. Baltes & O.G. Brim (Eds). *Life-span development and behavior* (Vol. 3).

Table 6.3 Life-event contexts (Reese & Smyer, 1983)

Superordinate set	*Context*	*Comments*
Family	Family	Family of origin: parents, siblings, etc.
	Love and marriage	Partner or mate
	Parenting	Children, or having and rearing children
	Residence	Dwelling place
Self	Health	Own health and biological functions
	Self	Predominant reference of event is to the self
Social relations	Community	Community relations and functions
	Friendships	Close friends and primary friendship networks
	Social relations	Psychosocial relations
Work	Finances	All contexts related to money (including household economics)
	School	Schooling, education and training
	Work	Occupation and career
Miscellaneous	Law	Reference is to crime and legal matters: perpetration of crime, legal consequences (for victim of crime, context is classified elsewhere)
	Miscellaneous	Contexts that do not fit elsewhere in the list

Reproduced with permission from Reese, H.W., & Smyer, M.A. (1983). The dimensionalization of life-events. In E.J. Callahan & K.A. McKluskey (Eds.). *Life-span developmental psychology: Nonnormative events*. Copyright © 1983 by Academic Press)

personal–psychological for 31.9 per cent, biological for 16.1 per cent, and physical–environmental for a mere 4 per cent. They suggest this probably reflects the interests of the researchers they sampled, who tended to be social scientists rather than biological or physical scientists. For researchers with an interest in life-span development, taxonomies such as this can be used, for example, to investigate fluctuations in the occurrence and significance of life events across the life course. When the objective is to compare and contrast a relatively small number of life events (rather than simply to classify a large number), then other dimensions from the list in Table 6.3 can be employed as well. Thus, Reese and Smyer selected two events from each of ten contexts and rated them on ten dimensions.

Several life-event taxonomies utilise only one dimension, with Holmes and Rahe's (1967) Social Readjustment Rating Scale perhaps being the best known. Respondents are asked to indicate which of forty-three events, rank ordered according to their estimated stressfulness (and listed in Table 6.4) they have experienced within (usually) the last 12 months. The sum of the stress ratings for these events is taken as an indicator of the amount

Table 6.4 Life events ordered for stressfulness (Holmes & Rahe, 1967)

Rank	*Life event*	*Rank*	*Life event*
1	Death of spouse	22	Change in responsibilities at work
2	Divorce	23	Son or daughter leaves home
3	Marital separation	24	Trouble with in-laws
4	Jail term	25	Outstanding personal achievement
5	Death of close family member	26	Spouse begins or stops work
6	Personal injury or illness	27	Begin or end school
7	Marriage	28	Change in living conditions
8	Fired at work	29	Revision of personal habits
9	Marital reconciliation	30	Trouble with boss
10	Retirement	31	Change in work hours or conditions
11	Change in health of family member	32	Change in residence
12	Pregnancy	33	Change in schools
13	Sex difficulties	34	Change in recreation
14	Gain of new family member	35	Change in church activities
15	Business readjustment	36	Change in social activities
16	Change in financial status	37	Moderate mortgage or loan
17	Death of close friend	38	Change in sleeping habits
18	Change to a different line of work	39	Change in number of family get-togethers
19	Change in number of arguments with spouse	40	Change in eating habits
		41	Vacation
20	Heavy mortgage repayments	42	Christmas
21	Foreclosure of mortgage or loan	43	Minor violations of the law

of stress experienced by individuals and used as a basis for predicting the likelihood of their suffering stress-related health problems. Including positive as well as negative events in the list acknowledges that both can be stressful. However, assigning fixed weightings to different events ignores individual differences in their impact and meaning for different respondents. Rescalings of the items in the Social Readjustment Rating Scale in 1977 and 1995 (Miller & Rahe, 1997) revealed both an increase in the level of self-reported stress engendered by the life events included in the inventory, and a degree of variation in the relative stressfulness associated with some of the items. With the exception of "marriage" (which fell from fifth to nineteenth in terms of stress level relative to other items), the items at the top of the original list retained more or less the same relative rank, although for many there was an increase in the absolute level of stress they were accorded. There was, for example, more anxiety than previously about death of close friends, major illness, marital separation, mortgage foreclosure, and work issues. Such changes can be understood as the outcome of changes in the way work and relationships are structured and valued, that is, as sociocultural changes reflecting history-graded influences on the life course.

Life events as processes: the dynamics of psychosocial transitions

When attention shifts from the characteristics of life events to the experiences of individuals undergoing them, a somewhat different line of research emerges. Originating primarily in the study of people's reactions to loss or crisis (e.g. Moos, 1986; Parkes, 1971, 1991), a body of research has accumulated that indicates how disruptions to our accustomed way of life trigger a relatively predictable cycle of reactions and feelings as shown in Figure 6.2.

It is not claimed that everyone's response follows an identical path in every instance. In particular, there may be differences, depending on whether or not the change is a desired and pleasurable change, resulting in the proposal of two alternative paths through the reaction phase of the cycle. None the less, the cycle is sufficiently generalisable for most people to recognise it in their own experience in relation to at least some significant life events. The cycle – known as the transition cycle – is a general pattern rather than a rigid sequence. It is set in motion when any event or non-event, "results in changed relationships, routines, assumptions, and roles" (Schlossberg et al., 1995, p. 27). The inclusion of non-events (that is, events we hoped or expected would occur, but which did not) in this discussion is important because failure to obtain an anticipated promotion or conceive a planned baby, let us say, can provoke as significant a transition as the new job or baby would have done. Put another way, both events and non-events can require us to modify our "assumptive world"

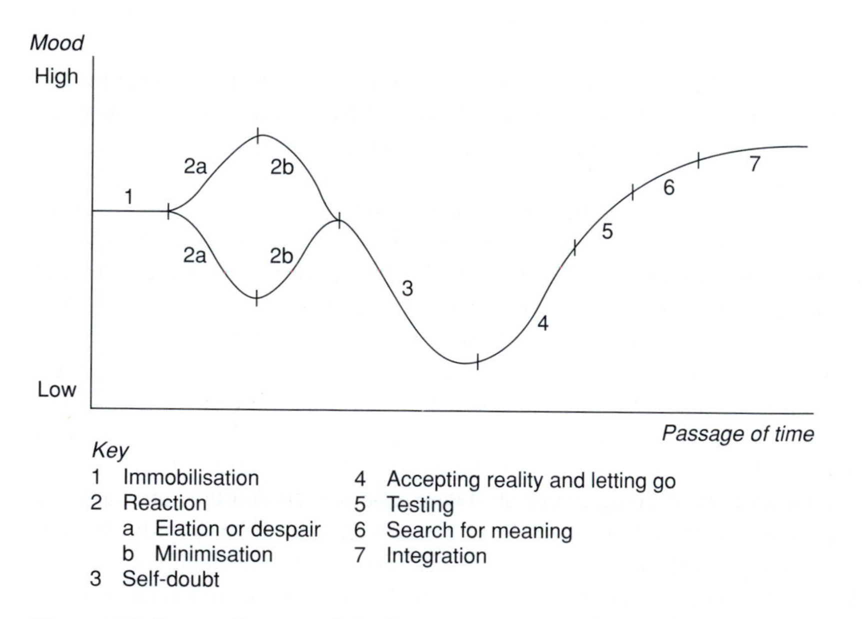

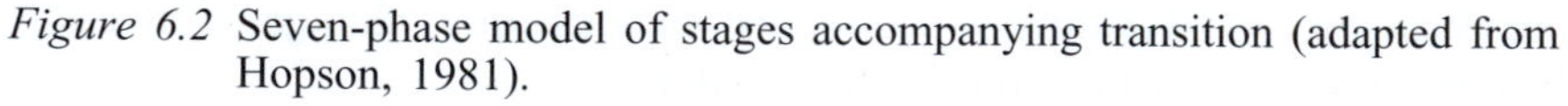
Figure 6.2 Seven-phase model of stages accompanying transition (adapted from Hopson, 1981).

(Parkes, 1971) – the largely taken-for-granted assumptions we make about ourselves and our world.

Units cannot be assigned to either the horizontal dimension of "time" or the vertical dimension of "mood". Individual differences are to be expected in the time taken to cope with any particular transition. Similarly, a person can cope very rapidly with one transition but, with another, never progress beyond the first or second stage. Queen Victoria is a well known example of someone who never came to terms with the death of her husband. She kept his room and his belongings as they had always been. She could not, or would not, "let go" of the world of which he had been a part. Furthermore, progress through the stages of the transition cycle is rarely smooth and continuous. Taking two steps forward and one step back is likely to be a more accurate description (Hopson, 1981). Indeed, someone may be working on several stages concurrently.

With regard to the vertical dimension, individual differences are to be expected in the degree of mood swing and in the level of the final plateau. For any particular individual going through any particular transition, the "peak" of elation might or might not be more extreme than the "trough" of despair. The final plateau might level out either above or below the individual's initial mood level. Even the labelling of this dimension is tentative. In an earlier version of the model shown in Figure 6.2 the vertical dimension was identified as "self-esteem" (Hopson & Adams, 1976). There is a long history of alternative, more specific labelling of this dimension, for example, "morale level" when talking about unemployment, or "competence" when discussing coping with promotion (Parker & Lewis, 1981).

Despite the caveats listed above, the seven stages discussed in the following sections represent a generally recognisable sequence of responses accompanying a wide range of transitions.

1. Immobilisation

How would you feel if one evening *all* your numbers came up on the National Lottery? How would you feel if you turned the corner of your road one day and found that your home had been burned to the ground? The chances are that initially you would not be able to comprehend the full implication of what had happened. Your initial response might be one of disbelief – "This can't be true". You might well be "stopped dead in your tracks". This is the stage of immobilisation or shock. It is characterised by a sense of being overwhelmed, of being "frozen up". Its duration and intensity tend to increase with the magnitude, the unexpectedness, and the negative valence of the event.

2. Reaction

(a) Elation or despair. After a greater or lesser time, the sense of shock gives way to a sharp swing of mood, the direction of which depends on the nature and circumstances of the transition. For positive or desired events the extent of the swing may range from mild pleasure to total elation, whilst for a negative or undesired event the mood shift might be anything from slight disappointment to despair.

(b) Minimisation. The initial post-shock reaction will almost always be followed by some form of minimisation. This might be in relation to the feelings associated with the event and/or the anticipated impact of the change. For a positive transition the feelings of elation become dampened as more ambiguous or less desirable concomitants of the transition become apparent or are confronted. This links in with the tenet of life-span developmental psychology (Baltes, 1987) that development involves both gains and losses. Thus the joy of obtaining a much sought after university place may be tempered by questions of, "Will I be able to cope?" or "Perhaps I will miss the folk at home after all". Similarly, the importance or likely impact of a negative event may be played down. The situation may be reassessed as being less dire than was originally thought. Thus, the person who fails to obtain a university place may say, "At least I won't have to take any more exams" or "I'm just as likely to get a job without a degree".

3. Self-doubt

The boundaries between the phases of the model are not distinct and the minimisation of the positive aspects of a desired event can slip almost imperceptibly into a period of self-doubt. With negative events, the minimisation phase may not be noticeable and the individual might seem to pass directly from despair to self-doubt. This dip in mood is associated with the growing realisation of the reality of the changes in one's life space. Originally, this third phase was labelled a period of depression (Hopson & Adams, 1976), but this was altered to self-doubt (Hopson, 1981) on the realisation that, whilst depression was a common response, it was not the only one. The underlying dimension of self-doubt might also be manifested in other ways, such as by anxiety, anger, or sadness. There might be fluctuations in energy level. The individual might alternate between phases of anger and phases of apathy.

4. Accepting reality and letting go

Until this point the individual has to a greater or lesser extent still been attached to the past in a way that inhibits him or her from beginning actively to cope with the new situation. At some point these attachments, or affectional bonds (Parkes, 1971), must be broken and reformed if the individual is to continue to develop and grow. The reality of the change must be accepted. The hold on the past must be loosened, but not necessarily totally relinquished. Thus, bereaved people might continue to describe themselves in relation to the deceased person in ways that imply a continuing relationship (Klass, Silverman, & Nickman, 1996). The dead person might continue to be a role model for the bereaved, thereby providing a source of both solace and guidance.

This process of "letting go" can be traumatic (Brammer & Abrego, 1981). There might be tears as the loss of the past is mourned; there might be anger at the perceived injustice of the demand for change. Emerging from the experience, however, is at least some degree of commitment to "put the past behind me" and face the future. In a sense, this phase of letting go is a watershed in coping with transitions. It is the point at which we can begin to convert the tragedies and disasters in our lives into growth points.

Letting go undoubtedly requires courage. It inevitably involves a plunge into the unknown. To use the analogy offered by Levinson and his colleagues (1978), it is a phase during which we have cast ourselves adrift from the past but cannot yet see the land of the future. To use Parkes' (1971) terminology, we have severed our old affectional bonds but not yet formed any new ones. It is the point at which the individual's orientation begins to turn away from the past towards the future.

Bridges (1980, p. 11) suggested that transitions actually begin with an ending: "We have to let go of the old thing before we can pick up the new – not just outwardly, but inwardly, where we keep our connections to the people and places that act as definitions of who we are". Bridges distinguished three stages in the transition process: an "ending", followed by a period of "confusion and distress", leading to a "new beginning": "Endings and beginnings, with emptiness and germination in between" (Bridges, 1980, p. 150). From this perspective, "letting go" is the first part of a transition, rather than the midpoint.

5. *Testing*

Once our relationship to the past has been at least partially renegotiated, we can begin to explore the new terrain. New options are tentatively considered and alternative ways of behaving are tried. This is an experimental period, reminiscent of Erikson's concept of the identity crisis (see Chapter 4), during which, as it were, new identities are tried on for size until gradually new affectional bonds or attachments to the new world are established. It may be accompanied by rapid mood changes as plans are considered and discarded, and as hopes are raised and dashed. None the less, the "low point" of the transition is past and, taken overall, the person's mood, morale, or level of self-esteem is on the rise.

6. Search for meaning

"Putting the past behind you" does not imply a pretence that the disruption or change never happened. Rather, this sixth phase in the transition cycle is characterised by a conscious striving to learn from the experience. It is a cognitive phase during which people seek to make sense of what has happened to them. It is a healthy form of reflective thinking without which the individual would not be able to develop a deep understanding of the meaning of the change in his or her life. It should not be interpreted as "morbid dwelling on the past". This perspective is consistent with Klass et al.'s (1996) questioning of whether a continuing relationship with a lost loved one is necessarily a symptom of unresolved grief. Rather than expunging the deceased person from our life structure, it may be healthier to find a new, albeit changed, place for them within our life (Walter, 1996).

7. Integration

Arguably, the transition process can be said to be complete when the individual feels "at home" in the new, post-transition reality. The new behaviours that may have been so painfully acquired, the new self-conceptions and understandings of events perhaps so agonisingly achieved, have become an integral part of the person's view of the world. The transition has become integrated into the life space and no longer dominates it. However, it is also possible to question whether transitions ever end. The dialectical perspective on the life course holds that developmental tasks are never completed: "At the very moment when completion seems to be achieved, new doubts arise in the individual" (Riegel, 1976, p. 697). This is compatible with the notion of the life course as a never ending story (see the discussion of narrative in Chapter 7) and of the inevitably temporary nature of life structures (see, here, the discussion of Levinson et al.'s model in Chapter 5).

Coping with transitions

It was emphasised earlier that individual differences exist in coping with transitions, despite the identification of "typical" patterns of response. But what produces this individual variation? Schlossberg et al. (1995) developed a framework that identified four major sets of factors (Activity 6.1) "that influence the individual's ability to cope during a transition" (p. 47). Only one set of factors – the situation – relate to the objective characteristics of transitions (and even here some judgements are involved). The other sets of factors – self, support, and strategies – refer to the people undergoing the transition (who they are and what they do) and the social and material contexts in which they are embedded. Individuals can then assess, or be assessed, in terms of what Schlossberg et al. refer to as their assets and liabilities in each of these domains. This follows Fiske and Chiriboga (1990), who rejected a degree-of-impairment model in favour of one that recognised that we all have both multiple assets, resources, and strengths, and multiple liabilities, deficits and limitations. Again there is this theme of "both/and" rather than "either/or", which characterises much life-span theorising. People's situation, self, support and strategies can then be construed as a balance of assets and liabilities, rather than as unambiguously "good" or "poor", with the recognition that the ratio between the two can change.

Activity 6.1 Coping with transitions (adapted from Schlossberg et al., 1995)

The "4-S" framework identifies four major factors that influence an individual's ability to cope during a transition:

- situation variable – what is happening? What sort of transition is it?
- self variable – to whom is it happening?
- support variable – what help is available?
- strategies variable – how does the person cope?

Schlossberg et al. (1995) suggest that we can assess our assets and liabilities (or strengths and weaknesses) in relation to each of these domains.

Think of a major life event or transition that you have been through. What were your assets and liabilities with regard to each of the "4-S" categories? If you were to experience a similar transition today, how would the balance between your assets and liabilities have changed?

The situation variable

From the large number of potential variables (see Table 6.1), Schlossberg et al. identify eight dimensions in people's transition situation likely to have particular impact on their ability to cope with change. These are summarised in Box 6.2 and elaborated in more detail below.

1. Trigger. What set off the transition? Schlossberg et al. identify several, frequently interrelated, dimensions along which events triggering a transition can vary. They can be anticipated or unanticipated, external (e.g. a friend dying suddenly) or internal (e.g. the gradual realisation that one is not going to gain promotion), an identifiable event or an intangible non-event. It is not the event *per se* that is important, rather it is the meaning of the event for the individual. A decade birthday indicates no greater passage of time than any other birthday, but its symbolic importance can be enormous.

Box 6.1 "Situation" factors influencing capacity to cope with transitions (adapted from Schlossberg et al., 1995)

Key dimensions along which transitions can vary and which can influence how we cope with them include:

- trigger – what set off the transition?
- timing – how does the transition relate to social norms and personal life stage?
- control – what aspects of the transition can the person control?
- role change – does the transition involve role change?
- duration – is the transition seen as permanent or temporary?
- previous experience – has the person met similar transitions in the past?
- concurrent stress – what and how great are the other stresses currently facing the person?
- assessment – does the person view the situation positively or negatively?

2. *Timing.* How does the transition relate to social norms and personal life stage? Despite the loosening of social norms regarding the timing of major life events, most of us still carry some sort of a "social time clock" in our head, and judge whether we are "early", "on time" or "late" with respect to a range of family, career and self issues. To be "off time" will still frequently leave us feeling uncomfortable. As well as being "on" or "off" time, transitions can occur at better or worse times, making them relatively easier or harder to manage. Thus, geographic relocation in the middle of studies for A-levels, or becoming pregnant when one has just obtained a new job, are likely to be judged as transitions occurring at "bad" times.

3. *Control.* What aspects of the transition can the person control? The issue here is the degree of actual and perceived control people feel they have over their significant life events. Enforced retirement through ill health or redundancy can be harder to cope with than if the decision had been made voluntarily. Rodin (1990) suggests that through middle age and into old age the domains over which we feel we have control are likely to diminish. None the less, even if the transition itself is beyond our control, our response to it can, at least to some degree, be within our power. This is also the rationale behind the view of successful ageing (Baltes, 1993; Baltes & Baltes, 1980, 1990) as involving selection, optimisation, and compensation (see Chapter 1).

4. *Role change.* Does the transition involve role change? The essence of transitions is the changes they engender in the individual's internal life structure. However, most also involve behavioural change, often involving

role loss, role gain or, perhaps most frequently, role exchange. Thus, in the role of new mother a woman's life structure expands to include the new baby (a role gain), but it can also contract, at least temporarily, through the relinquishment of a range of occupational and social activities (role loss). Roles will vary in the extent to which they are accompanied by normative expectations concerning how to behave. Such norms can ease entry to a new role by providing guidelines and reducing uncertainty. However, by the same token, they can also be experienced as restrictive – as, for example, when people feel obliged to relinquish a particular activity because "I'm too old for that sort of thing" – be it 12-year-olds who feel they should relinquish the role of "child" and are "too old" to play with dolls any longer, or 60-year-olds who feel it is time they sold their motor bikes for a more sedate form of transport more "in keeping" with the role of "senior citizen".

5. Duration. Is the transition seen as permanent or temporary? A change that is viewed as permanent will be regarded differently from one that is assumed to be temporary. In particular, negative aspects of a change can be easier to accept if it is known they will be of limited duration. However, the duration of a change can be uncertain, and this can be even more stressful and unsettling. Thus, parents of a sick or disabled child might experience relief when the condition is diagnosed, even if the prognosis is poor, because it represents something tangible to address rather than the intangible sense that "something is wrong". Furthermore, a change assumed initially to be temporary can turn out to be permanent, demonstrating how the assessment of a transition is a continuing, dynamic process rather than a once-and-for-all judgement.

6. Previous experience. Has the person met similar transitions in the past? In the main it is assumed that we learn from experience and, if we have successfully weathered a particular kind of transition in the past, this will give us both the skills and the confidence to do so again in the future. However, if we experienced past transitions as overwhelming and our attempts to resolve them as unsatisfactory, then this can decrease our perception of our ability to cope with future transitions, even if the balance between our assets and liabilities has shifted and in theory become more favourable.

7. Concurrent stress. What and how great are the stresses currently facing the person in other areas of life? It might be that once a person reaches the integration phase of the transition cycle they have the time and energy to handle another upheaval. Alternatively, they might be suffering from the equivalent of "combat fatigue", where any further demands for change and adaptation would be "the straw that broke the camel's back". In any case, transitions frequently do not occur in this sequential fashion and instead come tumbling one on top of the other. Indeed, a transition in one arena of life may be the trigger for numerous other transitions. Thus, the amount and nature of stresses elsewhere in the person's life will influence their experience of and ability to cope with any one particular transition.

8. Assessment. Does the person view the situation positively or negatively? The nature of a transition in terms of the person's assessment of its source, controllability, magnitude, duration, familiarity, and timing in relation to social norms, personal life stage, and other concurrent events, will all contribute to whether the transition is viewed as positive or negative. This assessment, whilst not necessarily being articulated, can still influence the person's passage through the transition cycle. These multiple factors in relation to which a transition can vary precludes the assessment of particular events in terms of their inherent difficulty or impact. The particular situation in which they occur and of which they form a part is of crucial importance.

The self variable

The self variable, as construed by Schlossberg et al., refers to the personal, demographic and the psychological characteristics a person brings to the situation. Key relevant factors are summarised in Box 6.3. They represent people's coping resources, that is, not what they actually do but rather, "what is available to them in developing their coping repertoires" (Pearlin & Schooler, 1978). For any particular transition they will represent a network of assets and liabilities.

Box 6.2 "Self" factors – or personal resources – influencing capacity to cope with transitions (adapted from Schlossberg et al., 1995)

"Self" factors refer to what people bring to the situation by virtue of "who they are". Factors particularly relevant for individuals as they cope with transitions include:

- *Personal and demographic resources*:
  - socioeconomic status
  - gender
  - ethnicity
  - age and life stage
  - state of health.
- *Psychological resources*:
  - psychological maturity
  - personality
  - commitment and values.

Personal and demographic resources. Age and life stage, plus other personal and demographic characteristics such as socioeconomic status, gender, ethnicity, and state of health, place people in different cultural contexts (see Bronfenbrenner's model, outlined in Chapter 1) with different resources. These cultural contexts bear directly on the opportunities and limitations available to people and also on how they perceive and assess their life.

Age and life stage influence the number and type of life events or transitions with which the individual is confronted (Fiske & Chiriboga, 1990). Thus, young adults must make decisions concerned with establishing an independent identity and life structure, the middle years of life are characterised by the occupancy of many highly salient roles (see the discussion of Super's life-career rainbow in Box 1.6), and older adults are likely to face transitions resulting from declining health and lost roles and relationships. It has been suggested (Fiske & Chiriboga, 1990; McLanahan & Sorensen, 1985; Pearlin, 1980) that early adulthood is the life stage characterised by the greatest number of stressful life events, although social and cultural changes leading to an increasingly "fluid" life cycle might render this conclusion outdated. However, events from early adulthood are listed most frequently when older adults are asked to identify the most important events in their whole lives (Martin & Smyer, 1990).

Psychological resources. Psychological resources are the personal characteristics that mediate between the demands on the individual and the individual's response to those demands (Pearlin & Schooler, 1978). They include psychological maturity, personality, commitments, and values (Schlossberg et al., 1995).

People approach the same transition differently depending on their level of maturity. Thus, children need to have reached Piaget's formal operations stage before they are capable of analysing transitions using abstract thinking. Similarly, people's goals during transitions will be influenced by whether they are operating at Loevinger's (1976) self-protective stage, where they are motivated to satisfy immediate needs; the conformist stage, where they are motivated to impress significant others and gain social approval; the conscientious stage, where they are motivated to achieve skills and competence; or the autonomous stage, where they seek to deepen understanding of themselves and others, be responsible for their own destiny, and develop their ability to tolerate ambiguity and uncertainty. People's location within other frameworks, for example, Erikson's psychosocial stages (Chapter 4) or Kohlberg's stage or moral reasoning (also Chapter 4), will, similarly, influence the way they experience and respond to transitions.

Personality refers to patterns of a person's behaviour, feelings, and attitudes that are relatively enduring and predictable in a given situation. The question of how enduring personality is has been a topic of much debate

– of which the discussion of stability and consistency in Chapter 3 forms a part. None the less, a cluster of somewhat overlapping personality characteristics has been linked with more effective coping, including self-esteem, self-efficacy, mastery, internal locus of control, self-confidence, and flexibility. A thread running through many of these constructs is the extent to which the individuals regard their life experiences as being under their own control. At a higher level of generality, concepts such as optimism and hardiness also invoke this theme of personal control.

Box 6.3 Values and priorities (adapted from Fiske & Chiriboga, 1990)

Fiske and Chiriboga (1990) asked: "What is your main purpose in life at the present time?" the participants in their longitudinal study of adulthood. From the answers, they developed the following seven-category typology of values (p. 216):

- achievement and work – economic competence, rewards, success, social status
- good personal relations – love and affection, happy marriage, friends
- philosophical and religious – including concern with the meaning of existence and adherence to an ethical code
- social service – helping others, community service, etc.
- ease and contentment – simple comforts, security, relaxation
- seeking enjoyment – recreation, exciting experiences
- personal growth – self-improvement, being creative.

Fiske and Chiriboga (1990) developed a seven-category value typology, summarised in Box 6.4. The significance of a particular life event or transition will be influenced by its relationship to our values, priorities, and commitments, and Schlossberg et al. suggest that a value system that contributes to our management of transitions characteristic of one life stage may be dysfunctional at another. As, over time, our values and preoccupations change, so too does our response to and ability to manage particular life events and transitions. Activity 6.1 encourages you to assess your own values and priorities in life.

The support variable

Social support can be defined as, "interpersonal transactions that include one or more of the following key elements: affect, affirmation, and aid" (Kahn & Antonucci, 1980, p. 267). Affective transactions involve expressions of liking, admiration, respect, or love; transactions involving affirmation confirm the appropriateness or rightness of some action or statement; whilst transactions expressing aid can offer any number of material and cognitive forms of

Activity 6.2 Your values and priorities

Take some time to reflect on the question that Fiske and Chiriboga (1990) asked their research participants: "What is your main purpose in life at the present time?"

To what extent can you fit your answer to the above question into one of the seven categories in Box 6.3?

- How does your value system relate to those transitions and life events you would regard as being of major significance?
- How have your values and priorities changed over the course of your life?
- What changes do you anticipate for the future?

assistance, including things, money, time, advice, guidance, and entitlements. There have been several broadly similar attempts to offer more detailed classifications of types of social support. One typical classification is shown in Box 6.4.

Whilst it is the benefits of social networks that is normally emphasised in the literature, it is also the case that such relationships can have negative (Antonucci & Depner, 1982) or stressful (Gottlieb, 1983) effects as well (Thoits, 1995). By their mere existence, social networks have a

Box 6.4 Functions of social support (based on Weiss, 1974)

- Reassurance of worth – the comfort and confidence provided by others' recognition of one's competence, skills and value.
- Opportunity for nurturance – responsible for the care of others and feeling needed by others.
- Attachment – emotional closeness, feelings of intimacy and security.
- Social integration – the sense of belonging to a group whose members share common interests and activities.
- Obtaining guidance and assistance – having relationships with people who can provide advice, expertise, and practical help.
- Sense of reliable alliance – knowing that one can count on receiving assistance in times of need.

Fulton (1990) arranged the above functions hierarchically. Lower level social support provisions focus on the individual recipient of the support (e.g. obtaining guidance and sense of reliable alliance); middle-level provisions focus on the relationship between the person and those within their network (e.g. attachment and social integration); and higher-order provisions include components beyond the person and their network, moving them into a world other than their own (e.g. reassurance of worth and opportunity for nurturance). Within a social support network exchanges occur at all three levels, vary over time, and are subject to changing relationship needs.

social integration effect (Antonucci & Depner, 1982) – we obtain a niche in society with concomitant norms, expectations, and obligations. We might appreciate this as a source of security, or spurn it as an unwelcome and unpalatable restriction. Family networks, for example, can be the source of both great succour and great stress. Furthermore, on entering a network we might welcome some linkages but not others. On marriage we generally join a network that includes all members of our partner's family, whether we would willingly choose to or not. Similarly, our workplace network can comprise both stress-assuaging and stress-producing relationships. In sum, interpersonal networks, "can scapegoat and intimidate as well as support, can reinforce dysfunctional behaviors and can isolate individuals from other constructive and normalizing influences" (Mechanic, 1999, p. 714). La Gaipa (1990) distinguishes between short-term and long-term negative effects of social support networks, emphasising that they have an impact on both individuals and the relationships between them. Short-term negative effects include feeling smothered and controlled, feeling obligated to conform, and a sense of inadequacy, whereas the long-term effects include low self-esteem and identity problems, resentment, and depression.

It is also possible that the support proffered within a network could be ineffective or inappropriate (La Gaipa, 1990). It might, for example, offer advice when it is emotional support that is needed. The support offered might be judged, at least by outsiders, as harmful rather than beneficial – as when parents are concerned to remove their adolescent child from the influence of what they perceive to be an undesirable peer support network.

Thus, both the sustaining and destructive potential of social networks must be recognised. Passing through transitions is likely to have an impact – for better or worse (or both) – on people's interpersonal relations. On the one hand, support networks can be mobilised in response to some life events – as when friends rally round to support the bereaved. On the other hand, established networks will be disrupted by such events as retirement or geographic relocation.

Sources of support

Intimate relationships, family units, and a network of friends are all important sources of social support during stressful transitions. These can be seen as elements in the person's environment, as defined by Bronfenbrenner (1977, 1979). Not all support need emanate from personal relationships, however. It can also come from the institutions, communities, and physical environments of which people are a part. This is encapsulated in the concept of stability zones (Toffler, 1970), that is, mental retreats and anchors that allow us to cope with change and complexity in other areas (Pedler, Burgoyne, & Boydell, 1978). Whilst interpersonal relationships frequently provide us with a range of very important stability zones, other kinds of stability zones may relate to ideas, places, things, and organisations (see Box 6.5 and Activity 6.3).

Box 6.5 Stability zones

Toffler (1970) suggests that we can cope with large amounts of change, pressure, complexity, and confusion provided at least one area of our life is relatively stable. Such stability zones are frequently associated with people, ideas, places, things, and organisations.

- *People* stability zones are sources of social support. They represent values and enduring relationships with others, for example, family, long-standing friends, and colleagues.
- *Ideas* that are stability zones could be a deeply felt religious belief or a strong personal and/or professional commitment to a philosophy, political ideology, or cause.
- *Places* of varying scale can comprise stability zones. They might be large scale (like a country) or small scale (e.g. a street or a particular room). "Home" is often a stability zone, a place with a comforting familiarity about it, perhaps where one grew up or has spent considerable time.
- *Things* as stability zones take the form of favourite, familiar, comforting possessions. They might range from family heirlooms, through particular objects to favourite items of clothes.
- *Organisations* as stability zones could be the work organisation, a professional body, a club, or any other organisation to which one belongs and with which one identifies.

Stability zones can overlap – "home" has elements of place, people, and things, for example; "books" have elements of things and ideas; and "the work place" might have elements of all stability zones.

The strategies variable

Whether we are aware of it or not, we all cope with transitions. When we say we can't cope what we mean is that we do not believe our coping is effective. Perhaps our strategies have not worked, or we do not know what strategies to employ, or we do not possess the skills or resources we believe to be necessary. None the less, we do all have a range of strategies or coping responses that we bring to bear on transition experiences. Furthermore, our repertoire of strategies can normally be expanded and/or used more effectively. Whereas Schlossberg et al.'s "self" variable refers to what individuals bring to transitions by virtue of who they are, and the "support" variable relates to the environmental and, in particular, the social resources people have available to them, strategies refer to what people actually do – their coping responses as opposed to their coping resources (Pearlin & Schooler, 1978).

In the face of life exigencies we might employ any number of specific responses. Think of all the different ways a couple might respond to

Activity 6.3 Your stability zones

Pedler et al. (1978) suggest working through the following questions in order to help clarify and nurture your own stability zones:

1. *What are your stability zones and how well do they serve you?*
   What "oases of stability" can you identify in the five areas of people, ideas, places, things, and organisations? Ask yourself what you would like to change and what you would like to retain.
2. *How stable are your stability zones?*
   Can you be sure the people you rely on will stay around? Are your basic ideas and beliefs sound? Can you count on staying in your "places" and will your places stay the same? Do your possessions continue to satisfy? Will they last or eventually wear out? Can you count on remaining a member of the organisations you want to belong to?
3. *Will your stability zones serve you in the future?*
   Things, situations, and roles change with time. Objects wear out, activities (such as sport) might become more difficult, houses become too big or too small, children grow up and leave home, organisations and places change, other people have their own lives to follow, ideas are sometimes found wanting or deficient. To what extent will your stability zones remain stable, and to what extent will they continue to meet your needs?
4. *Can you influence the existence of your stability zones?*
   To what extent are the people, ideas, places, things, and organisations that you depend on under your control?
5. *Do you invest enough in your stability zones?*
   Do you work on nurturing the relationships that are important to you, developing your ideas, looking after and maintaining your possessions?
6. *Are there any changes you want to make in your stability zones, and how you use and maintain them?*
   Write an action plan detailing what you would like your stability zones to be in 6 months' time, and how you could go about achieving them.

Adapted with permission from Pedler, M., Burgoyne, J., & Boydell, T. (1978). *A manager's guide to self-development.* London: McGraw-Hill.

relationship difficulties. They might seek advice from friends, family, or professional counsellors; they might talk matters through with each other in an attempt to resolve their conflict; they might change their expectations of what their life together should be like; they might develop additional interests; they might separate. Such specific tactics can be grouped according to their more general function (Lazarus & Folkman, 1984; Moos, 1986; Pearlin & Schooler, 1978). Whilst different researchers have grouped coping strategies in somewhat different, albeit overlapping, ways, four distinct goals can be identified – two directed at the environment (or situation) and two at the person (or self):

- Environment (or situation) focused coping, by:
  - modifying the situation and thereby the demands it makes on the individual, for example, negotiating a change in job specification, rescheduling payment of bills
  - escaping from or avoiding the situation – for example, walking out of a stressful relationship, not accepting additional responsibilities at work.
- Person (or self) focused coping, by:
  - developing additional coping strategies or personal resilience, for example, attending classes in yoga, relaxation, or assertiveness; developing new support systems
  - altering the way the situation is perceived and assessed, for example, cognitive restructuring in order to challenge unrealistic expectations or irrational beliefs.

Only coping strategies that involve modifying the environment act directly on the situation that is making the demands. These strategies are aimed at altering or eliminating the source of life strains and therefore represent the most direct way of coping with them. Attempts to resolve conflict through negotiation between the relevant parties would fall under this heading. However, in their study of responses to life strains, Pearlin and Schooler (1978) found that such direct actions comprised the minority of coping responses. They offered four possible explanations for this:

1. The individual might not recognise the situation as the source of the problem. Without such insight actions cannot consciously be mobilised towards altering it.
2. Even if the source of the problem is recognised, people could lack the knowledge or skills to change it.
3. People could resist changing the situation out of fear that the resulting situation would be worse.
4. The conditions producing the demands might be resistant and difficult to change, thus undermining motivation to try.

Classifying particular coping strategies as serving particular functions is somewhat arbitrary in that a particular strategy can serve more than one function and/or its effect might change over time. Thus, developing assertiveness skills increases our repertoire of coping skills (a person-focused function) and might enable us better to negotiate a more satisfactory work role (an environment-, problem-, or task-focused function). Similarly, effective time management both enables us to cope more efficiently with the demands placed upon us and changes the situation by reducing the amount of stress we experience. Furthermore, whilst, say, rescheduling payment of bills might be an effective short-term strategy for changing the situation, if the new schedule is not adhered to the result could be an increase rather than a decrease in actual and experienced stress.

The question of the relative effectiveness of different coping strategies is important, though not necessarily easy to answer. Most, if not all, strategies have their time and place, and, indeed, "effective coping means flexible utilization of a range of strategies as each situation demands" (Schlossberg et al., 1995, p. 74). Problem-focused strategies will be most appropriate and tend to be most used when the situation is one that can be changed, whilst emotion-focused strategies can be more effective when the situation must be adapted to rather than altered (Lazarus & Folkman, 1984).

Like transitions, coping is best thought of as a process rather than a single response. As the situation changes (possibly as a result of our response), so may the appropriateness of any particular coping strategy. This can be linked to the phases of transition management discussed earlier. During the initial stage of shock, denial may be an appropriate response, allowing the individual to come to terms gradually with the reality of the event. It is only when the denial becomes dysfunction that it is problematic. Likewise, emotion-focused coping responses – including the venting of feelings such as anger, grief, and fear – can be particularly important during the early stages of transition management. With time, these can be substituted or supplemented by more problem-focused strategies.

There is limited evidence about how people's strategies change across the life course. What evidence there is suggests that changes in children's coping strategies links in with cognitive developments, and that changes in the strategies used by older people may tie in with the nature of the stress they experience and their interpretation of it. Thus, infants and very young children will try to manage the stress of a medical examination by trying to escape the situation and/or preventing the examination taking place (Hyson, 1983), at the same time giving vociferous vent to their feelings. During the years of childhood, however, they learn to use cognitive strategies for coping (Brown, O'Keefe, Sanders, & Baker, 1986; Miller & Green, 1984), for example, distracting themselves by thinking of something else, or making positive self-statements such as "I can handle this" when about to undertake a stressful task.

In a study of age differences in stress and coping processes Folkman, Lazerus, Pimley, and Novacek (1987) found that the middle-aged subjects tended to use more problem-focused approaches to coping, whereas the older subjects employed more emotion-focused strategies. The older subjects perceived their stressors to be less changeable, making self-focused coping strategies seem more appropriate than situation-focused ones.

Despite this evidence for age differences in coping, a focus on transitions and life events diverts attention away from the concepts of age and life stage, such that the guiding light of the stage concept no longer shines so brightly in the firmament. Instead, adult life can be seen as a continuing process of coping with internal and external events and non-events. The task for life-span developmental psychology, from this standpoint, is to try to uncover basic processes of coping and adaptation that are valid for adults of any age (Bee, 1994). This is what both the transition dynamics model of Hopson and Adams and the '4-S' model of Schlossberg et al. strive to do.

7 Dynamic continuity through narrative

> We are the stories we tell and could tell.
> (Booth, 1983)

Key aspects of the work of theorists such Piaget, Freud, Erikson, Kohlberg, Havighurst, and Levinson can be described in terms of stages, sequences, or, at the least, phases. The theories of development proposed by those such as Kolb, Riegel, and Rogers, rather than suggesting a procession of stages through which we all pass, present development as progression along a path punctuated by pauses or resting places of indeterminate length. Some of us will travel far along this path; some of us will struggle to get much past the starting line. All of these models accept at least the possibility of ordered change within the life course – the orientation described in the 1970s (Gergen, 1977) as a dominant orientation within developmental psychology.

As the main alternative to the ordered-change approach, Gergen identified a "stability orientation", which has shunned the transitory and attempted to identify the consistent. However, as has been discussed earlier (Chapter 3), stability, or consistency, does not imply the total absence of change, but rather, particular types of change that follow certain rules or order.

There is also a third orientation to development identified by Gergen that, like the "ordered change" orientation, focuses explicitly on change, but which assumes that, far from being orderly and predictable, "there is little about human development that is 'preprogrammed'" (Gergen, 1977, p. 148). Gergen terms this the "aleatory-change" orientation and proposes that, whilst our biological systems establish the limit or range of our activities, the precise character of our life course is highly dependent on a variety of environmental factors, for example, economic, geographic, social, class, political. The aleatory-change orientation draws attention to the third tenet of the life-span perspective (as discussed in Chapter 1), namely, the plasticity of development. It emphasises how specific environmental influences vary across time and culture and how, therefore, the life courses of individuals are neither universal nor invariant. Despite this, however, individuals generally experience, if not a sense of stability, then a sense of continuity and coherence in their lives and in their definition of who they are, that is, something more compatible with the stability orientation. The present chapter reviews two explanations of how and why this happens. First, we consider the continuity theory of normal development proposed by Robert Atchley (1971, 1989, 1999) to accommodate the tensions between change and stability over the life course, and then there is a more general discussion of the notion of the life course as a narrative construction.

A continuity theory of the life course

Atchley (1989, p. 183), describing continuity as "an illusive concept", makes a distinction between static and dynamic continuity. Static continuity implies being unchanging, uniform, and remaining the same – not a notion that is very applicable to life-span development. Dynamic continuity, by contrast, starts with the idea of a basic structure, which persists over time but which allows for a variety of changes to occur within the context provided by that structure. Levinson's (1986; Levinson et al., 1978) concept of the life course as the evolution of a life structure, whilst discussed earlier under the heading of development as the management of a series of developmental tasks is, none the less, compatible with this perspective.

Atchley (1989) makes a distinction between internal (intrapsychic) and external (environmental) structures and proposes that in making adaptive choices, middle-aged and older adults attempt to preserve and maintain these structures, preferably through the use of continuity: "by applying familiar strategies in familiar arenas of life" (Atchley, 1989, p. 183). In this way we are able to maintain a continuous sense of who we are and explain our current behaviour and aspirations as in some way connected to what has come before.

External continuity

Whilst Gergen, in his aleatory change model of development, emphasised the ways in which external influences change and vary, continuity theory explores their continuities, that is, "the persistence of a structure of relationships and overt behavior" (Atchley, 1989, p. 185). External continuity is evidenced by being in familiar environments, undertaking familiar activities and skills, and interacting with familiar people (Caspi, Bem, & Elder, 1989). Key exemplifications include:

- *Continuity of environments*. This refers to the fact that we tend to choose environments that we believe will be compatible with our skills and disposition. In turn, our skills and disposition will have been honed by experience in particular environments. This notion underpins both Super's (1984, 1990) and Holland's (1996, 1997) theories of career choice and development. Thus, Super proposes that in choosing an occupation we strive to implement our self-concept. As most people's self-concept is assumed to remain fairly stable once adulthood is reached, people will tend to seek out broadly similar environments when making job changes, or else will strive to move into environments more compatible with their self-concept. Key aspects of Holland's theory are outlined in Box 7.1. Furthermore, environmental continuity also tends to result from the accumulation of particular types of experience and the development of particular skills. Such expertise often means that those environments in which we have the opportunity to operate are similar to those in which we have operated previously. We are "qualified for the job", as it were.

Box 7.1 Occupational choice as a process of person–environment fit (Holland, 1996, 1997)

Using a range of measures, but most notably the self-directed search (Holland, 1994; Holland, Fritzsche, & Powell, 1994), Holland characterises people according to their relative resemblance to six types:

Type	*Interests*
Realistic	Outdoor, technical, mechanical
Investigative	Scientific, inquiring, analytic
Artistic	Dramatic, musical, self-expressive
Social	Helping, guiding, group-oriented
Enterprising	Entrepreneurial, persuasive, political
Conventional	Methodical, organised, clerical

A person's interest profile is represented as a three-letter code reflecting the three interest types with which he or she expressed greatest affinity. Environments as well as people can be described according to this typology. A strongly "Realistic" environment, for example, is one that provides the opportunity for the expression of outdoor, technical, and mechanical interests, and, therefore, contains many members with "Realistic" scores on the self-directed search. It is assumed that people flourish in an environment that closely matches their type.

Holland, Sorenson, Clark, Nafziger, & Blum (1973) examined the work histories of nearly 900 men in their thirties and found that 79 per cent of the 5812 job transitions identified occurred within a single major category in the six-category system. At least in the 1970s, it would appear that people tended to move among similar jobs, that is, they maintained environmental continuity.

- *Continuity of relationships*. Finding limited evidence for the existence of a midlife crisis as a normative life event, Berger (1994) drew attention to the importance of continuity as well as change in our significant personal relationships. Kahn and Antonucci's (1980) concept of the social support convoy (discussed further in Chapter 8) points to the interpersonal or relationship aspects of external continuity. A person's convoy of support includes an "inner circle" of close family and friends whose support is not role dependent and may last a lifetime – "blood is thicker than water", as the saying goes.
- *Expectations and demands of environments and roles*. Consistencies in our physical, political, and social environment will all add to the external continuity of our lives, influencing the situations with which we "typically" have to cope, and the practical, intellectual, and interpersonal skills we need to survive and flourish in that environment. Although in Chapter 3 the sociocultural concept of stage was invoked primarily to account for predictable age-associated changes, the sequence of socially defined roles that a person is expected to fulfil across the life course has a logic of continuity, as well as change, that is often based on the notion of accumulated experience and learning. Thus we may be told not to "run before we can walk". If we decide to change the direction of our life by, for example, switching our educational path or changing to a markedly different career, we might be accused of "wasting" all the time and effort already expended in reaching our current position. In a work context, curriculum vitae are typically written so as to show how a person's current position is the logical cumulation of what has gone before. Activity 7.1 contains questions that encourage you to explore such external continuity in your own educational and career history.
- *Expectations and demands of others*. It is generally assumed by those with whom we interact that we will present ourselves in ways that are obviously tied to and connected with our past behaviours and presentation of ourself. The person who tries to renegotiate his or her role within the family could find resistance from other family members who like things the way they are. We might be encouraged "not to rock the boat", and be told "if it ain't broke, don't mend it". Like actors we can find ourselves "type-cast" into particular roles, and find it hard to break into new areas of endeavour.

A final point to emphasise is that individuals are not passive recipients of environmental continuities. Environments do not simply "happen" to people (Bee, 1994), shaping their behaviour in some automatic way. The intervening process, as Bee (1994, p. 502) points out, "is the individual's understanding of each experience". Whilst external continuity can be seen by others, it is only the individuals themselves who can ratify its existence through their own internal assessments of what is "typical" for them.

Activity 7.1 Curriculum vitae – spurious or real continuity?

Most people produce a curriculum vitae that shows development, progression, and direction. Make a list of key educational/career choices you have made to date – including such things as:

- GCSE (or O level) options
- A level/ BTec subject choices
- Choice of school, college, university, etc.
- Job/career decisions.

To what extent do these choices reflect external continuity, that is, "the persistence of a structure of relationships and overt behavior"?

Do they follow a step-wise linear path?

Is there a consistency of focus in the decisions you have made or have you changed direction markedly?

Do your extra-curricular activities add to or detract from any sense of external continuity? Is any coherence in your educational and career history spurious rather than real?

This brings us to the second, and in many ways more significant, prong of Atchley's (1989, 1999) continuity theory of ageing – that of internal continuity.

Internal continuity

Continuity of individuals' internal, as opposed to their external, basic structure concerns the maintenance of a consistent sense of who we are – of self and identity. It comprises our awareness of the persistence of an inner structure of "ideas, temperament, affect, experiences, preferences, dispositions, and skills" (Atchley, 1989, p. 185). Atchley emphasised how such awareness requires memory – a remembered past that enables the person to present and experience this continuity of self and identity. It allows inner change to be seen as connected to and both sustained and supported by the individual's past. Again we see how continuity cannot be viewed as the opposite of change. Rather, it describes a situation where change and evolution are played out within a stable directional context provided by the individual's past. It is points such as these on which the questions in Activity 7.2 invite you to reflect.

Activity 7.2 Personal values and priorities – constant or changing?

Consider the list of personal values or priorities listed below. Rank order their actual or anticipated importance to you at various ages.

Values				
	Ed	Education/learning	Fr	Friends
	Fa	Family	Ma	Marriage/intimates
	Ch	Children	Ca	Career
	Mo	Money	Re	Religion/spirituality
	Le	Leisure/recreation		

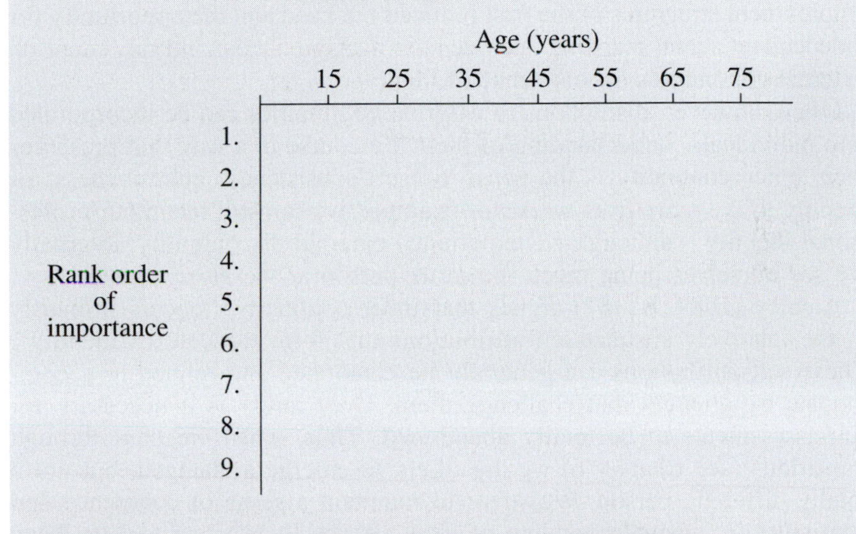

Look at the pattern of your answers. What changes do you notice? What explanations can you proffer for these changes?

Even more important in the present context are questions of continuity, specifically internal continuity. What evidence do you see of the persistence of an inner structure of "ideas, temperament, affect, experiences, preferences, dispositions, and skills" (Atchley, 1989, p. 185)?

To what extent does your profile represent a person who is "changing" in a very fundamental sense, as opposed to a person who is "finding themselves" or "becoming the self that one really is?"

Disruption of continuities

Both external and internal continuities may, however, be threatened, and, of the two, it is external continuities that are the more vulnerable. External continuities can be disrupted by such factors as role changes, geographic relocation, depletion of social support networks, and changes in health status. It is widely recognised, for example, that the stability and predictability of the workplace and, therefore, of career patterns has declined during recent decades (Arnold & Jackson, 1997). This increases the need for a sense of personal (or internal) identity (Holland, 1996) so that the individual can create a satisfying work and, indeed, recreational life. The stable employment structures of the past reduced the need and the opportunity for independent career planning and decision making – we could rely more on external continuities for our sense of identity.

Often, however, disruptions to external continuities can be incorporated into individuals' understanding of their life course in a way that preserves their inner continuity – the sense of self-consistency, cohesiveness, or identity. If we retire from work, for example, we can still retain our professional identity – although we experience external discontinuity, internally we see ourselves being much the same person as we always were.

Atchley (1989, p. 187) argues that inner continuity, "occurs primarily in the relatively abstract self-attributions that form the core of identity". These self-attributions can generally be elaborated and refined to accommodate experiences that challenge them. Only rarely is it necessary for self-assessments to be totally abandoned. Thus, when we pass through transitions (see Chapter 6) we are likely to emerge a changed, but not a totally different, person. We strive to maintain a sense of coherence and continuity in our understanding of who we are. Even if we feel we have changed significantly, we look to events or experiences in our past to "explain" and make sense of these changes.

Whilst the global assessments and attributions individuals make about themselves can persist, even in the face of substantial changes in the details of everyday life, crises of identity – experiences that require the reorganisation of individuals' definition of "who they are" – can disrupt this sense of internal continuity and be disconcerting and distressing. This can happen, for example, to people with dementia, AIDS, or other diseases with serious but uncertain outcomes (Atchley, 1989). Lacking a perception of continuity makes a person's life seem unpredictable and chaotic. If severe enough, it can destroy mental health. Severe discontinuity means that we have no standard against which to assess our life's integrity. The result can be extreme anxiety and depression, a lack of hope born of the inability to project one's future with any confidence. Thus, conditions that effect memory, such as amnesia and Alzheimer's disease, may result in sufferers no longer knowing who they are or were, not knowing who the other characters in their life story are, or even what the plot of the story might be (Atchley, 1989).

None the less, not all threats to either internal or external continuity are unwelcome. Indeed, many appear as desirable, anticipated, and/or "natural" stages or phases in accounts of the life course. We seek a balance between a sense of sameness on the one hand and challenge on the other. Furthermore, individuals differ in the extent to which they see the search for novelty or change as important, and the extent to which this experience of change is believed to be desirable (Cohler, 1982). The degree of continuity attributed by individuals to their lives can, therefore, be classified as too little, too much, or optimum (Atchley, 1989). If people experience too little continuity, life seems uncomfortably unpredictable. If they experience too much, then life seems dull and routine. Optimum continuity, "means that the individual sees the pace and degree of change to be in line with her or his coping capacity" (Atchley, 1989, p. 185). This links with Gergen and Gergen's (1988; Gergen, 1988) graphic representations of the life course (see Chapter 3), where we can judge our level of satisfaction with the "eventfulness" and "dramatic tension" of our lifelines. This, in turn, returns us to the narrative perspective on the life course. Here the basic internal structure that allows us both to experience continuity and accommodate change is that of a personal narrative. This is the stance elaborated in the remainder of this chapter.

The life course as narrative

Narrative theorists of the life course (for example Cohler, 1982; McAdams, 1997) take the idea of dynamic continuity one step further by focusing less on the existence of a consistent remembered past, and more on the process of re-interpreting the past in order to develop and maintain a coherent story. Rather than emphasising the process of continuity, the narrative perspective emphasises emplotment – the process of casting oneself as the main character in a narrative that is meaningful, productive, and fulfilling (Cochran, 1997). Activity 7.3 invites you to compose your own personal narrative, using as prompts the instructions employed by McAdams (1997) in his research. Self-narratives created in this way are not seen as evidence of people's stable and predictable personalities or behaviour patterns, but as temporary constructions, "that are shaped by such important factors as literary conventions, social norms, the context of the narrative, and self-determined goals" (Gergen, 1988, p. 100). As such, they share some of the assumed sources of developmental tasks (see Chapter 5).

The function of narratives

Personal narratives enable us to place order on the sometimes chaotic events in our lives and the desire to attain such order or coherence may lie behind the motivation to construe our lives in story form (Cohler, 1982). Perhaps most crucially, narrative construction provides a mechanism

Activity 7.3 "This is your life" (adapted from McAdams, 1997)

In his book, *The stories we live by,* McAdams (1997) encourages readers to tell their own life story as a way of enhancing self-understanding and promoting insight into their unique life course and personal journey. Whilst this can be done privately, McAdams recommends that readers find a sympathetic listener – ideally a friend who has not to date been significant in influencing their life – with whom to share the story. People often find this experience enlightening – something through which they learn a lot about themselves and think about things they don't usually think about. It tends to be an enjoyable experience, even if painful at times.

Perhaps you could explore your own life story using McAdams' interview schedule. It comprises seven sections designed to generate information about all key elements of a personal narrative.

Exploring your life story

Life chapters

Start by imagining your life as if it were a book, with each part of your life making up one chapter. Although the book is still unfinished, it probably already contains a number of interesting and well-defined chapters.

Divide your life into its major chapters and briefly describe each one. Whilst you may have as many or as few chapters as you like, McAdams does suggest a minimum of two or three and a maximum seven or eight. Think of this as a general table of contents for your book. Give each chapter a name and describe the overall contents of each chapter. Discuss briefly what makes for a transition from one chapter to the next. Although this first part of the interview could expand forever, try to keep it relatively brief, say within 30–45 minutes. Don't tell the "the whole story" here. Just give a sense of the story's outline. The goal of this section is to help:

- find an organising framework for your personal narrative
- reveal what you believe to be the major landmarks and developmental trends in your life
- generally express many different elements of your self-defining narrative, notably narrative tone and imagery.

Key events

The second part of the interview or exploration focuses on eight key events. A key event is, "a specific happening, a critical incident, a specific episode in your past set in a particular time and place" (pp. 257–8). It is a specific moment in your life that stands out for some reason – a particular moment in a particular time and place, complete with particular characters, actions, thoughts, and feelings. For each event, describe in detail what happened, where you were, who was involved, what you did, and what you were thinking and feeling during the event. Also, try to convey the impact this key event has had in your life story and what this event says about who you are or were as a person. Did this event change you in any way? If so, how?

The eight key events (or nuclear episodes) are:

1. *A peak experience* – a high point in your life story; the most wonderful moment in your life.
2. *A nadir experience* – a low point in your life story; the worst moment in your life.
3. *A turning point* – an episode wherein you underwent a significant change in your understanding of yourself. It is not necessary that you comprehended the turning point as a turning point when it in fact happened. What is important is that now, in retrospect, you see the event as a turning point, or at minimum as symbolising a significant change in your life.
4. *Your earliest memory* – one of the earliest memories you have of an event that is complete with setting, scene, characters, feelings, and thoughts.
5. *An important childhood memory* – any memory from your childhood, positive or negative, that stands out today.
6. *An important adolescent memory* – any memory from your teenage years that stands out today. Again, it can be either positive or negative.
7. *An important adult memory* – a memory, positive or negative, that stands out from age 21 onwards.
8. *Other important memory* – one other particular event from your past that stands out. It could be from long ago or from recent times. It can be positive or negative.

As well as providing information about tone and imagery, descriptions of key elements can be particularly powerful indicators concerning dominant themes in the personal narrative.

Significant people

In the third section of the interview focus on four of the most important people in your life story. They may include, but not necessarily be limited to, parents, children, siblings, spouses, lovers, friends, teachers, co-workers and mentors. At least one of the people selected should be someone to whom you are not related. "Please specify the kind of relationship you had or have with each person and the specific way he or she has had an impact on your life story" (p. 260). Following this, talk about any particular heroes or heroines you have had in your life.

The discussion of significant people is likely to throw light on the main characters, or imagoes, in the personal narrative.

Future script

Having talked about your past and your present, now consider your future. "What might be the script or plan for what is to happen next in your life?" (p. 260). Describe your present plan or dream for the future and then say in what ways it might enable you to be creative and/or to make a contribution to others.

The consideration of future scripts is likely to provide many different kinds of identity information. Like key events, it is especially sensitive to the revelation of motivational themes. It might also indicate a characteristic approach to generativity, and, "provide a glimpse of the sense of an ending" (p. 261) – that is, the denouement to the narrative.

Stresses and problems

By this point in the interview you have probably already touched on some problem areas in your life. Now consider in detail two areas in your life where you are currently experiencing at least one of the following:

- significant stress
- a major conflict.
- a difficult problem or challenge that must be addressed.

For each area, "describe the nature of the stress, problem or conflict in some detail, outlining the source of the concern, a brief history of its development, and your plan, if you have one, for dealing with it in the future" (p. 262).

Here may be signalled issues and conflicts that might need to be resolved in successive revisions of the personal narrative – perhaps, for example, allowing valued but hitherto underdeveloped imagoes or characters to flourish.

Personal ideology

Questions in this section relate to your fundamental beliefs and values, including:

- Any belief you might have in the existence of some kind of god, deity, or force that in some way influences or organises the universe.
- The essence of any such beliefs and the ways, if any, in which your beliefs differ from those of most people you know.
- Ways in which your religious beliefs have changed over time, including any period of rapid change.
- Your political position.
- What you consider to be the most important value in human living, plus anything else that would indicate your most fundamental beliefs and values about life and the world.

All these points impinge on the issue of the ideological setting of the personal narrative.

Overall life theme

As a finale to the interview, look back over your entire life story to see whether you can identify a central theme, message, or idea. This provides an explicit opportunity, at the end of what might be a lengthy period of reflection, to consider the overall meaning of the personal narrative.

Adapted version of the interview schedule for "Exploring your myth" reproduced with permission from McAdams, D. P. (1997). *Stories we live by: Personal myths and the making of the self.* New York: Guilford Press.

for developing and maintaining a sense of identity, as demonstrated in the discussion of McAdams' (1997) work in Chapter 4. Sacks (1985, pp. 105–6) elaborates this point: "each of us is a biography, a story. Each of us is a singular narrative, which is constructed, continually, unconsciously, by, through, and in us – through our perceptions, our feelings, our thoughts, our actions; and not least, our discourse, our spoken narrations". In effect, we are our stories.

Our stories can help fulfil a number of psychological functions, such as preserving self-esteem or allocating responsibility elsewhere (Viney & Bousefield, 1991). Our role as active agent in the telling of our stories can be empowering (Viney, 1993). It enables us to be better able to contribute to constructing how we and our community define ourselves.

We hear, as well as tell, stories about who we are. The stories that we hear in our family, school, and immediate community (our micro- and mesosystems, to use Bronfenbrenner's terms) teach us our place in the world and give our lives some order and predictability. Narratives help us normalise our experiences. Stories that mirror our own life reassure us that our experiences are normal – both in the sense of being understandable and in the sense of being shared by others. These stories will frequently reflect the "social clock" of our society and form the basis of our assessments of what we "should" be doing, and when. We evaluate ourselves either positively or negatively in relation to the events and timing of the social clock. Some elements of the social clock are less fixed than previously. Thus, for example, stories abound now of how, in our society, the upper age-limit for childbearing is being pushed ever higher – through the voluntary delaying of motherhood, through the production of "second families", and through technological advances involving fertility treatment, surrogacy, and the implanting of embryos into postmenopausal women.

There is considerable overlap between the social functions of narratives and the elements of social support, including reassurance of worth, opportunity for nurturance, attachment, social integration, obtaining guidance, and assistance, and a sense of reliable alliance (see Box 6.5 for further details).

At Bronfenbrenner's exo- and macrosystem level we can be said to, "inhabit the stories of our culture" (Mair, 1988). Howard (1991, p. 187) proposes that, "cultural differences might be rooted in the preferred stories habitually entertained by ethnic, class, racial, and cultural groups".

Although the narratives within our society can give guidance and directionality to our lives, they may, however, be imperfect guides (Cochran, 1997), as, for example, if we were to accept uncritically the "disengagement" narrative that it is normal and desirable to withdraw from significant roles as we age. Like an individual's life structure (Levinson et al., 1978; Levinson, 1986), cultural narratives can become out of date and no longer compatible with the prevailing conditions of life: "Lifted from conditions of life to which they did apply, these narratives might be described as anachronistic, impoverished, or distorted" (Cochran, 1997, p. 137). The notion of career choice as a once-and-for-all decision and of career development as a smooth, upward progression would constitute one such outmoded narrative.

In addition, narratives can conflict such that, to use Cochran's phrase, we can "be torn between two narratives" (Cochrane, 1997, p. 137). A Western narrative emphasising self-fulfilment might conflict with an Eastern one that emphasises family obligation, such that second generation immigrants in the West may feel they have to choose between isolation from their family and stultification of personal dreams.

Furthermore, there could be situations for which no adequate cultural narratives exist. For example, there might be no cultural narratives to guide women or ethnic minorities trying to move into careers that have traditionally been dominated by white, middle-class males. With time, the individual role models provided by pioneers who break through barriers through personally derived solutions will develop into cultural narratives.

Within any one community the cultural narratives of some subcultures may be more readily enacted than others. Gay and lesbian youth may, for example, find their narrative less easy to enact in the rampantly heterosexual ambience of many school and college communities.

Some authors (for example, Berne, 1975; Gustafson, 1992) propose that we each develop a core narrative, or personal myth, that is the central or singular (Spence, 1987) story behind the various stories we tell, and which we repeat in different relationships at different points across the life course. However, the narrative perspective in general assumes we are able to generate multiple storylines to accommodate and account for our experiences (McLeod, 1997). Any one account is likely to be only a provisional interpretation. Thus, Viney and Bousefield (1991) describe the core narrative as more like a suggestive hypothesis than a confirmed generalisation, likening it to a, "statement of best fit". It is not the only statement that could be made, but it is one that is plausible. Like Atchley's (1989, 1999) internal and external basic structures, the core narrative might be resilient, but it is not inviolable.

The following section first reviews briefly what we mean when we talk of a narrative, and then considers the life course from this perspective.

Narrative characteristics

A narrative, or story, offers a way of making sense of our experiences by ordering them in a sequence across time, according to a theme (Bruner, 1990, 1991). If events are described randomly they are likely to make little sense, and so a requirement of even the simplest coherent narrative is that it has, like a life, a beginning, a middle, and an end. From any one set of life experiences more than one story could be told, and accounts of the life course reflect decisions made concerning which events are sufficiently significant to include, what themes best provide a coherent and meaningful plot, and the degree and type of closure given to the story (Murray, 1986). These decisions reflect the different theoretical and value perspectives of a narrative's author, whether the author is an individual constructing a narrative of his or her own life or a researcher proposing a particular framework for considering life-span issues. Thus, stages, sequences, phases, and pauses can be subsumed under the umbrella of different narrative "plots".

Adopting a narrative stance does not necessitate severing all links with other perspectives. It can, for example, be consistent with the concept of life stages. Thus, whilst Cohler (1982) presents the life narrative as continually being reorganised on the basis of subsequent experiences, he also argues that three particular life transformations are especially likely to disrupt a person's narrative. These transformations accompany the transitions from early to middle childhood; from childhood to adolescence and young adulthood; and from early to middle adulthood. If narrative coherence cannot be maintained, the individual will experience, "feelings of fragmentation or personal disintegration" (Cohler, 1982, p. 215).

The first of these transformations is linked to the shift in cognitive and social processes that occurs between the ages of 5 and 7 years. The shift from egocentric to sociocentric thought, from preoperational to operational logic, and from dyadic to triadic relationships results in the development of a markedly different world view and triggers a profound transformation of the child's understanding of his or her place within it. The "old" stories, as it were, are no longer adequate explanations, and must be reformulated.

Cohler (1982) identifies adolescence – with its physiological changes, cognitive development of formal operations, and changed relationships within an increasingly complex social environment – as a second point of major transformation in the personal narrative. It is encapsulated in Erikson's notion of the identity crisis.

Both the early to middle childhood transformation and the transformation of the adolescent identity crisis are associated with maturation – both biological and psychological maturation and the socially shared understanding of the significance of such developments. In Cohler's third transformational period, which accompanies the transition from early to middle adulthood, maturation plays a far less significant part. Instead, its nature is largely socially determined and involves assessment and reassessment of the self in relation to the timing and passage of normatively defined social milestones. Its timing is also linked to the developing awareness of the reality of a finite lifetime. Not only is it the chronological "mid point" of the expected life cycle but both the expected and anticipated death of the older generation (in particular, parents) and the "untimely" death of contemporaries, serve as constant reminders of mortality. Cohler postulates, although does not develop to the same degree, the existence of a further transformation accompanying the transition from middle to old age. This is consistent with evidence of the particular importance of reminiscence in old age – "getting the story straight", and striving to rework events into a coherent, fulfilling life narrative.

Narrative forms

In Chapter 3 the idea of representing different narrative forms graphically was introduced. Distinction was made between progressive, regressive, and stability story lines, with the recognition that these simple forms will be combined within any one life course to produce a more complex structure. However, literary scholars have long suggested that there are only a limited number of story forms. Frye (1957), for example, distinguishes between comedy, romance, tragedy, and irony (or satire), relating them to the seasons of the year (see Gergen, 1988; Salmon, 1985):

- Comedy – a challenge or threat that is overcome to yield social harmony and a happy ending. Frye likens this to spring – the harmony experienced when the uprising of nature overcomes the threatening winter.
- Romance – the main character emerges victorious from a series of challenges and threats that are overcome by ardent idealism, love, and personal commitments. Frye relates this to the calm and wealth of summer, where, poetically, good triumphs over evil, light over darkness and virtue over vice.
- Tragedy – personal flaws and shortcomings lead to the defeat or demise of the main character. Happiness and position in society are lost. Frye likens this to autumn, where the fading away of life heralds the coming death of winter.
- Irony (or satire) – the main character is defeated by insurmountable hurdles and the hopelessness of the situation. Beyond hope, these narratives are the representations of unrealised expectations and dreams. Frye likens this to winter, which shows us that, ultimately, we are subject to, rather than master of, the force of death.

Whilst Frye's analogy between narrative forms and seasons of the year might seems fanciful and poetic rather than analytic (Gergen, 1988) his categories have been related both to the life course (Salmon, 1985) and to the models presented by life course researchers (Murray, 1986).

Salmon (1985) proposes that it is appropriate to construe the life course differently at different life stages. In childhood, we tend to see life as a comedy, in adolescence as a romance, and in adulthood as a more realistic, but less comfortable, tragedy or irony. The comic perspective describes life as basically safe and secure. It assumes that in the end all will be well, "that human affairs can be set right, [and] that problems can be laughed at, because they do not pose a final threat to happiness" (Salmon, 1985, p. 140). Whilst, as adults we see this as a naive view of the life course, it is one we frequently present to young children in story books, comics, films, and television. The comic vision is seen as appropriate to the innocence of childhood. It is compatible with the development of a positive narrative tone (McAdams, 1997) and a sense of basic trust (Erikson, 1980), as discussed in Chapter 5.

If it is appropriate for children to hold a happy-ever-after, comic vision of life, then, suggests Salmon (1985, p. 140), adolescence is the life stage for subscribing to an idealistic, romantic vision, whereby human affairs will be transformed by, "true love, by selfless commitment, [and] by personal integrity". This is a world view resting on the virtues resulting from successfully resolving Erikson's first five psychosocial crises and attaining the virtues of hope, will, purpose, competence, and fidelity.

Adult men and women who retain a romantic vision of life are likely to be perceived as naive and lacking in maturity. More sober world views, represented by the tragic and ironic story forms, are seen to reflect the more realistic, adult awareness that compromises must be made. There is recognition of the limits of human control and of the inevitable sufferings of human life: "The tragic view rests on the acceptance of pain and loss, the refusal to gloss over those aspects of living. The more detached ironic view offers a sense of the ultimate uncertainty of human life" (Salmon, 1985, p. 141).

The link between life stage and the narrative form employed to understand the life course is not absolute, however. When we use narratives to present ourselves to others, the form a story takes might vary according to the situation and goals of the storyteller. Thus, Gergen (1988) suggests that narratives told as a romance, with narrators overcoming obstacles to achieve a goal, might represent attempts by the narrators to present themselves as heroes who live in a world of treachery or danger. Listeners would be expected to be enthralled and admiring of such a protagonist. Similarly, the, "tragedy may be designed to elicit sympathy, and the comedy a companionable spirit of solidarity and harmony" (Gergen, 1988, p. 107). In these ways, narratives, although statements about ourselves, fulfil important social functions.

Story forms in accounts of midlife

Murray (1986) demonstrated how authors can tell different stories about the same life stage – in this case the midlife transition. He examined the narrative structures evident in accounts of the life course presented by three life course authors: Levinson (1986; Levinson et al., 1978) and Gould (1978, 1980) – both of whom theorised about the nature of life-span development – and Sheehy (1974), who aimed also to provide some sort of "life-manual" – guidelines as to how we could, and perhaps should, recast our own life story.

Sheehy's (1974) overall presentation of the adult life course is as a romance (Murray, 1986) involving coping with conflict between two forces within the self – "the Dream" (a positive force with origins in the fantasies of childhood) and "the inner custodian" (a negative force or "nasty tyrant" that originates in the demands that parents make of a child). This conflict reaches a peak in midlife and Sheehy advises people to face the conflict squarely, act bravely and be hopeful of the future: "The hope which Sheehy offers is a romantic one; there is an optimistic commitment to the self as the only force of authority in one's world" (Murray, 1986, p. 282). Structuring life according to alternative forms, for example as tragic – in which childhood hopes are destroyed by the cruel realities of adult life – or as a satire – where the idealistic dreams of childhood are disillusioned by the ironies and complexities of adulthood – would, in effect, be to engender despair. Critics arguing that for many people despair, rather than integrity, is a more realistic resolution of Erikson's final psychosocial crisis are seeing life as tragic or ironic rather than as a romance.

Sheehy, a journalist, draws on the more academic research of Levinson et al. (1978) and Gould (1978, 1980). Whilst all employ the image of the Dream as a primary force in human development, it is only Sheehy who presents such a romantic, optimistic view of the midlife struggle (Murray 1986).

Levinson's depiction of the midlife period as tragic is enshrined in the destruction–creation polarity that he sees as surfacing with especial force at midlife (see Chapter 5). In the reappraisal of life that typifies the midlife transition, "a man must come to a new understanding of his grievances against others for the real or imagined damage they have done him" (Levinson et al., 1978, p. 223). However, damage has not only been inflicted on him, but also by him, and this is his "tragic flaw". However, men differ in their readiness to face their own destructiveness. Some are unaware that they have done harm to others, or that they might wish to do so. Guilt about real or imagined damage they have inflicted makes others unable to consider the problems of destructiveness dispassionately and place them in broader perspective. Only some have a degree of understanding that they may feel both love and hate toward the same person, and be aware of the ambivalence in their own significant relationships. All, however, have work to do on addressing the destruction/creation polarity:

> Even the most mature or knowledgeable man has a great deal to learn at mid-life about the heritage of anger, against others and against himself, that he has carried within himself from childhood. He has to learn, also, about the angers he has accumulated over the course of adulthood, building on and amplifying the childhood sources. And

> he has to place these internal destructive forces within the wider context of his ongoing adult life, setting them against the creative, life-affirming forces and finding new ways to integrate them in middle adulthood.
>
> (Levinson et al., 1978, p. 225)

Acceptance and responsibility for one's own destructiveness transforms the disappointments and failures of our life from being merely a sad story to being a tragic one. In a sad story failure is the result of bad luck or external circumstances (a situation more akin to the ironic story form) and, in a sense, the people themselves are not to blame. In a tragedy, whilst there may be what Levinson et al. (1978, p. 226) describe as, "formidable external difficulties", failure "stems above all from an internal flaw, a quality of character" (p. 226). This does not, however, inevitably lend the person's personal narrative a pessimistic narrative tone (to use McAdams' [1997] term). Despair is not the inevitable outcome: "Although the hero does not attain his initial aspirations, he is ultimately victorious: he confronts his profound inner faults, accepts them as part of himself and of humanity, and is to some degree transformed into a nobler person" (Levinson et al., p. 226).

Gould (1978, 1980) employs yet another literary form in his representation of the process of life-span development, namely that of irony or satire. Gould depicts the process of "growing up" during adulthood as involving the sequential relinquishment of the childhood illusions that allowed us to believe the world to be ultimately a place of safety and harmony. In other words, the innocent trustfulness of the comic vision must be challenged: "To enjoy full access to our innermost self, we can no longer deny the ugly, demonic side of life, which our immature mind tried to protect against by enslaving itself to false illusions that absolute safety was possible" (Gould, 1978, p. 218). The truths to be faced are not, as in the tragic formulation, personal shortcomings. Whilst we could be accused of having been naive and innocent as children, this is not something for which we can be blamed or for which we can hold ourselves responsible. Rather, the unpalatable truths lie in the reality of the external world. Gould employs the metaphor of breaking a wild horse. The horse, through relentless exposure to the harsh realities of life, is tamed rather than defeated.

Murray describes Gould's interpretation of the life course as a process of demystification that, "strips away our last remaining illusion of safety and makes existentialists of us all" (Murray, 1986, pp. 284–5). This breaking down of illusions through experience conforms not to Sheehy's romantic hope of victory, nor to Levinson's tragic discovery of flaws, but to the literary form of irony, with its inescapable confrontation with and acceptance of "the real world". Murray's analysis demonstrates how different accounts of the life course can conform to different narrative structures and represent alternative ways of telling the same story. A particular narrative structure is chosen – implicitly or explicitly – to represent not some absolute truth but rather to reflect a particular philosophy about human existence.

Narrative themes

Narratives reflect not only a limited number of forms but also a limited number of significant motivational themes or recurrent patterns of human intention (McAdams, 1997). Theorists differ, however, in their propositions concerning the number and nature of these themes. Rogers (1961), for example, concentrates on a single motivational theme – the actualising tendency. Often, however, human motivation is construed in terms of two fundamental, contradictory motives. McAdams, whose theory was summarised in Chapter 4, drew upon Bakan's (1966) distinction between agency and communion. Other theorists invoke more than two themes. For example, Jacobs (1998) distinguishes three themes that are continually re-worked throughout the life span: trust and dependency, authority and autonomy, and co-operation and competition.

A single fundamental motive. Rogers (1961) is not alone in postulating a single, underlying motivational force – he alluded, for example, to the work of Angyal (1941), Goldstein (1940), Mowrer and Kluckhohn (1944), and Sullivan (1945). Rogers sees all organic and psychological needs as partial reflections of a person's actualising tendency, that is, a person's predisposition to become his or her potentialities. It reflects a person's fundamental need and striving for maintenance, enhancement, and actualisation of the self. It is a directional force evidenced by the tendency of an organism to move towards greater maturation. Physiologically the organism actualises itself in the direction of the greater differentiation of organs and of functions. In personal narratives, however, it is more likely that the actualising tendency will be reflected in psychological and emotional motives for self-government, self-regulation, and autonomy.

The path to self-actualisation is neither easy nor smooth, and personal narratives will record the struggles and pain of a person's movement towards self-enhancement and growth. None the less, Rogers (1961) is convinced of the enduring nature of this urge to express and activate all the capacities of the self: "it may become deeply buried under layer after layer of encrusted psychological defenses; it may be hidden behind elaborate facades which deny its existence; it is my belief, however, based on my experience, that it exists in every individual, and awaits only the proper conditions to be released and expressed" (Rogers, 1961, p. 351).

A two-pronged motivational system. In his account of the development of the "building blocks" of personal narratives, McAdams (1997) locates the emergence of recurrent patterns of intention, or thematic lines, within the middle years of childhood. These themes will subsequently be reflected in the personal narratives that people use to define and represent who they are. McAdams unites different story themes around the needs for power and love, corresponding to what he sees as the two central psychological motivations in human lives – agency and communion.

Agency motivation refers to strivings for power and control over the environment, for independence and autonomy, for status and for separateness from others. By contrast, communion motivation refers to the wish for love and intimacy, the wish to merge with others, and the desire to become part of something larger than the self. In the field of life-span development theories, this duality is reflected in Levinson's (1986; Levinson et al., 1978) repeated invocation of the tension between attachment and separateness. There is, for example, tension or conflict during the structure building phase of entering the adult world between, on the one hand, exploring possibilities through keeping options open and, on the other hand, creating a stable life structure through making choices and commitments.

A tripartite classification of themes. Jacobs (1998) replaces the linear representation of Erikson's theory with a cyclical image – that of a spiral rather than a straight staircase: "In effect we might then say that each of the eight 'treads' which Erikson calls the Eight Ages are repeated in each complete turn of the circular staircase: in each of the chronological ages therefore all the issues (of trust, autonomy, initiative, industry, identity, intimacy, generativity and integrity) are repeated. . . . Using this image, the issues of childhood are thereby reintroduced in the normal process of living, particularly in those crises of adult life through which nearly every person has to pass – but the issues identified as being part of adult life (such as intimacy, creativity and integrity) are also part of early experience" (Jacobs, 1998, p. 13). Jacobs (1998) develops most fully the themes enshrined in Erikson's first three psychosocial crises on the grounds that they are also the themes that almost inevitably emerge during counselling or psychotherapy. He draws out how these themes, "appear developmentally in childhood, adolescence and adult life" (p. 25), arguing that, "each age gives rise to occasions for reworking these basic themes and issues" (p. 25).

Issues of trust and dependency, whilst having their origins in the earliest weeks and months of life, are revisited at all others ages and life stages as the individual moves through a widening world of new and different relationships and experiences. Toddlers and children must learn that unquestioning trust in people or situations may be inappropriate – the world can also be a dangerous place and some people should be treated with suspicion rather than blind faith. Dependence – and its inevitable associate, independence – figure significantly in many life transitions and developmental tasks such as entering and leaving school; changing jobs; leaving the parental home; and establishing, maintaining, or terminating friendships and intimate relationships.

The theme of Erikson's second psychosocial crisis addresses issues of physical and personal autonomy and the balance between freedom and control that is reflected in people and institutions of authority. Whilst the themes of trust and dependency concern aspects of "being" and "who I am", the themes around authority and autonomy are more about "doing" – "what I can do" and "what I should do". During the second year of life the achievement of physical mobility paves the way for the emergence of issues concerning different aspects of control and independence that, "are played out not only at this young age, . . . but throughout life. Attitudes towards self and others over these important matters of doing, making, and acting, acquired in the early years, will be reinforced within the family in later childhood and adolescence, supported or challenged in school and become a major influence on the way in which learning, work, and relationships with authority in particular, are faced and worked with in adult life" (Jacobs, 1998, p. 98). Jacobs places a range of concerns under the rubric of authority and autonomy, including issues of control, of rigidity in oneself or towards others (authoritarianism), perfectionism, the expression of anger and loss of control with emotions generally, obsessional behaviours and attitudes, conditional love, and internalised authority figures.

The third recurring theme discussed by Jacobs (1998) – co-operation and competition – derives from Erikson's third psychosocial crisis. It revolves around the issue of whether relationships incorporate parity and equality, or whether they are characterised by rivalry and competition. Psychoanalytic theory highlights sex and sexuality as central to this theme. Throughout life individuals, "re-experience questions, anxieties and pleasures that first arose for them as children, as they encountered physical differences in gender, and as they explored birth and sex and relationships in the family" (Jacobs, 1998, p. 144). If the different aspects of co-operation and competition are negotiated satisfactorily, then relationships have a, "type of wholeness . . . in which we see others as complete persons, and not either as providers of care on the one hand or of rules on the other; instead they are people who have their own needs, to whom we may give, from whom we may receive, and with whom we may share, in acts of love, of friendship and of social cooperation" (Jacobs, 1998, p. 143).

Jacobs' three themes revolve, respectively, around issues of dependence, independence, and interdependence. The first theme is, at least in part, about symbiosis, the second about separateness, and the third about complementarity, that is, "togetherness with the acceptance of difference" (Jacobs, 1998, p. 143). These issues are not, however, addressed sequentially or completely. Instead, they re-emerge as individuals negotiate major transitions and relationships within various developmental domains such as family, work, and social and intimate relationships. There is what Jacobs (1998, p. 192) describes as a "circularity about development" that reflects "a process which is never completed, but is repeated in many forms and at different ages" (p. 192).

Narrative plots

The themes of our narratives are manifested in our story lines, or plots. Elsbree (1982), a literary critic, distinguished five generic plots: establishing or consecrating a home, engaging in a contest, taking a journey, enduring suffering, and pursuing consummation.

1. Establishing or consecrating a home. In the first of Elsbree's generic plots the basic image is that of building a home. General and specific evidence of this theme can be found throughout accounts of the life course. Creating a stable life structure, putting down roots, making commitments and establishing a more organised life are all recurrent themes in Levinson's (1986; 1996; Levinson et al., 1978) model of adult development, albeit that these tasks must often be worked on in the context of other, contradictory demands. Similarly, age-related norms and expectations concerning such events as taking on a mortgage or having children (Neugarten, 1977) are also evidence of this theme.

Elsbree's first generic plot is not only revealed in the literal act of home-building. Thus, whilst Erikson's (1980) task of generativity – establishing and guiding the next generation – is usually expressed through parenthood, it may also be expressed through other forms of creativity and altruistic concern. In general terms, the plot of establishing or consecrating a home is concerned with sustaining human community and creating order out of chaos.

2. Engaging in a contest. Elsbree's second generic plot is reflected in the image of engaging in a contest, or fighting a battle. Thus, Sheehy (1974) describes the task of the midlife period as being the achievement through battle of victory over the inner custodian – a "nasty tyrant" within the self, which commands that we meet the demands made of us by others, notably our parents. Erikson's depiction of life-span development as a sequence of "battles" or crises is illustrative of this theme on a grander scale. In similar vein, Levinson et al. (1978) see all stages of development being characterised by conflicting tasks.

3. Taking a journey. The image of the life course as a journey, Elsbree's third generic plot, is illustrated in Ford and Lerner's (1992) description of life-span development as a sea voyage (see Box 1.3). It recurs throughout Levinson et al.'s (1978) description of adult development as the evolution of a person's life structure through alternating structure-building and structure-changing phases. They talk, for example, of the early adult transition as, "a preliminary *step* into the adult world" (p. 56; emphasis added), and all major transitional phases as *bridges*, or *boundary zones*, between two *states* of greater stability. Unresolved problems are described as "*baggage* from the past" (p. 322; emphasis added). The image of journey permeates our thinking about the life course. Do we "know where we are going"? Is it "better to travel hopefully than to arrive"? It is one of the most pervasive images of life.

4. Enduring suffering. It is a *sine qua non* of accounts of the life course that at least some degree of suffering, the fourth of Elsbree's plots, ensues as the fidelity of our life choices is tested and we face mounting pressure to change. Transitions inevitably involve breaking at least some of the affectional bonds with which we are linked to the past. Similarly, Levinson et al.'s transitional phases are described as periods of upheaval, both exciting and frightening, during which we must, among other things, confront and come to terms with our limitations, flaws, and mistakes.

5. Pursuing consummation. Elsbree's final generic plot, that of pursuing consummation, is enshrined in many definitions of development proffered by life-span researchers. Thus Bühler (Bühler & Massarik, 1968), describes an "effective" person as one who leads a goal-directed life, striving for self-fulfilment and self-actualisation. Through this striving, basic needs can be transformed into life goals, and, ideally, "ultimate purpose". Likewise, you might recall (see Chapter 5) that Levinson et al. (1978, p. 91) describe the Dream as having, "the quality of a vision, an imagined possibility that generates excitement and vitality". That many life stories fall short of full consummation is indicated by the emphasis within life-span developmental psychology on the process rather than the end state of development – recall (in Chapter 1) Kaplan's (1983, p. 181) description of the concept of development as, "pertaining to a rarely, if ever, attained ideal".

These plots can be intertwined within the same story (see Box 7.2 for an example of this). Socially and personally plausible plots conform to particular structures (Gergen, 1988, p. 98): "If someone were to describe her life story as one in which each positive event was followed by a negative event, and *vice versa*, the narrative would be viewed with suspicion by contemporary listeners. Such a story would seem unreasonable by current social standards, as would a story in which one wonderful success followed upon another without end". Such accounts would not conform to what our cultural heritage has led us to expect in a life story.

The narrative perspective

As a conceptual tool, narratives provide a vehicle for understanding the life course in the same way as does, for example, the notion of stages.

Box 7.2 Generic plots in Gould's account of adult development

Gould's (1978, 1980) account of adult developments incorporates all of Elsbree's generic plots. He describes personal growth as a search for security (illustrating the plot of maintaining a home), as a conflict (engaging in a contest), and a journey (to arrive somewhere new) in which we must endure suffering (through the disturbance of safety patterns) in order to pursue consummation (the licence to be):

> As we expand our potential, we disturb the patterns within ourselves (our defensive system) and our relationship to those close to us. . . . That is why growth is a conflict – a disturbance of safety patterns; and that is why growth is more than learning and practising new activities or changing by will power. It is a transformation of self in which we enlarge the license to be, only after going through mythical dangers in order to arrive at a new secure place that in turn will be left when the feelings of stagnation and claustrophobia initiate another cycle.
>
> (Gould, 1980, p. 58)

Indeed, with the demise during recent decades of set paths through the educational, employment, and personal tasks of adulthood, the life stage model of the life course – and of adulthood in particular – has appeared less tenable. By the same token, the narrative perspective, with the centrality it accords to the individual as author of his or her own story, has achieved increasing prominence. As authors of our personal narrative, we select from our countless daily experiences what to include in the story and what to omit. We weave what we select into a narrative and link what is happening now with what has passed, and what might happen in the future: "If we do not exactly write the plots of our lives, nevertheless it is we alone who create our own stories. Agency lies not in governing what shall happen to us, but in creating what we make of what happens. We ourselves construct the meaning of our story" (Salmon, 1985, pp. 138–9).

8 Intervention

> If you don't know where you're going, you'll probably end up somewhere else.
>
> (Campbell, 1974)

Life-span developmental psychology was defined in Chapter 1 as the description, explanation, and modification of the life course. Intervention is concerned with the third of these goals. It is concerned with change – with promoting, facilitating, or preventing it. It is not, however, concerned with all change or, usually, with change *per se*. It is generally concerned with particular types of change for particular purposes.

Perhaps the most striking feature of Baltes' (1987) tenets of life-span developmental psychology is their inclusiveness. Above all they advocate a wide range of perspectives – on cause, on directionality, on evaluation of change (and, indeed, continuity). It follows, therefore, that a life-span perspective also leads to a similarly broad definition of appropriate interventions. Thus, Lerner and Ryff (1978) identified two major issues as characterising the life-span approach to intervention. There is, first, the assumption that the effect of any particular intervention procedure will vary between individuals, and, second, the consequent belief that intervenors must select from a wide array of possible procedures the one that is most appropriate for that particular intervention goal under those particular conditions. The impact of a particular procedure is recognised as being moderated by "the entire range of personological, cultural, and historical differences manifest in each individual" (Lerner & Ryff, 1978, p. 14). It is not possible, therefore, to offer fixed recommendations about ideal interventions. There is no single or unequivocal answer to the question of which behaviours should be the targets for intervention. Decisions must be made in the context of specific situations and persons.

Disease versus developmental approaches to life events

All interventions – like all definitions of development – are premised on notions of optimal, adequate, and deficient human functioning, and on how best to promote the former and/or avoid the latter. Rappaport (1977) labelled this the "conceptual" component of interventions. In the context of the present book, Danish et al.'s (1980) distinction between a developmental and a disease perspective on life events is a particularly salient way of construing the conceptual component of interventions.

The "disease" approach to life events and transitions sees such experiences as stresses or crises for the individual – hence the premise that scores on Holmes and Rahe's social readjustment rating scale (referred to in Chapter 6) are predictive of physical and/or psychological illness. Intervention from this conceptual standpoint is concerned with avoiding, eliminating or reducing stress so that the individual may pursue the path of "normal" development. The "developmental" perspective, in contrast, views life events not as pathological crises, but as states of imbalance that precede growth and may make growth possible. This is the assumption underlying Hopson's transition cycle (also referred to in Chapter 6). Life events can have either positive or negative outcomes (or both), and the goal of intervention is not the prevention of critical life events but rather the enhancement of the individual's ability to grow or develop as a result of the event.

The remainder of this chapter considers a number of parameters and frameworks that facilitate the conceptualisation and implementation of different intervention possibilities. First, it outlines the implications of assumptions made concerning the locus of responsibility for causing and resolving personal problems. Next, it addresses different possible sources of help (both individuals themselves and a range of external sources). Then what I have termed "technical" parameters of interventions are considered – including goals, timing, levels of analysis, mode, and style of interventions, and also different intervention taxonomies. Next, a generalised model of problem management and opportunity development is outlined as a framework for guiding life-span development interventions. Finally, a section addresses the development of life skills as a goal of life-span development interventions.

Attributions of responsibility

Issues of power, control, and responsibility are never far from the surface in any programmatic attempt at alteration. Who, for example, decides the intervention needs of a particular person, family, group, or community? Who decides the goals of an intervention? Who decides the mechanisms by which goals shall be addressed? Who is responsible for implementing the intervention? Who is responsible for the success of the programme? A typology of helping models proposed by Brickman et al. (1982; Karusa, Zevon, Rabinowitz, & Brickman, 1982) is organised around the issues of whether or not the patients/clients/participants of an intervention are held (retrospectively) responsible for creating the problem situation and/or (prospectively) for effecting a solution. Such implicit or explicit assumptions concerning the locus of responsibility are amongst the key factors determining the form of an intervention (Brickman et al.,1982; Yeo, 1993). Depending on what attributions of responsibility are made, interventions can take the form of material aid, instruction, exhortation, discipline, emotional support, advice and consultancy, or some other form of help.

By distinguishing between attributions of responsibility for causing problems and attributions of responsibility for finding solutions, four alternative general models of helping are derived, as shown in Box 8.1. First, general characteristics of the resulting typology will be reviewed. Then attention will turn to the four models it points to.

Box 8.1 Intervention typology based on attributions of responsibility for

		Attributions to self of responsibility for solution	
		High	Low
Attributions to self of responsibility for problem	High	Moral model	Enlightenment model
	Low	Compensatory model	Medical model

Two of the taxonomy's models, labelled the moral and the medical models in Box 8.1, are "symmetrical" models, in that in the former individuals are held to be responsible for both problem and solution, and in the latter they are held to be responsible for neither. The other two models, labelled the compensatory and the enlightenment models, are asymmetrical in this respect. In the compensatory model it is assumed that whilst individuals may not be responsible for problematic situations in which they find themselves, they are responsible for doing something about it. In the enlightenment model these assumptions are reversed. Individuals are held to be responsible for their problems but to be unable to effect a solution without some form of outside help. A number of corollaries, as summarised in Table 8.1, arise from the adoption of each position. They relate to the assessment made of the client and the consequent response or form of help. They comprise attributions made both by those experiencing the problem and by those offering the help. In any particular situation the attributions made by client and helper may or may not coincide. Thus counsellors can find clients wanting unequivocal advice, whereas their own goal is for clients to make their own decisions and choices, thereby accepting responsibility for themselves. The confrontation and resolution of such differences can constitute an important part of the early stages of the helper–client relationship.

The moral model conveys a stance in which helping others is neither an obligation (because everyone's troubles are of their own making) nor a feasible option (because everyone must find their own solutions). It is assumed, for example, that the unemployed could find jobs if only they tried hard enough. It is assumed that it is their own fault that they are unemployed and that the effort they have expended in trying to find work has been inadequate and/or misdirected. They are seen as lazy, and the only form of intervention deemed appropriate is to encourage or exhort the individual to change, improve and try harder – perhaps with reminders of how we are all responsible for our own fate and have a "moral duty" to help ourselves. Thus, the moral model places a strong emphasis on the self as a source of help.

The medical model derives its name from the traditional assumption of medical practice that people are responsible for neither the origin of nor the solution to their problems – or illnesses, as they would probably be called. This is an assumption much questioned in current medical practice, but the stereotype remains. The illness is not seen as the patient's "fault", nor is he or she expected to be responsible for prescribing the solution. It is seen as inappropriate either to blame people for their problems or to give them credit for finding solutions. The patient is, however, expected to take responsibility for following the expert's advice and for trying to get well – hence the debates over whether or not people who persist in maintaining unhealthy lifestyles (for example, with regard to smoking) should be allowed automatic access to scarce medical resources.

Table 8.1 Corollaries for helping and coping of attributions of responsibility for causing and solving problems (Brickman et al., 1982)

	Model of intervention			
	Moral	*Enlightenment*	*Compensatory*	*Medical*
Perception of self	Lazy	Guilty	Deprived	Ill
Action expected of self	Striving	Submission	Assertion	Acceptance
Others besides self who must act	Peers	Authorities	Subordinates	Experts
Actions expected of others	Exhortation	Discipline	Mobilisation	Treatment
Implicit view of human nature	Strong	Bad	Good	Weak
Potential pathology	Loneliness	Fanaticism	Alienation	Dependency

Adapted, with permission, from Brickman, P. et al. (1982). Models of helping and coping. *American Psychologist*, *37*(4), 368–374. Copyright © 1982 by the American Psychological Association.

Under the compensatory model people are seen as having to compensate by their own efforts for handicaps, obstacles or disadvantages resulting from the situation in which they find themselves. Thus, whilst individuals might not be seen as responsible for their inability to find employment, they are considered to be responsible for managing and coping with this situation. They are, in other words, assumed to be responsible for their response to, if not for the fact of, their unemployment. Helpers operating under the assumptions of this model see their help as compensating for resources or opportunities that their clients deserve or need but do not have. It is the recipient of the help, however, who is responsible for effectively using this help. The compensatory model is the model of helping people to help themselves. Rather than helpers simply providing what they believe the clients need, as under the medical model, under the compensatory model helpers assist clients to obtain the resources for themselves. Thus, it seeks to empower individuals to promote their own development.

Finally, the enlightenment model sees people as responsible for causing the problems that beset them, but as lacking the resources to find their own solutions. This model derives its name from the consequent efforts of those offering help to enlighten their clients as to what is really the problem and what they must do to deal with it. It assumes that clients need first to be made to see and accept the error of their ways, and then realise that they cannot solve their problems alone, but must follow the instructions of those who can help them. Once clients accept the premises of this model, great power accrues to those who are seen as being able to offer help. Clients view themselves as their own worst enemy and as powerless to change on their own. They see themselves as dependent on others for assistance and, lacking a sense of self-efficacy, might experience low self-esteem. Self-esteem can rise when, once "cured", clients seek with determination and possibly with fanaticism to enlighten others. The assumptive base of the enlightenment model is found in some mutual-help organisations and religious cults. Considerable commitment to the authority of the group and/or its leaders is actively encouraged. This allows for a high degree of social control, which may be efficient in terms of facilitating achievement of the organisation's goals, but which disregards personal autonomy and over-rides dissent.

As outlined above, each model of helping is something of a caricature. In reality, it is relative rather than absolute levels of responsibility that are attributed to self or others. In practice, responsibility is generally shared to some degree. Also, the appropriateness of the assumptions underlying each model can change over time. Thus, it might be appropriate to assume responsibility for a person immediately following a sudden trauma, gradually relinquishing this hold as the person emerges from the state of shock (to use the language of transition management). Likewise, it might be important for a helper initially to accept a client's denial of any culpability with regard to, say, a marital breakdown. Only with time, once a secure relationship with the helper has been established, might the client be able to explore and accept that the responsibility might be shared.

Despite these caveats, the generalised consequences, advantages, and pitfalls of adopting each of the different models can be identified. Attributions of responsibility to the self for causing problems (as in the moral and enlightenment models) engenders guilt, whilst attributions of responsibility to others for finding solutions (as in the medical and enlightenment models) engenders dependency. Application of the enlightenment model is, therefore, especially likely to promote negative self-images, with clients seeing themselves as doubly inadequate: first, because they allowed the problem to develop in the first place, and second, because of their perceived inability to do anything about it.

The medical model also tends to foster dependency in that people are not encouraged to believe they can do much for themselves. It may, however, make it easier for them to seek help in that their need for this help is not seen as evidence of personal culpability or blame. They can see themselves as "sick" rather than as "guilty" or "lazy". Modern medical practice frequently deviates at least to some degree from the assumptions of this model. Biofeedback techniques and imagery, for example, can be used in preference to drugs for controlling high blood pressure, thereby giving the individual responsibility for controlling his or her condition. It is generally accepted that achieving long-term behaviour change, for example, in the treatment of addictive behaviour, requires individuals to be motivated to change and to accept an active role in attaining and maintaining that change (Prochaska, DiClemente, & Norcross, 1992).

Models that credit individuals with the responsibility for dealing with their problems encourage an active stance – if we do not like things the way they are we should do something about it ourselves and not wait for somebody else to take the initiative. When this attitude is combined with the moral model's assumption that we are also responsible for having caused our problems in the first place, then unsuccessful attempts at coping can precipitate a deep sense of failure and inadequacy. An emphasis on self-reliance and self-responsibility can also foster feelings of isolation and loneliness.

The compensatory model, "allows people to direct their energies outward, working on trying to solve problems or transform their environment without berating themselves for their role in creating, or permitting others to create, these problems in the first place" (Brickman et al., 1982, p. 372). Taken to its extreme, the compensatory model is a reactive model – one is continually responding to problems not of one's own making. This can impose pressures on the lives of helpers and activists – seeing the same problem cropping up time and time again, feeling that as soon as one hurdle is surmounted there is another to be faced. If responsibility for solving problems is expanded to mean not simply coping with the immediate problem but attempting to prevent the problem recurring in the future, then this vicious cycle can be broken. It also implies accepting some responsibility for avoiding problems in the future, if not for causing the problems of the present. As such it represents a move towards the assumptions of the moral model. This emphasises how the attributions of responsibility can depend on the perspective taken rather than on some unequivocal "truth".

Box 8.2 Alcohol abuse viewed from the perspective of Brickman et al.'s (1982) models of helping

- Under the *medical model*, alcohol abuse would be seen as a physiologically based illness. Treatment would probably be medication. Certainly it would be under the control and direction of a professional expert.
- Interpretation of alcohol abuse under the *enlightenment model* is a harsh judgement. People are not allowed to plead excuses but must accept that it is their own weakness that has allowed the problem to get out of hand. Furthermore, they must accept their own inability to cope with the problem; claims to the contrary will be disbelieved. Clients must accept that they need the support and guidance of others – possibly recovered alcoholics who have been through the same process. Emphasis may be placed on the need to continue this contact and support in order to avoid relapse.
- Under the *compensatory model*, factors external to the individual, for example, pressure of work or the demands of a particular personal relationship, can be accepted as having "driven the person to drink". Individuals are expected, however, to become actively involved in changing the situation and/or modifying their response to it.
- Under the *moral model*, individuals would probably be urged to "pull themselves together" and be reminded of family or other responsibilities that are being neglected whilst they allow themselves to indulge in excessive drinking.

It is almost always possible to consider any particular problem from the perspective of more than one of the four models presented in this section. Unemployment has already been used to illustrate the attributions made under the moral and the compensatory models and Box 8.2 contains an illustrative example of alcohol abuse. In sum, Brickman et al.'s twin criteria of attributions of responsibility for causing and for solving problems provide a framework that helps to make explicit the assumptions, values, and implications of any particular intervention.

Sources of help

The multidisciplinary base of life-span developmental psychology (Baltes, 1987) ensures a role for many different professional groups in life course interventions. However, professional intervention of any sort is only one of several potential sources of help, and is frequently the source of last rather than first resort. Mental health professionals deal with only a minority of the developmental and mental health problems that people face (Goldberg & Huxley, 1980). There has long been evidence (Gottlieb, 1976; Gurin, Veroff, & Feld, 1960; Roberts, Prince, Gold, & Shiner, 1966; Ryan, 1969) that most people draw first upon their own resources and those of kith and kin before approaching official sources of assistance. Thus, Alonzo (1979) talked of a period of containment during which illnesses go unreported because people are able to contain the signs and symptoms of their condition. The illness or problem is acknowledged and assistance sought only when this containment breaks down. Furthermore, self-help groups might be the preferred method of treatment rather than the professional–client relationship characterising the therapy model more familiar to many psychologists and other mental health workers (Jacobs & Goodman, 1989).

Golan (1981) in an amalgam of several different classifications, distinguished five potential sources of assistance available to a person in need or distress:

- the self
- the natural help system
- the mutual help system
- the "non-professional" help system
- the professional help system.

The sources of help available to an individual form a part of the person's self, situation, support, and strategies, as discussed by Schlossberg et al. (1995) (see Chapter 7). Rarely does a person rely on just one source of help and support: "What we usually find is a weaving back and forth, an intricate combination of asking for and getting aid that merges into a pattern of multiple needs (or multiple aspects of the same need) attended to by various sources within the community" (Golan, 1981, p. 242).

The self as a source of help

Enshrined in many concepts of development is the notion of self-empowerment, defined by Hopson and Scally (1981, p. 57) as, "a process by which one increasingly takes greater charge of oneself and one's life". Accordingly, self-help materials have become a prime source of psychological guidance for many people (Norcross et al., 2000). This implies a shift away from dependence on externally defined or taken-for-granted goals or problem solutions, and an increased preparedness to take responsibility for one's own life. Nowhere is this clearer than in what might be termed the "self-improvement industry" – the plethora of self-help aids designed to help us decide who we are, where we want to go, and how we are going to get there. Whilst some are highly evangelical, with extravagant claims (Rosen, 1987), others are more measured, see, for example Ball's (1989) self-help guide to career planning that is discussed below.

There are texts designed to help us cope with almost every conceivable issue – buying a house, controlling drinking, improving personal relationships, for example. What they share is the characteristic that we are invited to draw on and develop our own resources (our self) to promote our own development or enhance our coping skills. The efficacy of such self-help treatments has been questioned (Rosen, 1987), with concerns being expressed about the reliability of self-diagnosis of problems, the risks of instructions being misunderstood or misapplied, and the high likelihood of non-completion of the programme. Furthermore, should the self-help efforts prove unsuccessful, there are risks of negative self-attributions, of anger towards the self or others, and of reduced belief in the value of other therapeutic techniques (Barrera, Rosen, & Glasgow, 1981).

Much of the section in Chapter 6 dealing with the management of transitions is concerned with the self as a source of help. Here, as it were, the individual is intervening in his or her own life. Most people will attempt to reach their own decisions and solve their own problems, either with or without the help of others. Furthermore, intervention by others might be directed at developing and mobilising the skills of self-dependence within the individual. Thus, others can teach the person generalisable problem-solving skills rather than offering specific solutions to a current problem. In this way the individual becomes more able, it is hoped, to resolve future difficulties without recourse to intervention from others. It is also a case of practice making perfect: it has long been accepted that successful coping through one's own actions promotes self-direction and self-dependence (Perlman, 1957) and enhances self-esteem and self-worth (Oxley, 1971).

The natural help system

Social support systems (see the discussion of Schlossberg et al.'s (1995) "support" factor in Chapter 7) are key components of people's natural help systems and of what Caplan (1974) refered to as the kith and kin system that is typically the first outside help to which an individual turns in times of difficulty or uncertainty. Relationships with friends can be substantial sources of support (Blieszner & Adams, 1992). Thus, for example, Heinemann and Evans (1990) found, in keeping with many others, that social support was pivotal in successful adaptation to widowhood, and also that this support was typically provided by family, friends, and other widows rather than professionals.

Golan adds "informal caregiver" to Caplan's categories, distinguishing between the "generalists" who are known for their overall wisdom and knowledge, and the "specialists" who have already coped successfully with particular demanding situations. Cowen (1982) showed how groups such as hairdressers and bartenders can proffer informal help by virtue of the circumstances and setting of their jobs. Whilst it is readily established that such informal help is both sought and provided, its precise function and/or effectiveness is less well documented.

The concept of a social support convoy (Antonucci, 1991; Kahn & Antonucci, 1980) provides a way of conceptualising the changing nature of the natural help system across the life course. Each person is thought of as moving through the life course, "surrounded by a set of other people to whom he or she is related by the giving or receiving of social support" (Kahn & Antonucci, 1980, p. 269). The members of this personal network will vary in the amount of support given or received, and the extent to which the support proffered is dependent on the role they occupy in relation to the person in question. In Figure 8.1 in Box 8.3, the smallest circle (P) represents this focal person and the three concentric circles represent the convoy that, metaphorically, "carries" or accompanies the person through transitions and other life experiences. Closeness and amount of support proffered are indicated by the distance between the focal person and the various convoy members.

Losses and gains in any circle of the convoy can occur in several ways. Kahn and Antonucci (1980) suggest that, during adulthood at least, loss in the innermost circle is likely to be the result of death or the kind of break experienced as a major betrayal. Changes in the second and third circle could simply reflect changes in role and/or location – we move to a different job or house and lose touch with at least some of our colleagues and neighbours who, until then, might have been a significant source of support. The boundaries between the circles of the network are permeable and, just as there can be flow into and out of the convoy, so, too, can there be movement across the circles as supportive relationships wax and wane. Those who become our partner or life long friend are likely to have entered our support convoy at the outermost circle and, over time, moved towards the centre. Similarly, as we "drift apart" from or "fall out" with convoy members, they will move to less central positions in our convoy, or perhaps leave it altogether.

The mutual-help system

Relationships within a social support convey can be reciprocal, that is, involve both the receiving and the giving of support. As such, they can be thought of as a mutual-help system. However, for the present purpose of distinguishing different sources of help across the life course, the term is applied here to relationships established with the explicit goal of providing mutual assistance.

Box 8.3 Social support convoys (Kahn & Antonucci, 1980)

A convoy does not include all people known to the focal person (P; Figure 8.1), but is limited to people who are important to him or her in terms of social support.

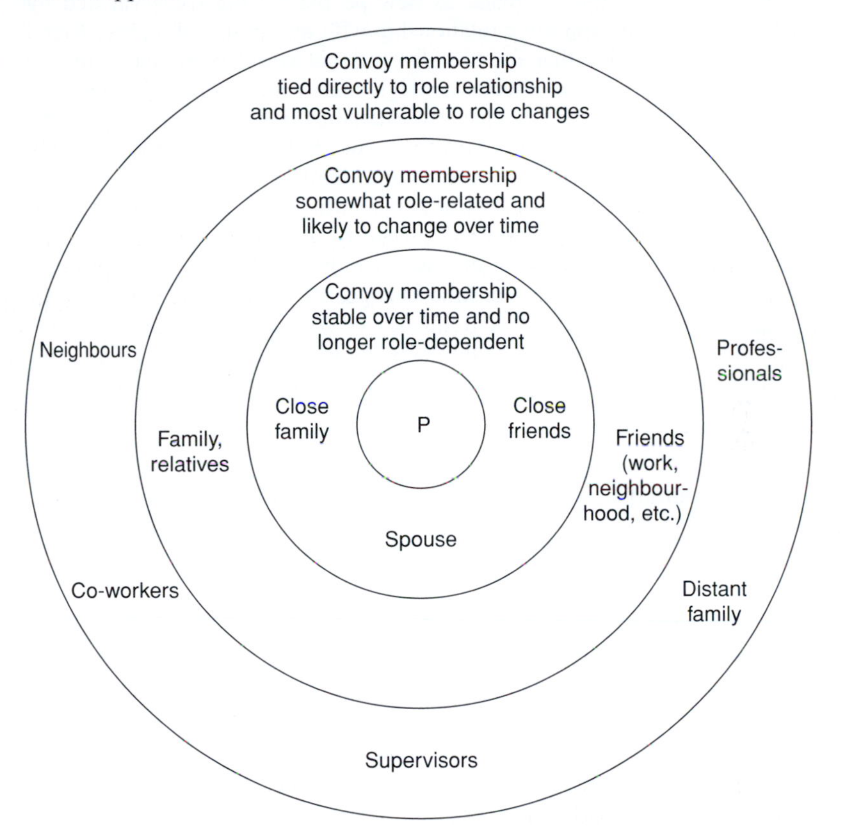

Figure 8.1 An example of a social support convoy (reproduced with permission from Kahn, R.L., & Antonucci, T.C. (1980). Convoys over the life course: Attachment, roles and social support. In P.B. Baltes & O.G. Brim (Eds). *Life-span development and behavior* (Vol. 3). Copyright © 1980 by Academic Press.)

- The outermost (third) concentric circle represents the convoy members who are least close to "P" and with whom the supportive relationship is likely to be role-dependent, of limited scope, and very vulnerable to role changes. Thus, "P" might have supportive work-related interactions with colleagues, but the relationships do not extend beyond the work setting and, if "P" or a colleague were to change jobs, the relationship would cease.
- The second concentric circle includes people with whom "P" feels some additional degree of closeness in that the support proffered is

less dependent on the roles that they fill in the person's life, and the time, place, and subjects of interaction extend beyond the boundaries of those roles. However, the relationship is not wholly independent of the role and might not be maintained if either member loses the role. Substitutions might be made as new people fill the roles vacated by others. Thus, a supportive relationship with the spouse of a close friend might not survive that friend's divorce, but could be replaced by the friend's new partner. Similarly, neighbours with whom "P" interacted daily and depended on extensively when they lived in an adjacent house could move out of the support convoy when they move away, possibly being replaced by whoever moves into their old house.

- The innermost circle consists of people who are very close to "P" and who are perceived as important providers of support. Because it is so highly valued, membership of this inner circle is likely to remain fairly stable through the years, despite changes of job or residence. Neither geographical proximity nor frequency of contact is necessarily a good indicator of membership of this closest circle, as when, in a crisis, we turn to an old friend who now lives far away and is seen only rarely.

There are mutual-help groups to support the entire life course (Katz & Hermalin, 1987). Groups exist, "for people who are infertile, who have had Caesarean deliveries, who have abused their children or who feel in danger of doing so, who have a disabled child, who have adolescent problems, who have any one of numerous problems of adult life, who are experiencing the transition to retirement, and who are adjusting to older age" (Orford, 1992, p. 234). Their defining characteristics are that they are made up of fellow sufferers (Kurtz, 1997) and believe in the efficacy of peer help (Katz & Bender, 1976; Stewart, 1990). Furthermore, self-help groups are committed to member governance, with leadership vested in selected members and/or professional representatives who, "serve at the pleasure of the group" (Jacobs & Goodman, 1989, p. 537).

It is likely that the members of a mutual-help system will be at different stages in relation to the life event or experience that links them. Thus, new members will be able to look to the system for details of how others have coped with a similar situation. They can look to and identify with individuals within the system as role models and as a source of hope for the future. Although these new members of mutual-help systems can gain a great deal, it has long been suggested (Riessman, 1965) that it is the helper who gains most. Thus, Skovholt (1974) identified four benefits that the helper might gain from the relationship: an increased sense of interpersonal competence from having successfully helped someone; an enhanced sense of personal adequacy from having given as well as received help; further self-insight gained through the process of working with others on their problems; and the gratitude and social approval of those who have been helped.

Although operable between dyads (as in co-counselling), mutual-help systems more usually involve groups of individuals with varying purposes and varying degrees and types of structure and formal organisation. Several typologies of different mutual help systems have been proposed. The one outlined in Box 8.4 focuses on the problem areas addressed and represents an amalgam of several.

Box 8.4 Types of mutual-help group (Borman, 1982; Katz & Hermalin, 1987; Levine & Perkins, 1987; Orford, 1992)

- *Groups organised around the experience of a particular crisis or transition.* Many mutual-help groups exist to support people who have experienced, or are experiencing, a specific traumatic life event, for example the death of a child, unemployment, divorce, or a particular type of surgery (e.g. colostomy). Alternatively, they could be undergoing a particular transition, such as the birth of a first child, or retirement. The purpose of the mutual-help system is generally to offer information and support during the crisis period. It is not normally expected that people will remain within the system on a permanent basis, although they might change their role to become a helper rather than a client. Alternatively, their activity could shift away from the receiving and/or giving of personal assistance, towards the more outward-looking activities of fund raising or political and consumer advocacy.
- *Groups for those with a permanent or long-term stigmatised condition.* This category includes a wide range of groups, including those whose members have a specific disability or condition (either physical or psychological) that renders them liable to "social isolation, stigmatisation, scorn, pity, or social punishment" (Levine & Perkins, 1987, p. 240). It also includes groups of social and minority group members who may experience social discrimination or disadvantage (Borman, 1982; Maton, 1988). It is likely that, as well as providing practical support and assistance, such groups will help members maintain a positive self-image and cope with the stigma, and might also campaign to attack prejudice and change the social attitudes that stigmatise group members.
- *Groups for people caught in a habit, addiction, or self-destructive way of life.* The most obvious examples of groups within this category would be those for people with drink- or drug-related problems, but organisations such as Weight Watchers and Gamblers Anonymous would also fall into this category. The main focus is on helping members behave differently and maintain a life style that enables them to avoid returning to their addictive or self-destructive habits.
- *Groups for family members or associates of those with physical, psychological, or stigmatised conditions.* These groups are for people who are "one step removed" (Gottlieb, 1983) from the problematic condition, but might be uncertain about how to cope and/or might themselves suffer stigma, social isolation or stress (Levine & Perkins, 1987; Orford, 1992).

- *Groups organised to counter specific social or community problems or threats.* These are groups that begin at the campaigning end of the spectrum of mutual-help group activities. They are often formed to meet a particular problem or threat to a community (Levine & Perkins, 1987), for example, the threatened closure of a local hospital or school, or a perceived environmental or health threat. As well as the attainment of specific goals, involvement in these campaigns can facilitate personal growth in the activists (Orford, 1992), providing a means of feeling more in control of otherwise uncontrollable events and a vehicle for expanding personal roles and activities.

All such typologies of mutual-help groups are somewhat crude because any one organisation can include a number of different types of groups. Similarly, groups can, as is indicated in Box 8.5, be involved in more than one type of activity. Thus Silverman (1978) distinguished four main activities of mutual-help groups: personal help, fund raising, consumer activity, and political action. A group can add one after the other of these activities to its repertoire, and an individual could become involved in all of them.

Mutual-help organisations vary considerably in their attitude towards and relationship with professional sources of help. Some are set up and organised by members of the professional help system whilst others are established in opposition to such systems and in response to their perceived inadequacies and limitations. Some groups consciously reject the involvement of professionals whilst in other instances professionals may have a directive, a facilitative, or a consultative role (Kurtz, 1997).

The non-professional help system

To talk of "non-professional" help does not imply that the help proffered is "unprofessional" or "amateurish". It might be that the help is unpaid, or that it is a subsidiary part of the helper's wider role responsibilities. Golan (1981), focusing specifically on sources of help during times of transition, distinguished between three categories of non-professional help: voluntary workers, community caregivers, and paraprofessionals.

Voluntary work tends, like mutual help, to be organised around specific problems, situations, or categories of people. It is often provided by people who have a particular interest, personal or professional, in the problem area or client group concerned. Voluntary workers can be highly trained, and, indeed "professional" helpers might undertake voluntary, unpaid work in addition to their salaried employment. Unlike the mutual-help system, however, with voluntary work not all helpers will have experienced the same problematic situation as the client. Nor is there the expectation that they will gain the same therapeutic benefit from the encounter as, say, the recovered alcoholic may gain from helping others with drink-related problems. Tutors in adult literacy schemes, for example, need not have suffered from literacy problems themselves. Nor would they look to their students for the same kind of support as they were offering to them. This is not to say, however, that there are no rewards for voluntary work. The benefits identified by Skovholt can appertain. Furthermore, voluntary work can be a mechanism for meeting generativity needs (see Erikson's theory, Chapter 4), for passing on the benefits of one's experience and knowledge to others.

Golan (1981) describes community caregivers as those who provide help and support to people in need either as part of their professional role or as an adjunct to it. Teachers, police officers, and the clergy, for example, can all fulfil such a function. They work in direct contact with various client groups in a number of types of relationships. Although they are professionals in their own right, their formal qualifications are not explicitly related to the field of helping. They might offer short-term assistance and/or operate as referral agencies, bringing clients to the attention of other sources of help and *vice versa*.

Paraprofessionals are personnel working within organisations that offer a helping service, but whose training is either more general or more specific, or at a more basic level than those categorised as professional helpers. Often the work of paraprofessionals will be concerned with relatively concrete, immediate interventions involving specific, defined activities. They frequently work in conjunction with or under the direction of members of the professional help system who, in turn, can rely heavily on their contribution. In some instances, voluntary workers and community caregivers come into the category of paraprofessionals.

The professional help system

Last in Golan's (1981) continuum of sources of help lie those individuals whose training and employment confer on them community or institutional sanction and responsibility for offering help to various client groups. Psychiatrists, clinical and educational psychologists, accredited counsellors, occupational therapists, social workers, and mental health nurses are amongst those in this category. Each group has its own professional identity, particular areas of competence, and modes of intervention.

The majority of research on the helping process has been conducted with members of the professional help system and their clients, despite this system being responsible for only a small proportion of the help sought or received for psychological or psychosocial problems. None the less, the aspects of helping interventions discussed in the remainder of this chapter can generally be applied to other sources of help as well. Help emanating from the self, and from the natural, mutual and "non-professional" help systems can be thought of in relation to parameters such as those discussed in the following sections.

The technical parameters of life-span development interventions

Defining intervention broadly as "programmatic attempts at alteration", Baltes (1973) indicated the diversity of possible intervention actions by grouping them under a number of key parameters. Target behaviours could include cognition, language, intellectual achievement, social interactions, motivational states, personality traits, and attitudes. The setting for the intervention might be the laboratory, the family, the classroom, the hospital, the organisation, or the community. The intervention mechanisms could range through psychotherapy, counselling, training, environmental change, health delivery, and economic support. Such examples are illustrative rather than exhaustive. The lists are limited only by our imagination and inventiveness. None the less, any one intervention can be described in relation to a number of key parameters including: goal, timing in relation to the target issue, level of analysis and intervention, mode of intervention, and style of delivery. These are discussed below.

The goals of life-span development interventions

If, as has been claimed, intervention is not directed at change *per se,* then it must be goal directed. Despite the varying definitions and terminology used by different authors over several decades (for example, Baltes, 1973; Caplan, 1964; Danish et al., 1980), distinctions are usually made between interventions directed at:

- treatment – through the alleviation or correction of existing problems
- prevention – through the counteracting of harmful circumstances before they have had a chance to produce illness or dysfunctioning
- adjustment – through helping the person come to terms with an illness, disability or other changed circumstances
- optimisation – through facilitating the best possible functioning, rather than merely the adequate.

Treatment is the first intervention goal that comes to most people's minds, although prevention is also widely recognised and advocated – hence the adage "prevention is better than cure". Adjustment is the cornerstone of much rehabilitation work. Optimisation stands out from the other intervention goals as being particularly compatible with a developmental rather than a disease perspective on life events (Danish et al., 1980). It assumes there is more to good health than the absence of disease. The distinction between adequate, successful, and optimal ageing is relevant here. Whereas an emphasis on prevention sees the world as being full of danger, an emphasis on optimisation sees it as being full of opportunity.

In practice, prevention and optimisation may well be linked, a reflection at least in part of the fact that preventive interventions, far from representing a single coherent approach, in fact comprise a wide and disparate range of strategies. Still amongst the most widely cited typologies of preventive interventions is Caplan's (1964) distinction between primary, secondary, and tertiary prevention:

- primary prevention is directed at reducing the incidence of a disorder within a community (possibly, therefore, paving the way for optimal rather than merely adequate or impaired development)
- secondary prevention aims at reducing the duration of those disorders that do occur
- tertiary prevention strives to reduce the impairment that may result from disorders (and possibly, thereby, including an "adjustment" as well as a "prevention" element).

Timing of interventions

Developmental interventions typically occur in relation to life events that, in turn, can be viewed as comprising a period of anticipation, a period of occurrence of the event, and an aftermath (Danish et al., 1980). Intervention can, therefore, occur before, during, or following the event. The timing of an intervention and its goals are related. Thus, interventions occurring before the onset of a particular life event will frequently be concerned with prevention. Those occurring during a life event will typically be concerned with treatment, and those occurring afterwards with adjustment. Accordingly, pre-marriage counselling will attempt to forestall the occurrence of marital difficulties; couple counselling is likely to be undertaken in response to problems that have already arisen; and support groups for the separated and divorced are likely to include amongst their goals the facilitation of adjustment to the marital break-up.

There is a less clear link between intervention timing and the goal of optimisation. Its basis in a developmental conception of human functioning means that optimisation can be thought of as a particular way of facilitating prevention, treatment or adjustment – looking for opportunities for personal growth rather than merely the re-establishment of some degree of equilibrium. This makes optimisation a possible goal irrespective of the timing of an intervention in relation to a critical life event.

Levels of analysis and intervention

The life-span perspective tends to stress the importance of adopting a contextual view of the person as embedded within an environment that both influences and is influenced by the individual. Bronfenbrenner's (1977, 1979) nested model of the person-in-context (see Box 1.8) reflects this viewpoint and suggests analysing individual problems in the context of the small group, organisation, institution, community, and/or culture.

At the individual level of analysis, one particular person is the focus of attention. His or her needs take priority, albeit that these needs may include taking into consideration other people within the person's interpersonal network. The small-group level of analysis looks to interpersonal rather intrapersonal dynamics. Group rather than individual deficits and difficulties are emphasised. This perspective leads to a focus on family, rather than individual, therapy, for example, and to an emphasis on such strategies as team building and interpersonal communication training within organisations.

Analysis at the organisational level begins from the assumption that the way in which organisations function and are structured will have an impact on individuals. For example, ineffective channels of communication can mean that a person cannot perform his or her job adequately. The solution is not, or not only, individual training or interpersonal skills training, it is also a problem of organisational design.

At the institutional and community level of analysis the emphasis is on broad social analysis. Social problems are seen as the products of social institutions rather than the fault of individuals, groups, or specific organisations. Blame is placed at the door of housing policy rather than particular housing departments, for example, or in the structure of the National Health Service rather than the workings of particular hospitals, staff groups, or patients.

Finally, analysis can look beyond institutions and communities to the way our thinking is influenced by such factors as the structure of a society's language and the mores of its operation. In the context of this book, it is ageist language use that is perhaps the most appropriate example. Language can also, however, either encourage or challenge sexism, racism, and cultural chauvinism.

Interventions can mirror these different levels of analysis, leading to programmes that include not just "client work" with individuals or small groups, but also what Lawton (1985) termed worker work and community work. This might involve working, as trainers or consultants, with groups such as teachers, social workers, and nurses, who themselves work directly with clients. It might also involve working at the level of programme-planning and policy-making – what has been termed "upstream" rather than "downstream" helping (Egan & Cowan, 1979; Rappaport, 1977). Gottlieb's typology of support interventions, as summarised in Box 8.5, similarly reflects this concern with multiple levels of intervention.

Mode of intervention

Another important consideration governing practice concerns the relative degree of control accorded to intervenor and recipient in deciding the goals and strategies of the intervention. This relates in part to Brickman et al.'s (1982) variable of the attributions of responsibility afforded to the

Box 8.5 Typology of support interventions (adapted from Gottlieb, 1988)

Gottlieb's intervention typology includes five major levels of support: individual, dyadic, group, social system, and community:

- The individual level of intervention includes both providing and receiving support. Providers of support promote attitudes and methods that invite the support of others. At this level, recipients are encouraged to manage their distress while interacting with and receiving support from others.
- There are two dimensions of dyadic intervention – support from a key person and the introduction of an outsider (e.g. buddy, coach, mentor, companion).
- Group interventions involve either support from a section within one's existing network or the development of support groups through what Gottlieb calls the "grafting of new ties".
- Social system intervention pertains to the larger context, including physical and sociocultural aspects. At this level the focus is on a reframing process that permits new approaches and new views on issues and problems. Also, emphasis is placed on structural change, which places people in different and more constructive relations to one another and to the institution.
- The final intervention is at the community level and pertains to widespread initiatives to promote social support through public campaigns.

self or others for managing problems. Beattie (1991) termed this the mode of intervention and identified a dimension ranging from authoritative to negotiated intervention. The authoritative mode is a "top-down" and expert-led mode, with the intervenor assuming responsibility for managing problems. By contrast, the negotiated mode is a "bottom-up" mode that values individual autonomy and where both goals and strategies for achieving them are agreed between intervenor and recipient. The client has far greater power in negotiated interventions to determine which problems should be addressed and how.

The choice of mode can be partly a pragmatic decision. Some clients might be unable to make decisions on their own behalf, thus requiring that intervenors adopt an authoritative stance. Others might refuse to co-operate with an authoritative intervenor, resisting the imposition from outside of either problem definition or problem solution. However, the choice of mode can also have a significant value-based component, reflecting views on issues such as the legitimacy and appropriateness of authority and control, and the wisdom and desirability of promoting personal autonomy and empowerment. In this sense, mode of intervention could have been discussed as a conceptual rather than a technical parameter of intervention.

Style of delivery

Styles of delivery refer to the ways in which services (interventions) are delivered to the target population. A broad distinction can be made (Rappaport, 1977) between the waiting mode and the seeking mode styles of delivery. The former is reactive, epitomised by the traditional relationship between doctor and patient, lawyer and client, or other expert and service recipient, whereby expert or other authority waits to be approached by the client for diagnosis and treatment. In contrast, seeking mode interventionists actively search out potential clients.

The style of delivery that is adopted will have a number of professional role implications for the intervenor. It can influence or logically be determined by the setting, level, target population, timing, and goal of intervention. Thus, with regard to intervention setting, services offered in the waiting mode are usually located in the office of the professional or other "expert" who is offering the service. Seeking mode interventions will typically be made within the micro- and mesosystems (Bronfenbrenner, 1979) of potential clients. Thus, in an attempt to reach more clients, a college counselling service might move its location from, say, the student health centre to the students' union. However, this alone would be insufficient to reach all those who might benefit from its services. Potential clients would still have to define themselves as such and take the initiative in approaching the counsellor's office; it is still a waiting mode style of delivery. Bringing intervention into the classroom by, for example, including self-development programmes as an integral part of the college curriculum might provide one way of breaking out of the waiting mode straitjacket. In this way, individuals who would benefit from personal counselling might be identified or identify themselves. It is a way of seeking out clients.

The seeking mode style of delivery is particularly well suited to preventive interventions. In the reactive waiting mode the expert responds to requests for treatment or for prevention. The seeking mode has the potential for dealing with issues before they are forced on the expert's or, indeed, the client's attention. It can also attempt to reach those who, for whatever reason, do not approach services operating through the waiting mode style of delivery. As a consequence of this strategy of searching out clients, the intervenor might well be taking responsibility for defining the client population, whereas with the waiting mode the clients are generally self-defined. It is possible that some clients will reject their label. Moves to add fluoride to drinking water to reduce tooth decay in children represents an attempt at preventive intervention using a seeking mode style of delivery. The compulsory wearing of seatbelts in cars is another example. Such interventions can be seen as violations of individual freedom, and can be ridiculed as examples of the "nanny state" at work. Those resisting such interventions are, in effect, objecting to being defined as clients. Simply prescribing or selling fluoride tablets for those children whose parents ask for them would constitute preventive intervention using a waiting mode style of delivery.

Seeking mode interventions were described by Rappaport (1977) as indicative of a "new attitude" to the role of the professional. This attitude is largely concerned with crossing traditional professional boundaries and role definitions. Seeking mode interventions can be delivered by any number of persons, either professional or non-professional helpers. The traditional expert, rather than delivering the service directly is more likely to assume the role of consultant, programme initiator, and/or evaluator.

Intervention taxonomies

Particular positions on the intervention parameters discussed above will often lead to particular intervention strategies, and several taxonomies of such strategies have been proposed using one or more of the dimensions. The dimensions selected reflect the particular interests of researcher or practitioner involved. Thus Danish et al. (1980) propose a six-cell typology of interventions based, along one dimension, on the conceptual distinction between a disease and a developmental approach to life events, and, along the other, on the timing of the intervention in relation to the target life event. Box 8.6 gives examples of intervention approaches falling within each of the six cells. Caplan's (1964) alternatives of primary prevention, secondary prevention (that is, treatment), and tertiary prevention (termed remedial services by Danish et al.) constitute interventions based on a disease model of human functioning. Enhancement efforts, support groups, and counselling are seen as exemplifying a developmental approach.

Box 8.6 Typology of intervention approaches based on conceptual component and timing (Danish et al., 1980)

	Timing of intervention in relation to event		
Conceptual component of intervention	*Before*	*During*	*After*
Disease	Primary prevention	Secondary prevention	Remedial services
Developmental	Enhancement efforts	Support groups	Counselling

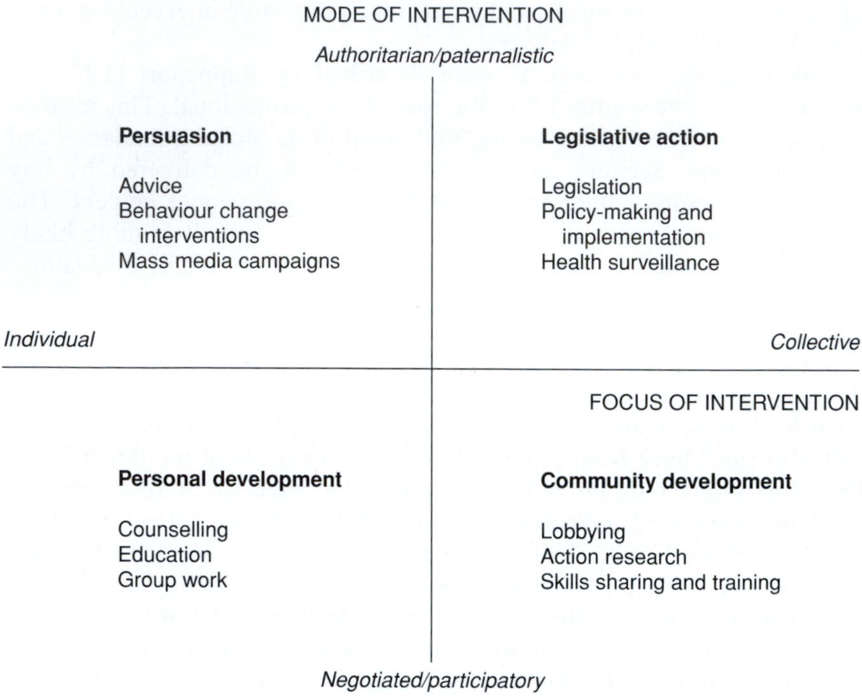

MODE OF INTERVENTION

Authoritarian/paternalistic

Persuasion	**Legislative action**
Advice Behaviour change interventions Mass media campaigns	Legislation Policy-making and implementation Health surveillance
Personal development	**Community development**
Counselling Education Group work	Lobbying Action research Skills sharing and training

Individual — *Collective*

FOCUS OF INTERVENTION

Negotiated/participatory

Figure 8.2 Four-fold grid of intervention strategies (reproduced with permission from Beattie, A. (1991). Knowledge and control in health promotion: A test case for social policy and social theory. In J. Gabe, M. Calan, & M. Bury (Eds.), *The Sociology of the health service*. London: Routledge).

In an alternative taxonomy (Figure 8.2), which was developed within the field of health promotion, Beattie (1991, 1995) proposed a four-fold typology of intervention strategies that distinguished, on the one hand, between authoritative and negotiated modes of intervention, and, on the other hand, between an intervention focus that is directed at the individual and one that is directed at the group or community level (called a collective focus by Beattie).

Choice of strategy is at least partly pragmatic, determined by what resources are available and when. However, it is also likely to reflect value-based decisions about the most appropriate way to define and address problems. In sum, interventions in life-span development can be described, compared, and contrasted with regard to a range of parameters and typologies such as those of Danish et al. (1980) and Beattie (1991) provide a clear framework for deciding on an intervention strategy.

A model of intervention practice

Interventions in keeping with the tenets of the life-span perspective endeavour to help people become more self-aware, more in control of their reactions to life, more empowered, and more able to use strategies that will get them where they want to go (Schlossberg et al., 1995). To achieve, this intervenors need to strive purposefully to stimulate conditions facilitating reflection and change. They are concerned with the processes of effective decision-making, problem management, and opportunity development – processes that have been investigated and developed in a wide range of specific situations.

A generalised model of problem management and opportunity development

One of the most fully developed discussions of a problem management approach to intervention is in the work of Gerard Egan (for example, 1993, 1998; Egan & Cowan, 1979). Most widely cited of Egan's work is the model of helping developed through the many editions of his book *The skilled helper* that have appeared over a period of more than 20 years. Egan sees the model as reflecting, "a natural process that plays itself out in any successful counselling, therapy, or other type of helping" (Sugarman, 1995, p. 276). The model can be used both reactively, in the handling of "problem situations", and proactively, in the development of opportunities. Because some problem situations will have to be adapted to rather than removed, Egan prefers to talk of "problem management" rather than "problem solving". He has also applied the model to the work setting (Egan, 1993), here presenting it as a systematic, unified model for initiating and managing change.

Egan argues (Sugarman, 1995) that this model is not his but merely the articulation of a "natural human process". Certainly it is a sequence that appears in a number of guises in a wide range of literatures. The emphasis given to particular phases can vary, as can the terminology used, but the basic dynamic is very similar. A generalised version of this model, adapted from Egan and Cowan's (1979) application of the model to community settings, is presented in Figure 8.3.

The core of the model rests on the proposition (Egan, 1998) that all comprehensive helping models help clients to address four fundamental and progressive issues, each of which can be divided into two steps:

- *Stage 1: Understanding the current scenario*. This involves addressing questions such as: "What is going on?", "What are the problems, issues, concerns, or undeveloped opportunities that I/we should be attending to?" It is a stage that can be subdivided into two steps: step 1a, exploration; step 1b, focusing.

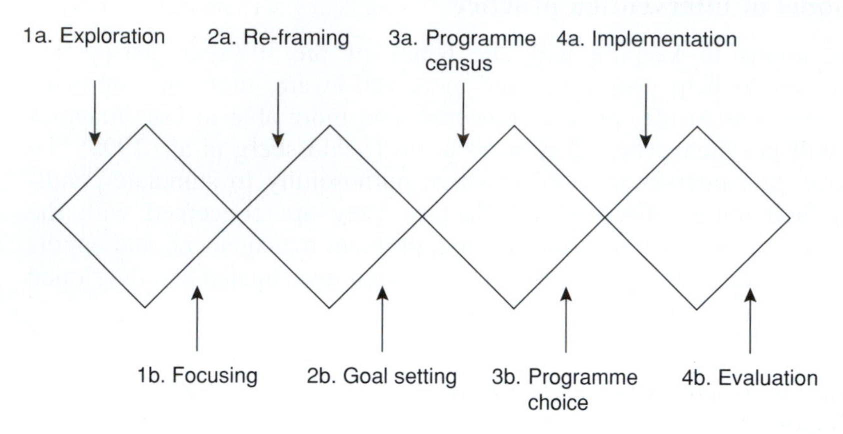

Figure 8.3 Steps in the process of problem management and opportunity development (reproduced with permission from Egan, G.E., & Cowan, M.A. (1979). *People in systems: A model for development in the human service professions and education*. Monterey, CA: Brooks/Cole).

- *Stage 2: Defining the preferred scenario*. Here the individual, group or community looks to the future and the ideal resolution: "What do I/we need or want in place of what is currently in place?" "What would things look like if they looked better?" This stage can be subdivided into the substages of: step 2a, re-framing; step 2b, goal-setting.
- *Stage 3: Developing a clear plan of action*. This stage is concerned with strategies: "What do I/we need to do to move from the current to the preferred scenario?" "What would be the best package of strategies?" Its two substages comprise: step 3a, programme census; step 3b, programme choice.
- *Stage 4: Implementing plan and evaluating progress*. This is the most active stage and addresses the question of, "How do I make this happen?" Its two steps are: step 4a, implementation; step 4b, evaluation.

A number of points about the model are worth particular note. First, the "diamonds" in Figure 8.2 reflect a characteristic of the model whereby the first step of each stage (that is, 1a, 2a, 3a, and 4a) is in one way or another a data collection step, and the second step of each stage (1b, 2b, 3b, and 4b) involves a process of decision making about this data. Thus, in stage 1 the first step is concerned with collecting data about the client's perception and understanding of the present situation, and the second step involves using this data to decide which part of the situation to focus on first. Similarly, in stage 4 the data collected in the first step concerns the experience of actually putting the plans into practice and the second step is concerned with deciding how effective this, and the whole sequence of earlier steps, has been.

Another key point is that, in two different ways, the model is cumulative. First, the stages are cumulative in that, generally speaking, later stages are successful only to the extent that earlier stages have also been addressed successfully. A frequent mistake in problem management and opportunity development is attempting to begin too far along the sequence, for example, taking the first course of action that occurs to us, without thinking of whether there may be more suitable alternatives or whether it really will address the issue we are concerned about. Second, the model is cumulative in the sense that the skills needed for each stage build on those needed for the previous stage. Thus the skills needed for achieving the goals of stage 2 include those needed to achieve the goals of stage 1, plus some more. The skills needed for stage 3 include those needed for stages 1 and 2, plus some more again. And so on.

This four-stage, diamond-shaped representation of the problem management and opportunity development (PM–OD) model was never incorporated into Egan's revisions of *The skilled helper*. Indeed, in the preface to the third edition, Egan (1986) expresses thanks to one of his graduate students for saving him from the temptation to do so, "by suggesting that I place evaluation at the centre of each stage". This is an important point – namely that evaluation should not merely be tagged on to the end of the process, but that there should be ongoing monitoring of progress, with regular reviewing and, if necessary, revision of objectives throughout. This is sometimes referred to as formative evaluation and is distinguished from summative evaluation, which is a final, overall assessment of what has been achieved. Step 4b in the four-stage, eight-step version of the model is primarily concerned with this summative evaluation and is an important component in the process of disengaging from the system. Its inclusion does not preclude ongoing formative evaluation but does risk obscuring its importance.

A risk in all step-wise presentations of sequences is that the processes can appear to be more linear and one-directional than is the case. The caveats that preceded the account of the model of transition dynamics (see Chapter 7) also apply here. Thus, there is no assumption that each step will be of equal significance or duration, nor that the individual, group, organisation, or community will pass smoothly from step 1a to step 4b. There is likely to be much back-tracking through earlier steps and blurring of the boundaries between different stages. Some steps might require disproportionate amounts of time, effort, and resources. Others might be far less demanding.

Although the PM–OD model is complex, it is built on simple principles: each individual's right to be different, the need for helpers to "earn the right" to help, and the need for clients to "own" their own problems and not be allowed to hand them to the helper who then takes responsibility for solving them. It is a joint problem-management model and requires the helper to understand the problem situation fully, and then help the client see the problem as objectively as possible, so that reasonable goals can be set to improve the situation. This may be enough, but the model goes on to build ways of helping clients to achieve their goals and to continue to build their self-confidence. The model is essentially a tool – it is not a prescription. It is built on the early stages and stage 1, which emphasises relationship-building skills in particular, is instrumental in earning the helper the right to help.

Applications of the PM–OD model

As described above, the PM–OD model is most readily applicable to one-to-one helping relationships. However, its sequence of stages can also be used by groups, organisations and communities to address a wide range of problem situations, and by individuals working alone on self-directed change.

The model has, for example, been applied to the facilitation of effective managerial problem solving (Francis, 1990), where it is presented under the acronym TOSIDPAR: Tuning in, Objective setting, Success measures, Information collection, Decision making, Planning, Action planning, Review to improve. A similar version appears in Woodcock and Francis (1993), where "inadequate problem solving skills" is identified as one of several blockages that can undermine managerial effectiveness.

An application of the PM–OD model to individual decision making in regard to career choice and change is discussed in more detail in the next section. This issue was selected in view of its important role within the process of life-span development

The PM–OD model in a self-help guide to career choice and change

Ball (1989) wrote his book, *Manage your own career*, for people of all ages who are thinking about their future employment. It is intended that readers work through the book on their own, although they are encouraged to seek constructive feedback from people around them, "family, friends and other people in and out of the workplace" (Ball, 1989, p. 1). They are encouraged, therefore, to implement the tenet of life-span developmental psychology to understand the self in context – in this instance at Bronfenbrenner's (1979) mesosystem level – and to utilise resources of the natural help system (Golan, 1981). Career planning is presented as a systematic process of preparing for one's next job move or career change. Specifically, career planning is described as implying three types of activity:

- Reviewing past experience of education, work and life events to identify what has been learned and achieved to date, and the people and events that have influenced the person's life.

- Understanding the present situation, current interests, skills, and values, and awareness of what it would be advantageous and desirable to change.
- Implementing ideas, setting goals for the future, and achieving the kind of change identified as desirable.

These activities demand that the reader becomes, sequentially, a designer, an explorer, a researcher, and a promoter – roles that will take the person through each stage of the generic model of opportunity development and problem management.

As a designer, the person is concerned with preparing, through the use of personal reflection and self-assessment questionnaires, a personal and career profile, that is, "a list of your qualities, your needs and the kind of things you would like to find in your work" (Ball, 1989, p. 23).

As an explorer, the person finds out about possible options: "Are you looking for a course of study/training or an immediate job?", "Which career options are possible?" "Which companies and organizations are recruiting?" (Ball, 1989, p. 24). It is specifically recommended that the person at this stage taps into his or her "social support convoy", to use Kahn and Antonucci's (1980) term, or what Ball refers to as the "grapevine".

Whereas as an explorer the person is concerned with generating a list of appropriate options, being a researcher involves investigating these possibilities in more detail. This includes not only the collection of information, but also decision making and evaluation skills. It can be thought of as a "mini-cycle" through all of the stages of the PM–OD model.

After this comes the promoter stage. Concerned with self-marketing, this involves making applications, meeting potential employers, and approaching training agencies or course centres.

It is assumed that, ideally, the promoter stage will result in an attractive job offer. Ball, warns, however, against seeing this as the end of the process. Implicitly he communicates the idea of the life course as involving regular re-evaluation:

> It is perhaps tempting to see the job offer as an end point in the career planning process and to view the prospect of a new job as a chance to relax and freewheel. . . . But even if you have been successful at starting out on your chosen career, returning to work after a break, or negotiating a career change, it is important to keep your career planning skills in play to watch that you are heading in a direction that is right for *you*. You will need to keep reviewing your goals. . . . The skills of self appraisal, researching opportunities for personal and career development and of marketing yourself can be brought into play time and again. They need to be rehearsed continually. In particular your career plan will require continual revision and updating, to encompass unforeseen events and situations. Career

planning thus becomes an ongoing, lifelong process, of which *you* are in control.

(Ball, 1989, p. 94, emphasis in original)

Planned change: a means to an end, not an end in itself

Systematic opportunity development and problem management does not necessitate the expunging of all that is spontaneous and creative. Thus, Bracht and Kingsbury (1990; Bracht, Kingsbury, & Rissel, 1999) emphasise that whilst they present a model of systematic, or planned, community change, they also "recognise the importance of grass-roots citizen responses to community issues" (Bracht & Kingsbury, 1990, p. 69). Similarly, Ball (1989, p. 1) points out on the opening page of his self-help guide that career planning, "is not, as it might seem, a way of planning away the next 35 years of your life, but quite simply a way of preparing for your next job move or career change".

Also, the model needs to be construed flexibly, not rigidly. The boundaries between stages are not watertight. People move backwards and forwards between stages, giving very variable amounts of attention to each of the key elements. Furthermore, clients may "dip in and out" of counselling, needing help with some stages in the PM–OD process, but not all.

Development of life skills

It has been emphasised how intervention in life-span development is concerned with promoting, facilitating, or preventing change. As was discussed in Chapter 1, however, change and development cannot necessarily be viewed as synonymous. It is possible, for example, for a person to change in ways that inhibit or prevent development. For change to be considered developmental there needs to be a movement towards a greater realisation of personal potential – a process involving the acquisition of new skills, the furtherance of self-awareness and the clarification of one's values (Hopson & Scally, 1980a). This operational definition of development is based on the notion of self-empowerment, namely, becoming, "more proactive, less dependent upon others, valuing the integrity of others as well as themselves, (and) more in charge of themselves and their lives" (Hopson & Scally, 1980a, p. 183).

In an approach similar to Schlossberg et al.'s (1995) identification of strategies for managing transitions (see Chapter 6), Hopson and Scally (1981) identify a range of teachable "life skills" that they see as necessary, although not sufficient, mechanisms of self-empowerment. Whilst recognising that any learning can potentially facilitate self-empowerment, Hopson and Scally have attempted to define those skills whose acquisition is most crucial. These skills, detailed in Figure 8.4, can be divided into four areas:

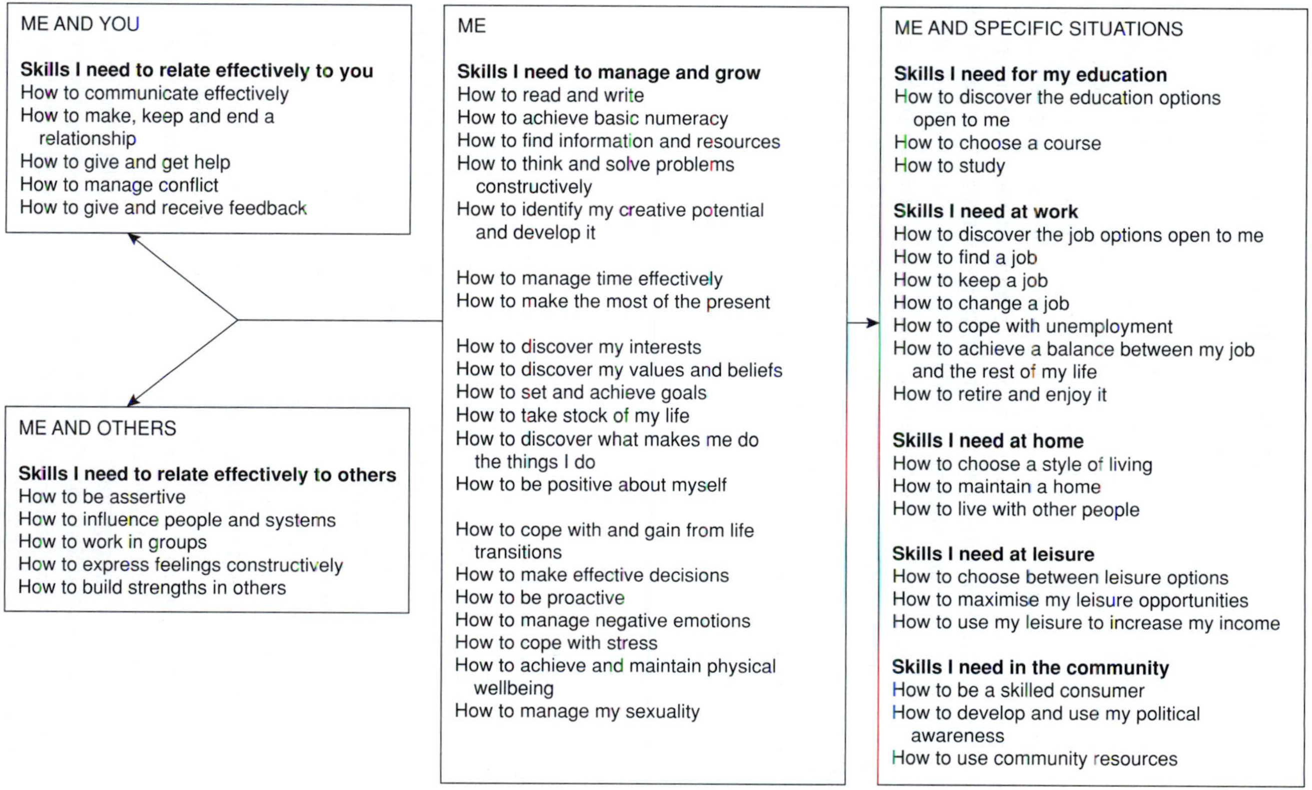

ME AND YOU

Skills I need to relate effectively to you
How to communicate effectively
How to make, keep and end a relationship
How to give and get help
How to manage conflict
How to give and receive feedback

ME AND OTHERS

Skills I need to relate effectively to others
How to be assertive
How to influence people and systems
How to work in groups
How to express feelings constructively
How to build strengths in others

ME

Skills I need to manage and grow
How to read and write
How to achieve basic numeracy
How to find information and resources
How to think and solve problems constructively
How to identify my creative potential and develop it

How to manage time effectively
How to make the most of the present

How to discover my interests
How to discover my values and beliefs
How to set and achieve goals
How to take stock of my life
How to discover what makes me do the things I do
How to be positive about myself

How to cope with and gain from life transitions
How to make effective decisions
How to be proactive
How to manage negative emotions
How to cope with stress
How to achieve and maintain physical wellbeing
How to manage my sexuality

ME AND SPECIFIC SITUATIONS

Skills I need for my education
How to discover the education options open to me
How to choose a course
How to study

Skills I need at work
How to discover the job options open to me
How to find a job
How to keep a job
How to change a job
How to cope with unemployment
How to achieve a balance between my job and the rest of my life
How to retire and enjoy it

Skills I need at home
How to choose a style of living
How to maintain a home
How to live with other people

Skills I need at leisure
How to choose between leisure options
How to maximise my leisure opportunities
How to use my leisure to increase my income

Skills I need in the community
How to be a skilled consumer
How to develop and use my political awareness
How to use community resources

Figure 8.4 Basic life skills (reproduced with permission from Hopson, B., & Scally, M. (1981). *Lifeskills teaching programme*. London: McGraw-Hill).

- *"Me" skills* – skills needed to survive and grow generally.
- *"Me and you" skills* – skills needed to relate effectively within one-to-one personal relationships.
- *"Me and others" skills* – skills needed to relate effectively to others within society.
- *"Me and specific situations" skills* – skills needed to operate effectively in particular microsystems.

Hopson and Scally (1981) discuss how the skills in their chart can be introduced and taught in schools and colleges, and have published a range of materials designed for teaching (and learning) a selection of these skills (Hopson & Scally, 1980b, 1982, 1985). In a similar vein, McCoy (1977) sought to identify educational programmes that would promote the achievement of the developmental tasks characterising each of the life stages of adulthood. Her suggested programmes for the post-retirement years, with their desired outcomes, are shown in Table 8.2. It is worth noting that she includes the final two developmental tasks – problem solving and managing the stress accompanying change – in her list of tasks for all life stages, thereby incorporating a cyclical as well as a linear model of development. At the more general level, Featherman et al. (1990) propose that successful ageing, defined as adaptive competence, can be increased by "learning to plan" – particularly in later years when, they suggest, an increasing proportion of developmental tasks become ill-defined. "Learning to plan" can, in turn, be conceptualised in terms of Kolb's experiential learning cycle, discussed earlier in this chapter.

Finale

Each chapter in this book considers aspects of life-span development in a somewhat different way. Chapter 1 provided an introduction and overview of some of the key concepts and issues that have exercised the minds of those interested in the topic. Chapter 2 reviewed some key methodological options and their assumptive base and implications. Chapter 3 reviewed, first, the cross-sectional (or age/life stage) approach to the life span, and then the longitudinal approach, with its range of meta-models for describing the life course. Chapters 4 to 7 considered different ways of construing the life course – as a cumulative sequence, as a series of developmental tasks, as organised around key life events and transitions, and as a process of narrative construction designed largely to create a sense of dynamic continuity. Chapter 8 considered intervention – conceptual parameters, technical parameters, and aspects of practice.

As we reach the final paragraphs of this book, it seems fitting to invoke the cyclical or spiral model of development and return to where the book started by inviting you to think back to the tenets of the life-span perspective summarised in Chapter 1 and to the lifeline you were invited to

Table 8.2 Developmental tasks, programme responses and desired outcomes for the post-retirement years (adapted from McCoy, 1977)

Tasks	*Programme responses*	*Desired outcomes*
1. Disengage from paid work 2. Search for new achievement outlets 3. Manage leisure time 4. Adjust to more constant marriage companion	1, 2, 3, 4. Workshops on retirement, volunteering, ageing; conferences on public issues affecting older people	1, 2, 3, 4. Creative, active retirement; successful coping; coping with role disengagement; public policies responsive to the needs of older people
5. Reassess finances	5. Financial management training	5. Freedom from financial fears
6. Be concerned with personal health care	6. Health care programmes	6. Appropriate health care
7. Search for meaning	7. Religious/spiritual exploration	7. Help in search for life's meaning, values of past life
8. Adjust to single state	8. Aloneness and loneliness workshops	8. Fulfilled single state
9. Be reconciled to death	9. Death and dying workshops	9. Philosophical acceptance of death, help in caring for the dying and handling of grief
10. Problem-solve	10. Creative problem-solving workshops	10. Successful problem solving
11. Manage stress accompanying change	11. Stress management, biofeedback, relaxation, meditation workshops	11. Successful stress management, personal growth

complete. To the questions asked in Box 1.1 can be added several that are relevant to the subject matter of the present chapter. For example:

- What sources of help were offered or sought at various points in your life course?
- What sources of help do you draw on habitually?
- On the basis of what assumptions was help proffered or accepted?
- How did this influence its effectiveness?
- For which particular aspects of the process of change do you most need assistance?

Those who seek consciously to "compose their own life" (Bateson, 1990) still need to obey the laws of the phases or sequences of development. As one author put it, "It is no good wanting to 'flower' before one has formed enough 'leaves', and leaf-formation is not a particularly spectacular activity!" (Lievegoed, 1979, p. 227). None the less, it is also important to avoid being unnecessarily constrained by the dictates of particular life stages, and to adopt a questioning approach to unspoken assumptions about the appropriateness and immutability of age-related and/or life-stage-related norms. Bee (1994) concluded that life satisfaction is predicted by essentially the same factors at every age – adequate social support, a sense of control, a low incidence of off-time or unplanned changes, and adequate financial conditions.

Despite the existence of both phases and themes, there remains an abundance of possibilities and life paths for the individual to create and follow. Making choices between different options will be inevitable, and preferably is carried out on the basis of sound knowledge and insight. This is where the parameters and practices of intervention come into the picture.

Rice (1995, p. 6) wrote, "*The goal of life-span developmental psychology is to help us live meaningful, productive lives.* The more we can learn about how and why we grow and change, and the more control we can have over the process, the more positive influences we can exert on the lives of our children, our adolescents and ourselves. Thus, the personal goal of the study of life-span development is *self-assessment* for the purpose of *self-improvement*, and *self-enhancement*" (emphasis in original). However, life-span development is not only about changes. It is also about continuities and stabilities. Creating and maintaining our stability zones (Toffler, 1970) or anchors (Schein, 1993) helps to provide the bases from which we can, whatever our life stage, move purposefully towards living in more self-empowered ways.

References

Allport, G.W. (1964). *Pattern and growth in personality*. New York: Holt, Reinhart and Winston.

Alonzo, A. (1979). Everyday illness behavior: A situational approach to health status deviations. *Social Science and Medicine*, *13*, 397–404.

American Psychological Association (1990). *Ethical principles in the conduct of research with human participants*. Washington, DC: American Psychological Association.

Angyal, A. (1941). *Foundations for a science of personality*. New York: Commonwealth Fund.

Antonucci, T.C. (1991). Attachment, social support, and coping with negative life events in mature adulthood. In E.M. Cummings, A.L. Greene, & K.H. Kramer (Eds.), *Life-span developmental psychology: Perspectives on stress and coping* Hillsdale, NJ: Lawrence Erlbaum.

Antonucci, T.C., & Depner, C.E. (1982). Social support and informal helping relationships. In T.A. Willis (Ed.), *Basic processes in helping relationships*. New York: Academic Press.

Arlin, P.K. (1975). Cognitive development in adulthood: A fifth stage? *Developmental Psychology*, *11*, 602–606.

Arlin, P.K. (1977). Piagetian operations in problem finding. *Developmental Psychology*, *13*, 297–298.

Arlin, P.K. (1989). Problem solving and problem finding in young artists and young scientists. In M.L. Commons, J.D. Sinnott, F.A. Richards, & C. Armon (Eds.), *Adult development: Vol. 1: Comparison and applications of developmental models*. New York: Praeger.

Arnold, J., & Jackson, C. (1997). The new career: Issues and challenges. *British Journal of Guidance and Counselling*, *25*(4), 427–433.

Arthur, M.B. (1994). The boundaryless career: A new perspective for organizational inquiry. *Journal of Organizational Behavior*, *15*, 295–306.

Assagioli, R. (1986). Self-realisation and psychological disturbance. *Revision*, *8*, 121–131.

Atchley, R.C. (1971). Retirement and leisure participation. *The Gerontologist*, *11*, 13–17.

Atchley, R.C. (1989). A continuity theory of normal aging. *The Gerontologist*, *29*, 183–190.

Atchley, R.C. (1999). *Continuity and adaptation in aging*. Baltimore, MD: Johns Hopkins University Press.

Baer, D.M. (1970). An age irrelevant concept of development. *Merrill Palmer Quarterly*, *16*, 230–245.

Bakan, D. (1966). *The duality of human existence: Isolation and communion in Western man*. Boston: Beacon Press.

Ball, B. (1989). *Manage your own career: A self-help guide to career choice and change*. London: Kogan Page and the British Psychological Society.

Baltes, P.B. (1968). Longitudinal and cross-sectional sequences in the study of age and generation effect. *Human Development*, *11*, 145–171.

Baltes, P.B. (1973). Strategies for psychological intervention in old age: A symposium. *The Gerontologist*, *13*, 4–38.

Baltes, P.B. (1979). Life-span developmental psychology: Some converging observations on history and theory. In P.B. Baltes & O.G. Brim (Eds.), *Life-span development and behavior* (Vol. 2). New York: Academic Press.

Baltes, P.B. (1987). Theoretical propositions of life-span developmental psychology. *Developmental Psychology*, *23*, 611–626.

Baltes, P.B. (1993). The aging mind: Potential and limits. *The Gerontologist*, *33*, 580–594.

Baltes, P.B., & Baltes, M.M. (1980). Plasticity and variability in psychological aging: Methodological and theoretical issues. In G.E. Gurski (Ed.), *Determining the effects of aging on the central nervous system*. Berlin: Schering.

Baltes, P.B., & Baltes, M.M. (1990). Psychological perspectives on successful aging: The model of selective optimization with compensation. In P.B. Baltes & M.M. Baltes (Eds.), *Successful aging: Perspectives from the behavioral sciences*. Hillsdale, NJ: Lawrence Erlbaum.

Baltes, P.B., Reese, H.W., & Lipsitt, L.P. (1980). Life-span developmental psychology. *Annual Review of Psychology*, *31*, 65–110.

Barak, B., & Schiffman, L.G. (1981). Cognitive age: A nonchronological age variable. In K.B. Monroe (Ed.), *Advances in consumer research* (Vol. 8). Ann Arbor: Association for Consumer Research.

Barrera, M., Rosen, G.M., & Glasgow, R.E. (1981). Rights, risks, and responsibilities in the use of self-help psychotherapy. In J.T. Hannah, R. Clark, & P. Christian (Eds.), *Preservation of client rights*. New York: Free Press.

Basseches, M. (1984). *Dialectical thinking and adult development*. Norwood, NJ: Ablex.

Bateson, M.C. (1990). *Composing a life*. New York: Plenum.

Beattie, A. (1991). Knowledge and control in health promotion: A test case for social policy and social theory. In J. Gabe, M. Calnan, & M. Bury (Eds.), *The sociology of the health service* (pp. 162–201). London: Routledge.

Beattie, A. (1995). The health promoting campus: A case study in project-based learning and competency profiling. In A. Edwards & P. Knight (Eds.), *Degrees of competence: The assessment of competence in higher education*. London: Kogan Page.

Bee, H. (1994). *Lifespan development*. New York: HarperCollins.

Bee, H.L., & Mitchell, S.K. (1984). *The developing person: A life-span approach* (2nd ed.). San Francisco, CA: Harper and Row.

Berger, K.S. (1994). *The developing person throughout the life span*. New York: Worth.

Berne, E. (1975). *What do you say after you say hello? The psychology of human destiny*. London: Corgi.

Biggs, S. (1998). *The mature imagination: Self and identity in midlife and beyond*. Buckingham: Open University Press.

Bijou, S.W. (1968). Ages, stages, and the naturalization of human development. *American Psychologist*, *23*, 419–427.

Birren, J.E., & Renner, J.V. (1977). Research on the psychology of aging: Principles and experimentation. In J.E. Birren & K.W. Schaie (Eds.), *Handbook of the psychology of aging*. New York: Van Nostrand Reinhold.

Blieszner, R., & Adams, R.G. (1992). *Adult friendship*. Newbury Park, CA: Sage.

Block, J., & Haan, N. (1971). *Lives through time*. Berkeley, CA: Bancroft Books.

Bond, J., Briggs, R., & Coleman, P. (1993). The study of ageing. In J. Bond, P. Coleman, & S. Peace (Eds.), *Ageing in society – an introduction to social gerontology* (2nd ed.). London: Sage.

Booth, W. (1983). *The rhetoric of fiction*. Chicago, IL: University of Chicago Press.

Borman, L. (1982). *Helping people to help themselves: Self-help and prevention*. New York: Haworth.

Bracht, N., & Kingsbury, L. (1990). Community organization principles in health promotion: A five stage model. In N. Bracht (Ed.), *Health promotion at the community level*. London: Sage.

Bracht, N., Kingsbury, L., & Rissel, C. (1999). A five-stage community organization model for health promotion. In N. Bracht (Ed.), *Health promotion at the community level 2: New advances*. London: Sage.

Brainerd, C.J. (1978). The stage question in cognitive–developmental theory. *Behavioral and Brain Science*, *1*, 173–182.

Brammer, L.M., & Abrego, P.J. (1981). Intervention strategies for coping with transitions. *Counseling Psychologist*, *9*, 19–36.

Breakwell, G.M. (1995). Interviewing. In G.M. Breakwell, S. Hammond, & C. Fife-Schaw (Eds.), *Research methods in psychology*. London: Sage.

Brewin, C.R., Andrews, B., & Gotlib, I.H. (1993). Psychopathology and early experience. *Psychological Bulletin*, *113*, 82–98.

Brickman, P., Rabinowitz, V.C., Karuza, J., Coates, D., Cohn, E., & Kidder, L. (1982). Models of helping and coping. *American Psychologist*, *37*, 368–384.

Bridges, W. (1980). *Transitions: Making sense of life's changes*. New York: Addison-Wesley.

Brim, O. (1975). Macro-structural influences on child development and the need for childhood social indicators. *American Journal of Orthopsychiatry*, *45*, 516–524.

Brim, O.G., & Ryff, C.D. (1980). On the properties of life events. In P.B. Baltes & O.G. Brim (Eds.), *Life-span development and behavior* (Vol. 3). New York: Academic Press.

British Psychological Society (1998). *Code of conduct, ethical principles and guidelines*. Leicester: British Psychological Society.

Bronfenbrenner, U. (1977). Toward an experimental ecology of human development. *American Psychologist*, *32*, 513–531.

Bronfenbrenner, U. (1979). *The ecology of human development*. Cambridge, MA: Harvard University Press.

Bronfenbrenner, U. (1986). Ecology of the family as a context for human development: Research perspectives. *Developmental Psychology*, *22*, 723–742.

Bronfenbrenner, U. (1992). Ecological systems theory. In R. Vasta (Ed.), *Six theories of child development: Revised formulations and current issues*. London: Jessica Kingsley.

Bronfenbrenner, U., & Crouter, A. (1983). The evolution of environmental methods in developmental research. In E. Kessen (Ed.), *Handbook of child psychology: Vol. 1. History, theory and methods* (4th ed.). New York: Wiley.

Brown, B.B. (1990). Peer groups and peer cultures. In S.S. Feldman & G.R. Elliott (Eds.), *At the threshold: The developing adolescent*. Cambridge, MA: Harvard University Press.

Brown, B.B., Mory, M.S., & Kinney, D. (1994). Casting adolescent crowds in relational perspective: Caricature, channel, and context. In R. Montmayor, G.R. Adams, & T.P. Gulotta (Eds.), *Personal relationships during adolescence*. Thousand Oaks, CA: Sage.

Brown, J.M., O'Keefe, J., Sanders, S.H., & Baker, B. (1986). Developmental changes in children's cognitions to stressful and painful situations. *Journal of Paediatric Psychology*, *11*, 343–357.

Bruner, J.S. (1990). *Acts of meaning*. Cambridge, MA: Harvard University Press.

Bruner, J.S. (1991). The narrative construction of reality. *Critical Inquiry*, *18*, 1–21.

Bühler, C. (1933). *Der Menschliche Lebenslauf als Psychologisches Problem*. Leipzig: Hirzel.

Bühler, C., & Massarik, F. (Eds.). (1968). *The course of human life: A study of goals in the humanistic perspective*. New York: Springer.

Buss, A.R. (1979). Dialectics, history and development: The historical roots of the individual-society dialectic. In P.B. Baltes & O.G. Brim (Eds.), *Life-span development and behavior* (Vol. 2). New York: Academic Press.

Butler, R.N. (1987). Ageism. In *The encyclopedia of aging*. New York: Springer.

Butler, R.N., & Lewis, M.I. (1973). *Aging and mental health*. St Louis, MO: Mosby.

Bytheway, B. (1995). *Ageism*. Buckingham: Open University Press.

Campbell, D. (1974). *If you don't know where you're going, you'll probably end up somewhere else*. Niles, IL: Argus Communications.

Caplan, G. (1964). *Principles of preventive psychiatry*. New York: Basic Books.

Caplan, G. (1974). Support systems. In G. Caplan (Ed.), *Support systems and community mental health*. New York: Behavioral Publications.

Caspi, A., Bem, D.J. & Elder, G.H. (1989). Continuities and consequences of interactional styles across the life course. *Journal of Personality*, *57*, 375–406.

Chaplin, J. (1988). Feminist therapy. In J. Rowan & W. Dryden (Eds.), *Innovative therapy in Britain*. Buckingham: Open University Press.

Chickering, A.W., & Havighurst, R.J. (1981). The life cycle. In A. Chickering & associates (Eds.), *The modern American college: Responding to the new realities of diverse students and a changing society*. San Francisco, CA: Jossey-Bass.

Chiriboga, D.A. (1989). Mental health at the midpoint: Crisis, challenge, or relief? In S. Hunter & M. Sundel (Eds.), *Midlife myths: Issues, findings and practice implications*. Newbury Park, CA: Sage.

Chodrow, N. (1978). *The reproduction of mothering*. Los Angeles, CA: University of California Press.

Clausen, J.A. (1993). *American lives: Looking back at the children of the great depression*. New York: Free Press.

Cochran, L. (1997). *Career counselling: A narrative approach*. Thousand Oaks, CA: Sage.

Cohler, B.J. (1982). Personal narrative and the life course. In P.B. Baltes & O.G. Brim (Eds.), *Life-span development and behavior* (Vol. 4). New York: Academic Press.

Colby, A., & Kohlberg, L. (1984). Invariance sequence and internal consistency in moral judgement stages. In W.M. Kertines & J.L. Gewirtz (Eds.), *Morality, moral behaviour, and moral development*. New York: John Wiley.

Commons, M.L., Sinnott, J.D., Richards, F.A., & Armon, C. (Eds.). (1989). *Adult development: Vol. 1. Comparison and applications of developmental models*. New York: Praeger.

Compas, B.E., Hinden, B.R., & Gerhardt, C.A. (1995). Adolescent development: Pathways and processes of risk and resilience. *Annual Review of Psychology, 46*, 265–293.

Costa, P.T., & McCrae, R.R. (1997). Longitudinal stability of adult personality. In R. Hogan, J. Johnson, & S. Briggs (Eds.), *Handbook of Personality Psychology*. New York: Academic Press.

Cowen, E.L. (1982). Help is where you find it: Four informal helping groups. *American Psychologist, 37*, 385–395.

Crawford, M. (1971). Retirement and disengagement. *Human Relations, 24*, 255–278.

Crawford, M. (1972). Retirement and role playing. *Sociology, 6*, 217–236.

Cumming, E. (1975). Engagement with an old theory. *International Journal of Aging and Human Development, 6*, 187–191.

Cumming, E., & Henry, W. (1961). *Growing old: The process of disengagement*. New York: Basic Books.

Dalton, G.W., Thompson, P.H., & Price, R. (1977). The four stages of professional careers. *Organisational Dynamics* (Summer), 19–42.

Dan, A.J., & Bernhard, L.A. (1989). Menopause and other health issues for midlife women. In S. Hunter & M. Sundel (Eds.), *Midlife myths: Issues, findings and practice implications*. Newbury Park, CA: Sage.

Danish, S.J., Smyer, M.A., & Nowak, C. (1980). Developmental intervention: enhancing life-event processes. In P.B. Baltes & O.G. Brim (Eds.), *Life-span development and behavior* (Vol. 3). New York: Academic Press.

Datan, N. (1983). Normative or not? Confessions of a fallen epistemologist. In E.J. Callahan & K.A. McKluskey (Eds.), *Life-span developmental psychology: Non-normative life crises*. New York: Academic Press.

Datan, N., Rodeaver, D., & Hughes, F. (1987). Adult development and aging. *Annual Review of Psychology, 38*, 153–180.

Denzin, N.K. (1978). *Sociological methods*. New York: McGraw-Hill.

Denzin, N.K., & Lincoln, Y.S. (Eds.). (1994). *The handbook of qualitative research*. Thousand Oaks, CA: Sage.

DePoy, E., & Gitlin, L.N. (1998). *Introduction to research: Understanding and applying multiple strategies* (2nd ed.). St Louis, MO: Mosby.

Dreyer, P.H. (1989). Postretirement life satisfaction. In S. Spacapan & S. Oskamp (Eds.), *The social psychology of aging*. Newbury Park, CA: Sage.

Dunphy, D.C. (1963). The social structure of urban adolescent peer groups. *Sociometry, 26*, 230–246.

Egan, G. (1986). *The skilled helper: A systematic approach to effective helping* (3rd ed.). Monterey, CA: Brooks/Cole.

Egan, G. (1993). *Adding value: A systematic guide to business-driven management and leadership*. Monterey, CA: Brooks/Cole.

Egan, G. (1998). *The skilled helper: A problem-management approach to helping* (6th ed.). Pacific Grove, CA: Brooks/Cole.

Egan, G.E., & Cowan, M.A. (1979). *People in systems: A model for development in the human-service professions and education*. Monterey, CA: Brooks/Cole.

Elkind, D. (1967). Egocentrism in adolescence. *Child Development*, *38*, 1025–1034.

Elkind, D., & Bowen, R. (1979). Imaginary audience behavior in children and adolescents. *Developmental Psychology*, *15*, 38–44.

Elsbree, L. (1982). *The rituals of life: Patterns in narrative*. New York: Kennikat.

Erikson, E.H. (1950). *Childhood and society*. New York: Norton.

Erikson, E.H. (1959). Identity and the life cycle. *Psychological Issues*, *1*(1), 1–171.

Erikson, E.H. (1963). Childhood and society (revised ed.). Harmondsworth: Penguin.

Erikson, E.H. (1980). *Identity and the life cycle: A reissue*. New York: Norton.

Estes, C.P. (1993). *Women who run with wolves: Contacting the power of the wild woman*. London: Rider.

Featherman, D.L., Smith, J., & Peterson, J.G. (1990). Successful aging in a post-retired society. In P. Baltes & M.M. Baltes (Eds.), *Successful aging: Perspectives from the behavioral sciences*. Hillsdale, NJ: Lawrence Erlbaum.

Fife-Schaw, C. (1995). Questionnaire design. In G.M. Breakwell, S. Hammond, & C. Fife-Schaw (Eds.), *Research methods in psychology*. London: Sage.

Fiske, M., & Chiriboga, D.A. (1990). *Change and continuity in adult life*. San Francisco, CA: Jossey-Bass.

Folkman, S., Lazarus, R.S., Pimley, S., & Novacek, J. (1987). Age differences in stress and coping processes. *Psychology and Aging*, *2*, 171–184.

Ford, D.H., & Lerner, R.M. (1992). *Developmental systems theory: An integrative approach*. Newbury Park, CA: Sage.

Fowler, J.W. (1981). *Stages of faith*. San Francisco, CA: Harper and Row.

Francis, D. (1990). *Effective problem solving: A structured approach*. London: Routledge.

Fry, C.L. (1976). The ages of adulthood: A question of numbers. *Journal of Gerontology*, *31*, 170–177.

Frye, N. (1957). *Anatomy of criticism*. Princeton, NJ: Princeton University Press.

Fulton, B.J. (1990). Coping and social support in older people's experience of chronic illness. In M.A.P. Stevens, J.H. Crowther, S.E. Hobfell, & T.L. Tannenbaum (Eds.), *Stress and coping in later-life families*. New York: Hemisphere.

Geertz, C. (1973). Thick description: Toward an interpretative theory of culture. In C. Geertz (Ed.), *The interpretation of culture*. New York: Basic Books.

Gergen, K.J. (1977). Stability, change and chance in understanding human development. In N. Datan & H.W. Reese (Eds.), *Life-span developmental psychology: Dialectical perspectives on experimental research*. New York: Academic Press.

Gergen, K.J., & Gergen, M.M. (1988). Narrative and the self as relationship. *Advances in Experimental Social Psychology*, *21*, 17–56.

Gergen, M.M. (1988). Narrative structures in social explanation. In C. Antaki (Ed.), *Analysing everyday explanation: A casebook of methods*. London: Sage.

Gilligan, C. (1982). *In a different voice: Psychological theory and women's development*. Cambridge, MA: Harvard University Press.

Gilligan, C., & Attanucci, J. (1988). Two moral considerations: Gender differences and similarities. *Merrill-Palmer Quarterly*, *34*, 223–237.

Golan, N. (1981). *Passing through transitions: A guide for practitioners*. New York: Free Press.

Goldberg, D., & Huxley, P. (1980). *Mental illness in the community: The pathway to psychiatric care*. London: Tavistock.

Goldstein, K. (1940). *Human nature in the light of psychotherapy*. Cambridge, MA: Harvard University Press.

Gooden, W.E. (1989). Development of Black men in early adulthood. In R.L. Jones (Ed.), *Black adult development and aging*. Berkeley, CA: Cobb and Henry.

Gottleib, B.H. (1976). Lay influences on the utilization and provision of health services: A review. *Canadian Psychological Review*, *17*, 126–136.

Gottlieb, B.H. (1983). *Social support strategies: Guidelines for mental health practice*. Beverly Hills, CA: Sage.

Gottlieb, G.H. (1988). Support interventions: A typology and agenda for research. In S. Duck (Ed.), *Handbook of personal relationships*. Chichester: Wiley.

Gould, R.L. (1978). *Transformations: Growth and change in adult life*. New York: Simon and Schuster.

Gould, R.L. (1980). Transformational tasks in adulthood. In S.I. Greenspan & G.H. Pollock (Eds.), *The course of life: Psychoanalytic contributions toward understanding personality development: Vol. 3. Adulthood and the aging process*. Washington, DC: National Institute for Mental Health.

Gross, R. (1996). *Psychology: The science of mind and behaviour* (3rd ed.). London: Hodder and Stoughton.

Guba, E.G. (1981). Criteria for assessing the trustworthiness of naturalistic inquiries. *Educational Communication and Technology Journal*, *29*, 75–92.

Guba, E.G., & Lincoln, Y.S. (1989). *Fourth generation evaluation*. Newbury Park, CA: Sage.

Gurin, G., Veroff, J., & Feld, S. (1960). *Americans view their mental health: A nationwide interview survey*. New York: Basic Books.

Gustafson, J.P. (1992). *Self-delight in a harsh world: The main stories of individual, marital and family psychotherapy*. New York: Norton.

Haan, N. (1972). Personality development from adolescence to adulthood in the Oakland Growth and Guidance Studies. *Seminars in Psychiatry*, *4*, 399–414.

Hammond, S. (1995). Using psychometric tests. In G.M. Breakwell, S. Hammond, & C. Fife-Schaw (Eds.), *Research methods in psychology*. London: Sage.

Hancock, T., & Perkins, F. (1985). The mandala of health: A conceptual model and teaching tool. *Health Promotion*, *10*, 8–10.

Handy, C. (1989). *The age of unreason*. London: Arrow.

Harris, R.L., Ellicott, A.M., & Holmes, D.S. (1986). The timing of psychosocial transitions and changes in women's lives: An examination of women aged 45 to 60. *Journal of Personality and Social Psychology*, *51*, 409–416.

Harrison, R. (1976). The demoralising experience of prolonged unemployment. *Department of Employment Gazette*, (April), 1–10.

Havighurst, R.J. (1953). *Human development and education*. New York: Longmans.

Havighurst, R.J. (1956). Research on the developmental task concept. *School Review*, *64*, 215–223.

Havighurst, R.J. (1963). Successful aging. In R. Williams, C. Tibbitts, & W. Donahue (Eds.), *Process of aging* (Vol. 1). New York, NY: Atherton.

Havighurst, R.J. (1972). *Developmental tasks and education* (3rd ed., 1st ed. 1948). New York: David McKay.

Havighurst, R.J. (1973). History of developmental psychology: Socialization and personality development through the life span. In P.B. Baltes & K.W. Schaie (Eds.), *Life-span developmental psychology: Personality and socialization*. New York: Academic Press.

Havighurst, R.J. (1982). The world of work. In B.B. Wolman (Ed.), *Handbook of developmental psychology*. Englewood Cliffs, NJ: Prentice-Hall.

Havighurst, R.J., Neugarten, B.L., & Tobin, S.S. (1968). Disengagement and patterns of aging. In B.L. Neugarten (Ed.), *Middle age and aging*. Chicago, IL: University of Chicago Press.

Heckhausen, J. (1999). *Developmental regulation in adulthood: Age-normative and sociostructural constraints as adaptive strategies*. Cambridge: Cambridge University Press.

Heckhausen, J., & Schulz, R. (1993). Optimization by selection and compensation: Balancing primary and secondary control in life span development. *International Journal of Behavioral Development*, *16*, 287–303.

Heckhausen, J., & Schulz, R. (1995). A life-span theory of control. *Psychological Review*, *102*, 284–304.

Heinemann, G.D., & Evans, P.L. (1990). Widowhood: Loss, change, and adaptation. In T.H. Brubaker (Ed.), *Family relationships in later life*. Newbury Park, CA: Sage.

Hirschhorn, L. (1977). Social policy and the life cycle: A developmental perspective. *Social Service Review*, *51*, 434–450.

Hochschild, A.R. (1975). Disengagement theory: A critique and proposal. *American Sociological Review*, *40*, 553–569.

Hochschild, A.R. (1976). Disengagement theory: A logical, empirical, and phenomenological critique. In J.F. Gubrium (Ed.), *Time, roles, and self in old age*. New York: Human Sciences Press.

Holland, J.L. (1994). *The self-directed search*. Odessa, FL: Psychological Assessment Resources.

Holland, J.L. (1996). Exploring careers with a typology: What we have learned and some new directions. *American Psychologist*, *51*, 397–406.

Holland, J.L. (1997). *Making vocational choices* (3rd ed.). Odessa, FL: Psychological Assessment Resources.

Holland, J.L., Fritzsche, B.A., & Powell, A.B. (1994). *The self-directed search: Technical manual – 1994 edition*. Odessa, FL: Psychological Assessment Resources.

Holland, J.L., Sorenson, A.B., Clark, J.P., Nafziger, D.H., & Blum, Z.D. (1973). Applying an occupational classification to a representative sample of work histories. *Journal of Applied Psychology*, *58*, 34–41.

Holmes, T.H., & Rahe, R.H. (1967). The social readjustment rating scale. *Journal of Psychosomatic Research*, *11*, 213–218.

Hopson, B. (1981). Response to the papers by Schlossberg, Brammer and Abrego. *Counselling Psychologist*, *9*, 36–39.

Hopson, B., & Adams, J. (1976). Towards an understanding of transition: Defining some boundaries of transition dynamics. In J. Adams, J. Hayes, & B. Hopson (Eds.), *Transition: Understanding and managing personal change*. London: Martin Robertson.

Hopson, B., & Scally, M. (1980a). Change and development in adult life: Some implications for helpers. *British Journal of Guidance and Counselling*, *8*(2), 175–187.
Hopson, B., & Scally, M. (1980b). *Lifeskills teaching programme. No. 1*. Leeds: Lifeskills Associates.
Hopson, B., & Scally, M. (1981). *Lifeskills teaching*. London: McGraw-Hill.
Hopson, B., & Scally, M. (1982). *Lifeskills teaching programme. No. 2*. Leeds: Lifeskills Associates.
Hopson, B., & Scally, M. (1985). *Lifeskills teaching programme. No. 3*. Leeds: Lifeskills Associates.
Hopson, B., Scally, M., & Stafford, K. (1988). *Transitions: The challenge of change*. Leeds: Lifeskills Associates.
Howard, G.S. (1991). Culture tales: A narrative approach to thinking, cross-cultural psychology and psychotherapy. *American Psychologist*, *46*, 187–197.
Hyson, M.C. (1983). Going to the doctor: A developmental study of stress and coping. *Journal of Child Psychology and Psychiatry*, *24*, 247–259.
Inhelder, B., & Piaget, J. (1958). *The growth of logical thinking from childhood to adolescence*. New York: Basic Books.
Itzin, C. (1986). Ageism awareness training: a model for group work. In C. Phillipson, M. Bernard, & P. Strang (Eds.), *Dependency and interdependency in old age: Theoretical perspectives and policy alternatives*. London: Croom Helm.
Jacobs, M. (1998). *The presenting past: The core of psychodynamic counselling and therapy* (2nd ed.). Buckingham: Open University Press.
Jacobs, M.K., & Goodman, G. (1989). Psychology and self-help groups: Predictions on a partnership. *American Psychologist*, *44*, 536–544.
Janesick, V.J. (1994). The dance of qualitative research design: Metaphor, methodolatry, and meaning. In N.K. Denzin & Y.S. Lincoln (Eds.), *The handbook of qualitative research*. Thousand Oaks, CA: Sage.
Jaques, E. (1965). Death and the mid-life crisis. *International Journal of Psychoanalysis*, *46*, 502–514.
Jaques, E. (1980). The mid-life crisis. In S.I. Greenspan & G.H. Pollock (Eds.), *The course of life: Psychoanalytic contributions toward understanding personality development: Vol. 3. Adulthood and aging*. Washington, DC: National Institute of Mental Health.
Johnson, J., & Bytheway, B. (1993). Ageism: Concept and definition. In J. Johnson & R. Slater (Eds.), *Ageing and later life*. London: Sage.
Jourard, S.M. (1974). *The healthy personality: An approach from the viewpoint of humanistic psychology*. New York: Macmillan.
Jung, C.G. (1972). The transcendent function. In H. Read, M. Fordham, G. Adler, & W. McGuire (Eds.), *The structure and dynamics of the psyche: Vol. 8. The collected works of C G Jung* (2nd ed.). London: Routledge and Kegan Paul.
Kagan, J. (1980). Perspectives on continuity. In O.G. Brim & J. Kagan (Eds.), *Constancy and change in human development*. Cambridge, MA: Harvard University Press.
Kahana, E., Kiyak, A., & Liang, J. (1980). Menopause in the context of other life events. In A.J. Dan, E.A. Graham, & C.P. Beecher (Eds.), *The menstrual cycle: A synthesis of interdisciplinary research*. New York: Springer.

Kahn, R.L., & Antonucci, T.C. (1980). Convoys over the life course: Attachment, roles and social support. In P.B. Baltes & O.G. Brim (Eds.), *Life-span development and behavior* (Vol. 3). New York: Academic Press.

Kalish, R. (1979). The new ageism and the failure model: A polemic. *The Gerontologist, 19*, 398–402.

Kaplan, B. (1983). A trio of trials. In R.M. Lerner (Ed.), *Developmental psychology: Historical and philosophical perspectives*. Hillsdale, NJ: Lawrence Erlbaum.

Karusa, J., Zevon, M.A., Rabinowitz, V.C., & Brickman, P. (1982). Attributions of responsibility by helpers and recipients. In T. Willis (Ed.), *Basic processes in helping relationships*. New York: Academic Press.

Katz, A., & Bender, E. (1976). Self-help groups in western society: History and prospects. *Journal of Applied Behavioral Science, 12*, 265–282.

Katz, A., & Hermalin, J. (1987). Self-help and prevention. In J. Hermalin & J. Morell (Eds.), *Prevention planning in mental health*. Newbury Park, CA: Sage.

Kimmel, D.C. (1974). *Adulthood and aging*. New York: Wiley.

Kindermann, T.A., & Valsiner, J. (1995). Individual development, changing contexts, and the co-construction of person–context relations in human development. In T.A. Kindermann & J. Valsiner (Eds.), *Development of person–context relations*. Hillsdale, NJ: Lawrence Erlbaum.

Kirschenbaum, H., & Henderson, V.L. (Eds.). (1989). *The Carl Rogers reader*. London: Constable.

Kitchener, K.S. (1986). The reflective judgement model: Characteristics, evidence, and measurement. In R.A. Mines & K.S. Kitchener (Eds.), *Adult cognitive development*. New York: Praeger.

Kitchener, K.S., & King, P. (1981). Reflective judgement: Concepts of justification and their relationship to age and education. *Journal of Applied Developmental Psychology, 2*, 89–116.

Kitchener, K.S., & King, P.M. (1990). The reflective judgement model: Ten years of research. In M.L. Commons, C. Armon, L. Kohlberg, F.A. Richards, T.A. Grotzer, & J.D. Sinnott (Eds.), *Adult development: Models and methods in the study of adolescent and adult thought*. New York: Praeger.

Klass, D., Silverman, P., & Nickman, S. (Eds.). (1996). *Continuing bonds: New understandings of grief*. London: Taylor and Francis.

Kleemeier, R.W. (1962). Intellectual changes in the senium. *Proceedings of the American Statistical Association, 1*, 290–295.

Kohlberg, L. (1969). *Stages in the development of moral thought and action*. New York: Holt, Reinhart and Winston.

Kohlberg, L. (1973a). Stages and aging in moral development – some speculations. *The Gerontologist, 13*, 497–502.

Kohlberg, L. (1973b). Continuities in childhood and adult moral development revisited. In P.B. Baltes & K.W. Schaie (Eds.), *Life-span developmental psychology: Personality and socialization*. New York: Academic Press.

Kohlberg, L. (1978). Revisions in the theory and practice of moral development. In W. Damon (Ed.), *Moral development: New directions for child development*. San Francisco, CA: Jossey-Bass.

Kohlberg, L. (1980). *The meaning and measurement of moral development*. Worcester, MA: Clark University Press.

Kohlberg, L., & Turiel, E. (Eds.). (1973). *Recent research in moral development*. New York: Holt, Reinhart and Winston.

Kohli, M., & Meyer, J.W. (1986). Social structure and social construction of life stages. *Human Development*, *29*, 145–149.

Kolb, D. (1984). *Experiential learning: Experience as the source of learning and development*. Englewood Cliffs, NJ: Prentice-Hall.

Kramer, D.A. (1989). Development of an awareness of contradiction across the life span and the question of postformal operations. In M.L. Commons, J.D. Sinnott, F.F. Richards, & C. Armon (Eds.), *Adult development: Comparisons and applications of development models*. New York: Praeger.

Kurtz, L.F. (1997). *Self-help and support groups*. London: Sage.

Labouvie-Vief, G. (1980). Beyond formal operations: Uses and limits of pure logic in life-span development. *Human Development*, *23*, 141–161.

Labouvie-Vief, G., & Hakim-Larson, J. (1989). Developmental shifts in adult thought. In S. Hunter & M. Sundel (Eds.), *Midlife myths: Issues, findings and practical implications*. Newbury Park, CA: Sage.

Labouvie-Vief, G., & Lawrence, R. (1985). Object knowledge, personal knowledge, and processes of equilibration in adult cognition. *Human Development*, *28*, 25–39.

La Gaipa, J.J. (1990). The negative effects of informal support systems. In S. Duck & R.C. Silver (Eds.), *Personal relationships and social support*. London: Sage.

Langer, E.J. (1989). *Mindfulness*. Reading, MA: Addison-Wesley.

Lawton, A. (1985). Youth counselling. *British Journal of Guidance and Counselling*, *13*, 35–48.

Lazarus, R.S., & Folkman, S. (1984). *Stress, appraisal and coping*. New York: Springer.

Lefrancois, G.R. (1996). *The lifespan* (5th ed.). Belmont, CA: Wadsworth.

Lerner, R.M. (1976). *Concepts and theories of human development*. Reading, MA: Addison-Wesley.

Lerner, R.M. (1995). Developing individuals within changing contexts: Implications of developmental contextualism for human development research, policy and programs. In T.A. Kindermann & J. Valsiner (Eds.), *Development of personcontext relations*. Hillsdale, NJ: Lawrence Erlbaum Associates.

Lerner, R.M., & Ryff, C.D. (1978). Implementation of the life-span view of human development: the sample case of attachment. In P.B. Baltes (Ed.), *Life-span development and behavior* (Vol. 1). New York: Academic Press.

Levine, M., & Perkins, D. (1987). *Principles of community psychology: Perspectives and applications*. New York: Oxford University Press.

Levinson, D.J. (1986). A conception of adult development. *American Psychologist*, *42*, 3–13.

Levinson, D.J. (1996). *The seasons of a woman's life*. New York: Ballantine Books.

Levinson, D.J., Darrow, D.N., Klein, E.B., Levinson, M.H., & McKee, B. (1978). *The seasons of a man's life*. New York: AA Knopf.

Lievegoed, B. (1979). *Phases: Crisis and development in the individual*. London: Rudolf Steiner Press.

Lincoln, Y.S., & Guba, E.G. (1985). *Naturalistic inquiry*. Beverly Hills, CA: Sage.

Lincoln, Y.S., & Guba, E.G. (1986). But is it rigorous? Trustworthiness and authenticity in naturalistic evaluation. In D.D. Williams (Ed.), *Naturalistic evaluation*. San Francisco, CA: Jossey-Bass.

Linde, C. (1993). *Life stories: The creation of coherence.* Oxford: Oxford University Press.

Loevinger, J. (1976). *Ego development.* San Francisco, CA: Jossey-Bass.

Lowenthal, M.F., & Chiriboga, D.A. (1972). Transition to the empty nest: Crisis, challenge or relief? *Archives of General Psychiatry, 26*, 8–14.

Lowenthal, M.F., Thurnher, M.T., & Chiriboga, D. (1975). *Four stages of life: A comparative study of women and men facing transitions.* San Francisco, CA: Jossey-Bass.

Maas, H.S. (1989). Social responsibility in middle age: Prospects and preconditions. In S. Hunter & M. Sundel, (Eds.), *Midlife myths: Issues, findings and practice implications.* Newbury Park, CA: Sage.

McAdams, D.P. (1985). *Power, intimacy, and the life story: Personological inquiries into identity.* Homewood, IL: Dow Jones-Irwin.

McAdams, D.P. (1997). *Stories we live by: Personal myths and the making of the self.* New York: Guilford Press.

McCandless, B.R., & Evans, E.D. (1973). *Children and youth: Psychosocial development.* Hillsdale, IL: Dryden Press.

McCoy, V.R. (1977). *Lifelong learning: The adult years.* Washington, DC: Adult Education Association.

McCrae, R.R., & Costa, P.T. (1984). *Emerging lives, enduring dispositions: Personality in adulthood.* Boston: Little Brown.

McCrae, R.R., & Costa, P.T. (1990). *Personality in adulthood.* New York: Guilford.

McLanahan, S.S., & Sorensen, A.B. (1985). Life events and psychological well-being over the life course. In G.H. Elder (Ed.), *Life course dynamics: Trajectories and transitions, 1968–1980.* Ithaca, NY: Cornell University Press.

McLeod, J. (1997). *Narrative and psychotherapy.* London: Sage.

Maddox, G., & Eisdorfer, C. (1962). Some correlates of activity and morale among the elderly. *Social Forces, 41*, 254–260.

Magnusson, D. (1989). Individual development: A holistic, integrated model. In P. Moen, G.H. Elder, & K. Lüscher (Eds.), *Examining lives in context: Perspectives on the ecology of human development.* Washington, DC: American Psychological Association.

Mair, M. (1988). Psychology as storytelling. *International Journal of Personal Construct Psychology, 3*, 121–135.

Malim, T., & Birch, A. (1998). *Introductory psychology.* London: MacMillan.

Marsiske, M., Lang, F.R., Baltes, P.B., & Baltes, M.M. (1995). Selective optimization with compensation: Life-span perspectives on successful human development. In R.A. Dickson & L. Backman (Eds.), *Psychological compensation: Managing losses and promoting gains.* Hillsdale, NJ: Erlbaum.

Martin, P., & Smyer, M.A. (1990). The experience of micro- and macroevents: A life span analysis. *Research on Aging, 12*, 294–310.

Maslow, A.H. (1970). *Motivation and personality* (2nd ed.). New York: Harper and Rowe.

Maton, K. (1988). Social support, organizational characteristics, psychological well-being, and group appraisal in three self-help group populations. *American Journal of Community Psychology, 16*, 53–78.

Mechanic, D. (1999). Issues in promoting health. *Social Science and Medicine, 48*, 711–718.

Miller, D., & Form, W. (1951). *Industrial sociology*. New York: Harper.

Miller, M.A., & Rahe, R.H. (1997). Life change scaling for the 1990s. *Journal of Psychosomatic Research, 43*, 279–291.

Miller, S.M., & Green, M.L. (1984). Coping with stress and frustration: Origins, nature, and development. In M. Lewis & C. Saarni (Eds.), *Origins of behavior* (Vol. 5). New York: Plenum.

Moos, R.H. (1986). *Coping with life crises: An integrated approach*. New York: Plenum.

Mortimer, J.T., Finch, M.D., & Kumka, D. (1982). Persistence and change in development: The multidimensional self-concept. In P.B. Baltes & O.G. Brim (Eds.), *Life-span development and behavior* (Vol. 4). New York: Academic Press.

Mowrer, O.H., & Kluckhohn, C. (1944). A dynamic theory of personality. In J.M. Hunt (Ed.), *Personality and the behavior disorder* (Vol. 1). New York: Ronald Press.

Murray, K. (1986). Literary pathfinding: The work of popular life constructors. In T.R. Sarbin (Ed.), *Narrative psychology: The storied nature of human conduct*. New York: Praeger.

Neugarten, B.L. (1965). A developmental view of adult personality. In J.E. Birren (Ed.), *Relations of development and aging*. Springfield, IL: C.C. Thomas.

Neugarten, B.L. (1968). *Middle age and aging: A reader in social psychology*. Chicago, IL: University of Chicago Press.

Neugarten, B.L. (1974). Age groups in society and the rise of the young-old. *Annals of the American Society of Political Science, 415*, 187–198. (Reprinted in D.A. Neugarten (Ed.). (1996). *The meaning of age: Selected papers of Bernice L. Neugarten*. Chicago, IL: Chicago University Press.)

Neugarten, B.L. (1977). Adaptation and the life cycle. In N.K. Schlossberg & A.D. Entine (Eds.), *Counseling adults*. Monterey, CA: Brooks/Cole.

Neugarten, B.L. (1979). Time, age and the life cycle. *American Journal of the American Psychiatric Association, 136*, 887–894. (Reprinted in D.A. Neugarten, (Ed.). (1996). *The meaning of age: Selected papers of Bernice L. Neugarten*. Chicago, IL: Chicago University Press.)

Neugarten, B.L., & Datan, N. (1973). Sociological perspectives on the life cycle. In P.B. Baltes & K.W. Schaie (Eds.), *Life-span developmental psychology: Personality and socialization*. New York: Academic Press. (Reprinted in D.A. Neugarten (Ed.). (1996). *The meaning of age: Selected papers of Bernice L. Neugarten*. Chicago, IL: University of Chicago Press.)

Neugarten, B.L., Moore, J.W., & Lowe, J.C. (1965). Age norms, age constraints, and adult socialization. *American Journal of Sociology, 70*(6), 710–717. (Reprinted in D.A. Neugarten (Ed.). (1996). *The meaning of age: Selected papers of Bernice L. Neugarten*. Chicago, IL: University of Chicago Press.)

Neugarten, B.L., Wood, V., Kraines, R., & Loomis, B. (1963). Women's attitudes toward the menopause. *Vita humana, 6*, 140–151. (Reprinted in D.A. Neugarten, (Ed.). (1996). *The meaning of age: Selected papers of Bernice L. Neugarten* Chicago, IL: Chicago University Press.)

Newman, B., & Newman, P. (1995). *Development through life: A psychosocial approach* (6th ed.). Pacific Grove, CA: Brooks/Cole.

Norcross, J.C., Santrock, J.W., Campbell, L.F., Smith, T.P., Sommer, R., & Zuckerman, E.L. (2000). *Authoritative guide to self-help resources in mental health*. New York: Guilford Press.

Nunnally, J.C. (1973). Research strategies and measurement methods for investigating human development. In J.R. Nesselroade & H.W. Reese (Eds.), *Life-span developmental psychology: Methodological issues*. NY: Academic Press.

Oden, M.H., & Terman, L.M. (1968). The fulfilment of promise – 40-year follow-up of the Terman Gifted Group. *Genetic Psychology Monographs*, *77*, 3–90.

Oerter, R. (1986). Developmental tasks through the life span: A new approach to an old concept. In P.B. Baltes, D.L. Featherman, & R.M. Lerner (Eds.), *Life-span development and behavior* (Vol. 7). Hillsdale, NJ: Lawrence Erlbaum.

Oppenheim, A.N. (1992). *Questionnaire design, interviewing and attitude measurement*. London: Pinter Publishers.

Orford, J. (1992). *Community psychology: Theory and practice*. Chichester: Wiley.

Oxley, G. (1971). A life-model approach to change. *Social Casework*, *52*, 627–633.

Parker, C., & Lewis, R. (1981). Beyond the Peter Principle: managing successful transitions. *Journal of European Industrial Training*, 5, 17–21.

Parkes, C.M. (1971). Psycho-social transitions: A field for study. *Social Science and Medicine*, *5*, 101–105.

Parkes, C.M. (1991). *Bereavement studies of grief in adult life*. London: Penguin.

Pearlin, L.I. (1980). Life strains and psychological distress among adults. In N.J. Smesler & E.H. Erikson (Eds.), *Themes of work and love in adulthood*. Cambridge, MA: Harvard University Press.

Pearlin, L.I., & Schooler, C. (1978). The structure of coping. *Journal of Health and Social Behavior*, *19*, 2–21.

Pearsall, M. (1970). Participant observation as role and method in behavioural research. In W.J. Filstead (Ed.), *Qualitative methodology: Firsthand involvement with the social world*. Chicago, IL: Rand McNally.

Peck, R. (1968). Psychological developments in the second half of life. In B.L. Neugarten (Ed.), *Middle age and aging*. Chicago, IL: University of Chicago Press.

Pedler, M., Burgoyne, J., & Boydell, T. (1978). *A manager's guide to self-development*. London: McGraw-Hill.

Perlman, H. (1957). *Social casework: A problem-solving process*. Chicago, IL: University of Chicago Press.

Perlmutter, E., & Bart, P.B. (1982). "Changing views of the change": A critical review and suggestions for an attributional approach. In A.M. Voda, M. Dinnerstein, & S.R. O'Donnell (Eds.), *Changing perspectives on menopause*. Austin, TX: University of Texas Press.

Pervin, L.A., & Lewis, M. (1978). Overview of the internal–external issue. In L.A. Pervin & M. Lewis (Eds.), *Perspectives in interactional psychology*. New York: Plenum Press.

Phinney, J.S. (1990). Ethnic identity in adolescents and adults: Review and research. *Psychological Bulletin*, *108*, 499–514.

Phinney, J.S., & Rosenthal, D.A. (1992). Ethnic identity in adolescence: Process, context and outcome. In G.R. Adams, T.P. Gullotta, & R. Montemayor (Eds.), *Adolescent identity formation*. Newbury Park, CA: Sage.

Pilgrim, D. (1997). *Psychotherapy and society*. London: Sage.

Ponzo, Z. (1978). Age prejudice of "Act your age". *Personnel and Guidance Journal*, *57*, 140–144.

Prochaska, J.O., DiClemente, C.C., & Norcross, J. (1992). In search of how people change: Application to addictive behaviors. *American Psychologist*, *47*, 1102–1114.

Pryor, R.G.L. (1989). Conflicting responsibilities: A case study of an ethical dilemma for psychologists working in organisations. *Australian Psychologist*, *24*, 293–305.

Rapoport, R., & Rapoport, R. (1980). *Growing through life*. London: Harper and Row.

Rappaport, J. (1977). *Community psychology: Values, research and action*. New York: Holt Reinhart and Winston.

Reese, H.W., & Overton, W.F. (1970). Models of development and theories of development. In L.R. Goutlet & P. Baltes (Eds.), *Life-span developmental psychology: Research and theory*. New York: Academic Press.

Reese, H.W., & Smyer, M.A. (1983). The dimensionalization of life-events. In E.J. Callahan & K.A. McCluskey (Eds.), *Life-span developmental psychology: Nonnormative life events*. New York: Academic Press.

Reinert, G. (1980). Educational psychology in the context of the human life span. In P.B. Baltes & O.G. Brin (Eds.), *Life-span development and behavior* (Vol. 3). New York: Academic Press.

Reinke, B., Holmes, D.S., & Harris, R.L. (1985). The timing of psychosocial changes in women's lives: The years 25–45. *Journal of Personality and Social Psychology*, *48*, 1353–1364.

Rice, F.P. (1995). *Human development: A life-span approach* (2nd ed.). Englewood Cliffs, NJ: Prentice-Hall.

Richardson, L. (1994). Writing: A method of inquiry. In N.K. Denzin & Y.S. Lincoln (Eds.), *Handbook of Qualitative Research*. Thousand Oaks, CA: Sage.

Riegel, K.F. (1973). Dialectical operations: The final period of cognitive development. *Human Development*, *16*, 346–370.

Riegel, K. (1975). Adult life-crises: A dialectical interpretation of development. In N. Datan & L. Ginsberg (Eds.), *Life-span developmental psychology: Normative life-crises*. New York: Academic Press.

Riegel, K.F. (1976). The dialectics of human development. *American Psychologist*, *31*, 689–700.

Riegel, K.F., & Riegel, R.M. (1972). Development, drop and death. *Developmental Psychology*, *6*, 306–319.

Riessman, F. (1965). The "helper" therapy principle. *Social Work*, *10*, 27–32.

Rindfuss, R.R., Swicegood, C.G., & Rosenfeld, R.A. (1987). Disorder in the life course: How common is it and does it matter? *American Sociological Review*, *52*, 785–801.

Roazen, P. (1976). *Erik H. Erikson*. New York: Free Press.

Roberts, J., Prince, R., Gold, B., & Shiner, E. (1966). *Social and mental health survey: Summary report*. Montreal: Mental Hygiene Institute.

Roberts, K. (1977). The social conditions, consequences and limitations of careers guidance. *British Journal of Guidance and Counselling*, *5*, 1–9.

Roberts, K. (1997). Prolonged transitions to uncertain destinations: The implications for careers guidance. *British Journal of Guidance and Counselling*, *25*, 345–360.

Roberts, P., & Newton, P.M. (1987). Levinsonian studies of women's adult development. *Psychology and Aging*, *2*, 154–163.

Rodgers, R.F. (1984). Theories of adult development: Research status and counseling implications. In S.D. Brown & R.W. Lent (Eds.), *Handbook of Counseling Psychology*. New York: Wiley.

Rodin, J. (1990). Control by any other name: Definitions, concepts and processes. In J. Rodin, C. Schooler, & K.W. Schaie (Eds.), *Self directedness: Cause and effects throughout the life course*. Hillsdale, NJ: Lawrence Erlbaum.

Rogers, C.R. (1961). *On becoming a person*. Boston: Houghton Mifflin.

Rogers, C.R. (1980). *A way of being*. Boston: Houghton Mifflin.

Rose, A.M., & Peterson, W.A. (Eds.). (1965). *Older people and their social world*. Philadelphia: F.A. Davis.

Rosen, G.M. (1987). Self-help treatment books and the commercialization of psychotherapy. *American Psychologist*, *42*, 46–51.

Ross, D.B. (1984). A cross-cultural comparison of adult development. *Personnel and Guidance Journal*, *62*, 418–421.

Ruffin, J.E. (1989). Stages of adult development in Black professional women. In R.L. Jones (Ed.), *Black adult development and aging*. Berkeley, CA: Cobb and Henry.

Runyan, W.M. (1978). The life course as a theoretical orientation: Sequences of person–situation interaction. *Journal of Personality*, *46*, 569–593.

Rutter, M. (1989). Pathways from childhood to adult life. *Journal of Child Psychology and Psychiatry*, *30*, 23–51.

Rutter, M. (1996). Transitions and turning points in developmental psychopathology: As applied to the age span between childhood and mid-adulthood. *International Journal of Behavioral Development*, *19*, 603–626.

Rutter, M., & Rutter, M. (1993). *Developing minds: Challenge and continuity across the lifespan*. Harmondsworth: Penguin.

Ryan, W. (Ed.). (1969). *Distress in the city: Essays on the design and administration of urban mental health services*. Cleveland, OH: Case Western Reserve University Press.

Ryff, C.D. (1989). Beyond Ponce de Leon and life satisfaction: New directions in quest of successful ageing. *International Journal of Behavioral Development*, *12*, 35–55.

Sacks, O. (1985). *The man who mistook his wife for a hat*. London: Duckworth.

Salmon, P. (1985). *Living in time: A new look at personal development*. London: Dent.

Schaie, K.W. (1965). A general model for the study of developmental problems. *Psychological Bulletin*, *64*, 92–107.

Schaie, K.W. (1986). Beyond calendar definitions of age, time and cohort: The general developmental model revisited. *Developmental Review*, *6*, 252–277.

Schein, E. (1993). *Career anchors: Discovering your real value*. San Francisco, CA: Jossey-Bass.

Schlossberg, N.K. (1981). A model for analysing human adaptation to transition. *Counseling Psychologist*, *9*, 2–18.

Schlossberg, N.K., Waters, E.B., & Goodman, J. (1995). *Counselling adults in transition: Linking practice with theory*. New York: Springer.

Schonfield, D. (1982). Who is stereotyping whom and why? *The Gerontologist*, *22*, 267–272.

Shannan, J., & Kedar, H.S. (1979–80). Phenomenological structuring of the adult life span as a function of age and sex. *International Journal of Aging and Human Development*, *10*, 343–357.

Sheehy, G. (1974). *Passages: Predictable crises of adult life*. New York: E.P. Dutton.

Sheehy, G. (1996). *New passages: Mapping your life across time*. London: Harper-Collins.

Sigelman, C.K., & Shaffer, D.R. (1995). *Life-span human development* (2nd ed.). Belmont, CA: Brooks/Cole.

Silverman, P.R. (1978). Mutual help: An alternative framework. In Select Committee on Aging, US House of Representatives (Ed.), *Women in midlife – security and fulfilment*. Washington, DC: US Government Printing Office.

Skovholt, T.M. (1974). The client as helper: A means to promote psychological growth. *Counseling Psychologist*, *4*, 58–64.

Smith, L.M., & Klein, P.G. (1986). Qualitative research and evaluation: Triangulation and multi-methods reconsidered. In D.D. Williams (Ed.), *Naturalistic evaluation*. San Francisco: CA: Jossey-Bass.

Spence, D.P. (1987). *The Freudian metaphor: Toward paradigm change in psychoanalysis*. New York: Norton.

Staude, J.-R. (1981). *The adult development of C.G. Jung*. Boston, MA: Routledge.

Stevens-Long, L. (1990). Adult development: Theories past and future. In R.A. Nemiroff & C.A. Colarusso (Eds.), *New dimensions in adult development*. New York: Basic Books.

Stewart, A.J., & Healy, J.M. (1989). Linking individual development and social changes. *American Psychologist, 44*, 30–42.

Stewart, M.J. (1990). Expanding theoretical conceptualizations of self-help groups. *Social Science and Medicine*, *31*, 1057–1066.

Sudman, S., & Bradburn, N.M. (1982). *Asking questions: A practical guide to questionnaire design*. San Francisco, CA: Jossey-Bass.

Sugarman, L. (1995). Action man: An interview with Gerard Egan. *British Journal of Guidance and Counselling*, *23*, 275–286.

Sugarman, L. (1996). Narratives of theory and practice: The psychology of life-span development. In R. Woolfe & W. Dryden (Eds.), *Handbook of counselling psychology*. London: Sage.

Sullivan, H.S. (1945). *Conceptions of modern psychiatry*. Washington, DC: W.A. White Foundation.

Super, D.E. (1957). *The psychology of careers*. New York: Harper.

Super, D.E. (1980). A life-span, life-space approach to career development. *Journal of Vocational Behavior*, *16*, 282–298.

Super, D.E. (1984). Career and life development. In D. Brown, L. Brooks, & Associates (Eds.), *Career choice and development*. San Francisco, CA: Jossey-Bass.

Super, D.E. (1990). A life-span, life-space approach to career development. In D. Brown, L. Brooks, & Associates (Eds.), *Career choice and development* (2nd ed.). San Francisco, CA: Jossey-Bass.

Tamir, L.M. (1989). Modern myths about men at midlife: An assessment. In S. Hunter & M. Sundel (Eds.), *Midlife myths: Issues, findings and practice implications*. Newbury Park, CA: Sage.

Tennyson, W.W., & Strom, S.M. (1986). Beyond professional standards: Developing responsibleness. *Journal of Counseling and Development, 64*, 298–302.

Thoits, P.A. (1995). Stress, coping and social support processes: Where are we? What next? *Journal of Health and Social Behavior, 36*(Extra issue), 53–79.

Thomas, R.M. (1990). *Counseling and life-span development*. London: Sage.

Toffler, A. (1970). *Future shock*. London: Pan.

Turner, J.S., & Helms, D.B. (1979). *Life span development*. Philadelphia: W.B. Saunders.

Vaillant, G.E. (1977). *Adaptation to life: How the brightest and best come of age*. Boston, MA: Little Brown.

Vygotsky, L. (1994). The problem of the environment. In R.V. D. Veer & J. Valsiner (Eds.), *The Vygotsky reader*. Oxford: Blackwell.

Viney, L. (1993). *Life stories: Personal construct therapy with the elderly*. Chichester: John Wiley and Sons.

Viney, L.L., & Bousfield, L. (1991). Narrative analysis: A method of psychosocial research for AIDS-affected people. *Social Science and Medicine, 32*, 757–765.

Walter, T. (1996). A new model of grief: Bereavement and biography. *Mortality*, 1, 7–25.

Weick, A. (1989). Patterns of change and processes of power in adulthood. In S. Hunter & M. Sundel (Eds.), *Midlife myths: Issues, findings and practice implications* (pp. 235–52). Newbury Park, CA: Sage.

Weiss, R.S. (1974). The provisions of social relationships. In Z. Rubin (Ed.), *Doing unto others*. Englewood Cliffs, NJ: Prentice-Hall.

Wethington, E., Cooper, H., & Holmes, C.S. (1997). Turning points in midlife. In I.H. Gotlib & B. Wheaton (Eds.), *Stress and adversity over the life course: Trajectories and turning points*. Cambridge: Cambridge University Press.

Wilber, K. (1979). A developmental view of consciousness. *Journal of Transpersonal Psychology, 11*, 1–21.

Wilkinson, J. (1995). Direct observation. In G.M. Breakwell, S. Hammond, & C. Fife-Shaw (Eds.), *Research methods in psychology*. London: Sage.

Wohlwill, J.F. (1980). Cognitive development in children. In O.G. Brim & J. Kagan (Eds.), *Constancy and change in human development*. Cambridge, MA: Harvard University Press.

Woodcock, M., & Francis, D. (1993). *The unblocked manager: A practical guide to self-development*. Aldershot: Gower.

Wright, H.F. (1960). Observational child study. In P.H. Mussen (Ed.), *Handbook of research methods in child development*. New York: Wiley.

Yeo, M. (1993). Toward an ethic of empowerment for health promotion. *Health Promotion International, 8*, 225–235.

Index

Note: Page references in *italics* refer to Figures; those in **bold** refer to Tables